LUCY:
THE BITTERSWEET LIFE
OF LUCILLE BALL

By the Same Authors

JUDY: The Films and Career of Judy Garland
REBELS: The Rebel Hero in Films
LANA: The Public and Private Lives of Miss Turner

LUCY:
THE BITTERSWEET
LIFE OF LUCILLE BALL

by Joe Morella and Edward Z. Epstein

LYLE STUART, INC. • SECAUCUS, NEW JERSEY

To our families.

*Our sincere gratitude to the many
individuals who granted interviews
in connection with this book.*

*Special thanks to:
Patrick B. Clark, David C. L'Heureux
and Buddy*

LUCY:
THE BITTERSWEET LIFE
OF LUCILLE BALL

1

DOES EVERYONE really love Lucy? Hardly. She's been too successful too long to be liked by many outside her immediate circle, which consists mostly of family and people on her payroll. Since Hollywood is a town where jealousy is a universal ailment, many rumors about Lucille Ball's private life have reached fantastic proportions: Lucy is the mother of an illegitimate child raised in Jamestown, New York; Lucy shot and crippled a boy for life forty-five years ago; Lucy was "a gangland moll."

The bittersweet life of Lucille Ball is an incredible story. It does not require phony embellishments—the true story is exciting enough to stand on its own.

It's been a long trek for the orange-redhead from upstate New York who learned early that "Life takes guts." Her life has been characterized by a devout belief in God and in herself; a tempestuous, all-consuming love affair with a man as intense and volatile as she; an extraordinary and sustained drive for success, coupled with an unlimited capacity for hard work.

Even her detractors cannot dispute her talent, but her rise to stardom has been a tough, tear-stained uphill climb. While some are of the opinion that the long struggle has "turned her into a man," the chief qualities Lucille Ball projects in her TV characterizations are vulnerability and femininity.

Lucille Ball: Actress. Lover. Wife. Mother. Business Tycoon. She wasn't discovered sitting at a soda fountain or spotted in an elevator, resulting in instantaneous fame. Her achievements are no such accident of fate. She has had to overcome obstacles; they have left their scars.

"Even her relaxing is intense," notes a friend today. "If she doesn't know you she's cold as ice," observes a former CBS employee. "Naturally, you feel *you* know *her*, and you *love* her, as a result of the 'Lucy' shows. But it's a shock to realize she's not the childlike 'Lucy' character she plays. She's diamond-hard, extremely bright and extremely cautious with people. Unfriendly. My initial reaction was 'Wow, what a hard-nosed bitch.' "

As far as most people are concerned, Lucille Ball's life began on October 15, 1951, when the first "I Love Lucy" episode was broadcast over the CBS television network. Within six weeks, the names Lucille Ball and Desi Arnaz were household words; the love affair and marriage of Lucy and Desi finally took its place in show-business history.

It had taken "the battling Arnazes" eighteen years to achieve "overnight" super-stardom, and "the wild little girl" from the dull little upstate New York town, after years of struggling as a model, chorus girl, extra, bit player, supporting actress, leading lady in "B" films, glamour girl, dramatic actress and radio comedienne, had found her niche at last.

For a generation, the public and Lucy have had a love affair. As with a favorite child, the public has always forgiven her when a personal crisis placed her—or any member

2

of her family—in a less than flattering light. In the early 1950s, millions forgave her a youthful political indiscretion when it was revealed, at the height of the "Red Scare," that Lucille was suspected of having Communist ties back in the 1930s. More recently, mothers across the land sympathized with her when her son, Desi Arnaz, Jr., made headlines with his love affairs and an illegitimate child.

Lucille Ball has endured bad publicity, personal crises, spiteful rumors and the breakup of "the world's happiest and most successful marriage." She is a woman who, with faith, chutzpa and talent, has determined her own fate. Lucy now looks down on life from the lofty heights of money, influence and position. But it was not always that way.

Celoron, such an obscure little town in upstate New York that it is not even on most maps, is a suburb of Jamestown and was Lucille Ball's unlikely birthplace on August 6, 1911. Shortly after her birth, her mother, Desiree Hunt, and father, Henry Ball, moved from the Jamestown area and settled in Butte, Montana.

Desiree, nicknamed DeDe, was a pretty, vivacious young woman. "She had a lot of spunk and personality," recalls a Jamestown friend. "It sure as hell took a spirit of adventure to pick up and move to the wilds of Montana, but DeDe came from a long line of American pioneers."

In Montana, DeDe became pregnant with her second child. Then tragedy struck—a typhoid epidemic took the life of Henry Ball. Lucille remembers everything that happened that terrible day: hanging out the window, begging to play with the kids next door . . . the doctor coming . . . her mother weeping . . . a bird that flew in the window . . . a picture that fell off the wall.

Lucille was almost four.

Pregnant and alone, Desiree took Lucille and moved back with her father, "Grandpa" Fred Hunt. It was 1915.

Lucy's grandfather resumed the position of family patriarch. He was a character, a jack-of-all-trades, a one-time woodcutter, mailman, bon vivant, hotel owner and a Jamestown furniture factory worker. He was interested in politics, social reform and would later campaign for labor leader and Socialist candidate Eugene V. Debs and read the *Daily Worker*.

His attitudes about life, especially about family closeness and survival, determined the manner of Lucille's upbringing and her outlook on life.

He was, in the words of his other granddaughter, Cleo, "An enormously earthy, humorous man with a great sense of roots and heritage." A neighbor remembers him differently. "He was a bit of a nut, always pushing some kind of cause to better people's lives. Lots of energy and drive. I liked him."

What kind of child was Lucille? "A very original, dynamic, unusual child," remembered cousin Cleo. "She saw things in a way nobody else did."

Lucille's flair for acting emerged at a very early age. On one occasion a few months after her father's death, Lucille insisted on running next door to visit some kids who had the measles. DeDe looped a rope around Lucy's waist and hooked it by a trolley to the clothesline so that "Miss Busybody" could run freely back and forth, still harnessed. Suddenly, DeDe realized the trolley had stopped jingling. She looked out the window and overheard her daughter charming the milkman: "Oh, mister, *somehow* I happened to get caught in this silly old clothesline. Do you think you could get me loose?"

A few months later Lucille had a baby brother. Desiree named him Fred, after her father. "Even to this day," according to Cleo, "Lucy suspects Fred is her mother's favorite, although DeDe has devoted her entire life to Lucille."

"My brother Fred was always very, very good," remembered Lucille. "He never did anything wrong—he was too

4

much to bear. I was always in trouble, a real pain in the ass. I suppose I wasn't much fun to be around."

DeDe and her younger sister Lola (whose daughter Cleo would be Lucille's lifelong friend and business associate) were the only children of Fred C. Hunt and Flora Belle Orchutt.

Lucille's memories of Grandma Flora Belle are vivid, "A real pioneer woman and pillar of the family. She was a nurse and a midwife, an orphan who brought up four pairs of twin sisters and brothers all by herself." Grandpa first met Grandma when he owned a hotel and Flora Belle worked there as a maid.

The Hunts were a close-knit family. It was a blow to all when Grandma died. Lucy has recalled, "When she died at fifty-one, it was almost too much to bear. All I remember is holding onto my brother Freddie's hand, walking to the funeral."

Grandpa Hunt had an insatiable love of life which found its greatest expression through his grandchildren:

"He got us up early, otherwise we might miss something. Sunsets. He loved them and made us love them. He wore an old cardigan sweater and a wide-brimmed hat always on the tilt. Played rickey-tick piano and sang naughty ditties.

"He always made things—playhouses in trees, teeter-totters, doll houses, tents, bobsleds, stilts. In the winter it was skating and sledding and fishing through the ice for muskie. In the summer, boat rides and groaning picnic baskets."

Her early years had their share of happy memories. "Suppose I give you a few quick items from my childhood," Lucille mused to a friend. "There was, for example, the time when a skunk got into the tent in our back yard where my brother and I were sleeping. On another occasion we had a tragedy. The chicken coop back of our house caught fire, and I've never gotten over the fact that the hens roasted rather

5

than leave their chicks. Then pretty soon I was twelve years old and playing basketball and softball and doing an Apache dance in a Masonic revue. I hurled myself into the dance so enthusiastically I threw one arm out of joint, but I finished the performance. . . .

"Yeah, I guess I am real mid-America, growing up as a mix of French-Scotch-Irish-English, living on credit like everyone else, paying $1.25 a week to the insurance man, buying furniture on time. But it was a good full life. Grandpa took us camping, fishing, picking mushrooms, made us bobsleds. We always had goodies. I had the first boyish bob in town and the first open galoshes."

Her childhood had its unhappy memories as well. Lucy's mother had married a sheet metal worker, Ed Peterson, described by Lucy as "a handsome-ugly man, very well read. He was good to me and Freddie, but he drank too much."

For a while, Ed, DeDe and the children lived in Jamestown, but when times got rough they returned to Grandpa's house in Celoron. Lucy recalls, "When I was about seven, Ed and mother moved to Detroit, leaving me with his old-fashioned Swedish parents, who were very strict. I had to be in bed at 6:30, hearing all the other kids playing outside in the summer daylight. Maybe it wasn't that traumatic, but I realize now it was a bad time for me. I felt as if I'd been deserted."

Although this period might have seemed forever to Lucy, DeDe said it lasted "more like three weeks than three years."

Lucy's happiest memories have been of her childhood with Grandpa. Life at Grandpa Hunt's was hectic, not unlike the zany family of *You Can't Take It With You*.

The most important part of her childhood, at least from Lucy's point of view, was Grandpa's love of vaudeville. "There were those five-cent streetcar rides into Jamestown to 'do things.' See the vaudeville show, which he loved. Every week something new. It gave us a closeness, let us know someone cared."

6

At the vaudeville shows with Grandpa, Lucy saw Tom Mix movies and Pearl White serials. "Wow! I knew I had to be a part of it," Lucy remembered. "I tried out every year for the Scottish Rite revue. I got with the Jamestown Players."

Young Lucy did a play entitled *Within the Law*, which had a Sadie Thompson-like plot. The local reviews compared the youngster with Jeanne Eagles—"someone I had never heard of."

Desiree's marriage to Ed Peterson didn't endure, but the man had an important effect on young Lucy's life. "It was my stepfather who introduced me to the Chautauqua circuit, then at its height as a platform for lecturers, musicians, actors," Lucy later recalled. Her mother and stepfather drove her miles through the snow to the theater. "One night a monologist named Julian Eltinge was appearing. A female impersonator yet. Ed insisted I go. There sat this man with one light bulb, a little table and a glass of water, creating a whole world out of nothing, making people laugh and cry. It was magic. I can still see him, lank and tall. He looked like Lincoln."

Like many youngsters, Lucy had feelings of frustration and of reaching-out-and-trying-to-please. "I found the quickest and easiest way to do that was to make people laugh."

She discovered at the age of twelve that she could make people laugh. "Bernard Drake, the principal of my school, recognized my urge for approval," remembered Lucy. "I'd do anything for a smile—sell tickets, fix the stage, clean the office—and, recognizing my need, he saw to it that I had a part in school plays and operettas. My mother and stepfather also encouraged me to act, dance and sing."

Wanting to be an actress was considered a rather dubious goal in Celoron, New York, especially in the 1920s. The word actress still had a "wicked" connotation.

A young man who later became an M.D. and practiced in nearby Olean, New York, "used to walk Lucy home from school" when they were classmates at Jamestown High. His

7

mother, however, made him stop seeing Lucille because she had become known as "the Jamestown hussy."

Cleo remembers, "Lucille was always a wild, tempestuous, exciting child . . . with enormous energy, flair, style. She took us all over, particularly me, who was eight years younger . . . She was a reactor—she reacted to everything. Always conning us to be in her plays and was always in hot water with somebody. Running away was reacting. She'd inveigle me into going with her—I had a piggy bank. It was always very dramatic when we were caught. And that was the point. What she really wanted was to play a scene."

For example, "One summer, she conned me into running away. It was only to nearby Fredonia, but in her sneaky way she really wanted to catch up to a groovy high school principal who was teaching there. He played it very cool, calling Mom and telling her we were staying overnight in a boarding house. On his advice, when we got home DeDe acted as if we hadn't been away. That devastated Lucille, no reaction, nothing."

DeDe Ball was obviously a remarkably understanding and modern woman for the 1920s. If Lucille wanted to be an actress, then that's what she could be. In Cleo's words, "DeDe was never bound by the social conventions of the day. She didn't mind the ridicule of the neighbors. Lucy said she wanted to play the saxophone? She got a saxophone. Freddie a cello? He got a cello. She never cried poor." (Lucy had taken up the saxophone in high school not because of an interest in music but simply because she had a crush on a football player and wanted to get into the school band so she could go on the team's out-of-town trips.)

Continuing her recollections of DeDe, Cleo also stated, "She allowed us to express ourselves. She taught us character, values, involvement. She operated on the theory that none of us would ever disgrace Grandpa. It was a relationship based on trust."

8

DeDe even allowed Lucille to drop out of high school at fifteen and enroll at the John Murray Anderson–Robert Milton Dramatic School in New York City, though she wasn't overjoyed about it. But go to New York Lucy did. Not once, but many times, between 1926 and 1933.

Before tackling Broadway, Lucy had had some minor stage experience in Jamestown. In addition to attending the Chautauqua Institute of Music, she had appeared in local Masonic revues and played a lead in the Jamestown High School production of *Charley's Aunt.*

"I played the lead, directed it, cast it, sold the tickets, printed the posters and hauled furniture to the school for scenery and props." A portent of things to come.

Her enrollment at the Anderson-Milton Dramatic School wasn't a momentous event. Shortly after Lucille began, DeDe was notified that she was "wasting her money." A school official recommended that Lucille withdraw, since it was obviously futile to attempt to make "this gawky girl" into an actress.

"This dope—that's how I thought of him then—couldn't see what I had to offer," Lucy remembered. "I wasn't discouraged—delayed, yes, but not discouraged. I was struck by the lightning of show business."

Discussing the school, Lucy subsequently said, "I was shy, terrified. I was terribly frightened. I never put forth my personality. I just stood there rigid. Bette Davis was the star pupil. There was nothing shy about her. I can see her now, starring in plays while I hid behind the scenery. And I took elocution, and Robert Milton made me repeat 'water' and 'horses' because I pronounced them 'worter' and 'hasses.' I was so miserable mother brought me home, and I spent the next few months writing. Poetry."

During her stays in New York City, Lucille often got homesick. "I grew physically ill," she remembered. "I'd run

9

home for a while, then gather up my courage and go back. For years, I never even got inside a theater. But I sure managed to burn up a lot in train fare."

Years later, giving insight to her character, she confided: "Ever since I was fifteen years old and the director of the school told me to forget about acting and apply my energies to some other field, I've been determined to make him eat his words. I told myself, 'Someday, I'll have writers turning out material just for me.'"

Tragedy struck Grandpa Hunt's household in 1927. Freddie had received a .22 rifle as a Christmas gift. "You can shoot it on your twelfth birthday," he was promised. On the birthday, Grandpa set up a target in the back yard. Naturally, all the neighbor kids were there to watch. Suddenly, a six-year-old child ran across the line of fire and was accidentally hit by a bullet.

The child was crippled for life. The embittered parents took Grandpa Hunt to court and charged that he had "made a target" of the boy.

The court ruled that Fred Hunt had to await trial in Mayville, the county seat. Grandpa was forbidden to leave the city limits while the trial was pending. The house in Celoron had to be sold to pay for legal fees. This tragic incident changed all their lives, but most affected was Grandpa, and Lucy noted, "It broke his heart and spirit."

This shooting incident in Celoron provided the basis for countless rumors which plagued Lucy for years. One far-fetched story widely circulated is that Lucille, as "a wild young girl," had been hanging around with a group of "rowdies" and for fun they shot a boy from a moving car.

Ed and DeDe, along with DeDe's sister Lola, now separated from her husband, moved Grandpa and the children into a rented house in Jamestown. Ed still had his job at the factory. DeDe went to work in a department store and Lola took up nursing. To help out, Lucy, now a gawky teen-ager, got a job as a soda jerker in Jamestown. She was fired because she always forgot to put the bananas in the banana splits.

"This is no kidding," she recalled years later. "I've told this story hundreds of times but nobody's ever used it—maybe because it sounds so phony. But it's true. It's just that so much junk went into the split that by the time the bananas came due I'd forget them every time."

Times were rough for the family in the late 1920s and in 1929, after Lola died, Cleo went to live with her father in Buffalo. Lucille continued her treks to New York City, where DeDe arranged for her to stay with some friends.

Lucy's version of these early years of struggle was, "I never even finished night school. I couldn't wait to get into show business, and at that time show business meant vaudeville to me." But getting her break presented a problem. "I never met anybody who knew how to get into vaudeville, so I decided to be a show girl and I answered a call for an Earl Carroll tryout. I was tall and thin, but measurements weren't the whole bit then. Other things counted too, although I can't remember what. I rehearsed for two weeks, then a man said to me, 'Miss Belmont! (that's who I decided to be) You're through.'

"He didn't say why, but I found out later that I was so young and so dumb I wasn't contributing anything . . . I don't know why they picked me in the first place. Earl Carroll's show girls had great bodies, which looked fine in abbreviated costumes. I didn't. I went home and cried. I asked some of the girls I'd met, 'What'll I do now?' and they said, 'There'll be other calls. Maybe there'll be a Shubert call, but, of course, you won't make that.' I was a teen-ager and Shubert girls were *femmes fatales*, dripping diamonds and

11

minks, but I was picked for a Shubert show anyhow. We rehearsed for two weeks, and I was fired again. That time I really suffered."

Life as a show girl in New York in the 1920s was rough. Lucy recalled, "Shubert girls were the living, bitchy end. They didn't want any fresh competition. They'd say, 'Think you're pretty cute, don't you?' 'Call that a figure?' 'Go home!' Horrible things to say to a kid self-conscious about being skinny anyhow. I planned ways to kill myself so I wouldn't have to go home and tell everybody I'd lost another job. I thought, 'I'll get killed faster in Central Park because cars go faster there. But I want to get hit by a big car—with a handsome man in it.' Then I had a flash of sanity. I said to myself, 'If I'm thinking this way, maybe I don't want to die.' So I regrouped my forces."

Discussing struggling kids of later generations: "I don't understand kids today who get easily discouraged and yap about 'doing their own thing.' Don't they know what hard work is? Where are their morals? I always knew when I did wrong and paid penance." Comments like these reflect Lucy's simple philosophy of life.

Recalling her show-girl days, "I also had a grab on respectability. My grandparents raised me to have a conscience. I was very observant. I watched the other girls make their mistakes. I turned down a lot of so-called 'opportunities' because they were only 'maneuvers.' My ambition wasn't high. I just wanted to work."

While trying out for chorus girl jobs, Lucy invented a glamorous autobiography. She said that she had been born in Butte, Montana, which to her seemed a cut above Jamestown. To gather information for her Montana background, she wrote to any town in Montana big enough to have a Chamber of Commerce and memorized all their handouts. "I think I knew more about Montana than lots of the natives."

The Montana birthplace also provided her with nicknames

easy for casting directors to remember—they labeled her "Montana" or "the Buttean."

Lucy managed to wangle a chorus job in the third road company of Ziegfeld's *Rio Rita*. However, during rehearsals the stage manager told her, "It's no use, Montana. Go home. You ain't meant for show business."

Although she did go home a number of times, she wouldn't give up. She kept returning to New York, supporting herself with odd jobs: soda jerking, clerking, anything to keep going. At one point she was so broke that she only had four cents to her name, a penny short of the then five-cent subway fare. "So I panhandled for a penny," she has related. "A man offered me ten dollars, but I said firmly, '*Mister, I only need one cent!*'"

She landed a job in the chorus of the Broadway musical *Stepping Stones*, but the job lasted only a few weeks. Then came a chorus job in *Step Lively*, but she was fired two weeks later when the choreographer decided he only wanted girls who could do toe work. ("Toe work? I couldn't even do heel work!")

At first Lucille hated the casting directors and choreographers who couldn't see through the façade to the talent she knew was inside her. But she learned that burning up energy by hating was hurting no one but herself . . . especially since the people she hated weren't even aware of how she felt, nor could they have cared. Lucy later philosophized, "I loathe bitterness. It shows in everything you do and eats the liver right out of you."

This was a time when Lucille literally didn't have a nickel for a cup of coffee. She was eating only when she could find a "one-doughnut man." "This," she has explained, "is a guy who sits at a counter and orders doughnuts and coffee. He drinks his coffee, eats one doughnut and puts down a nickel tip. I'd do a fast slide onto his stool, yell for a cup of coffee, pay for it with his nickel, and eat the other doughnut.

13

"I was still trying to get into show business, but in the meantime I had taken a cheap, dark, dismal room of my own and I was starving to death," she said of this period. "Then one morning I picked up a paper and saw the word 'model.' I said 'Okay, I'll model.' I looked up a place that needed models for size ten to fourteen coats. 'Coats will cover my missing figure,' I thought, and I got the job."

She alternated between modeling and chorus girl jobs. "I tried starvation in all its forms," Lucy subsequently said, "and none of them was satisfactory. In a show, five weeks rehearsal without pay was the rule, and that's too long for a girl to fast.

"I had a hall room, fifth floor back and would sometimes try to prepare food over the gas jet. I would save up a little money from modeling and get a show job. For a week or two I'd live on hope and ambition and hoard my money. Then hunger would prove too much for me. I'd eat hearty, run out of funds and leave the show before the money started coming in. It never occurred to me to ask for an advance, so I don't know whether I could have gotten one or not.

"After repeating that experience two or three times, I made up my mind there was nothing to the hunger theory, so I decided to stick to modeling and really learn the business."

Finally working steadily, Lucy met another model who told her, "My husband's a commercial photographer and you're the type he needs for an assignment." So in addition to earning twenty-five dollars a week as a model in the garment district, Lucy picked up extra money by modeling in fashionable department stores and becoming a commercial photographer's model. She also posed for artists. Then she got a job at Hattie Carnegie's.

While modeling at Carnegie's was a step up in prestige, it only increased her salary to thirty-five dollars a week, so she continued her other assignments with illustrators such as

14

McClelland Barclay and John Lagata, while still trying to break into show business.

The strain was too much but she wouldn't slacken her pace. "Slow down, honey," advised a fellow model, "you look kinda pale." But Lucille had no time to waste. She was working. Then one afternoon at Carnegie's she was stricken with pains "which pierced my insides." The diagnosis was malnutrition and fatigue. Once again Lucy had to return to Jamestown.

Lucy learned from the experience. "I worked hard and I was ill for two years from the work and missed out on everything," she later said. "I was only eighteen, but I even learned from that. It taught me that without your health, you ain't got nothin'. Remember that, kiddo. I had no survival technique, so I didn't survive. But where I was different from the other dumb show girls is that I learned from every experience, and some of them don't."

Lucy recovered her health in Jamestown and became friendly with a girl named Gert Kratzert, a hairdresser. The two girls talked of "the big city," Lucille longing to return to New York, and Gert dreaming of the city's excitement. One afternoon, they stopped talking and boarded a bus for New York City.

They took a room at the Hotel Kimberly at 74th Street and Broadway. Gert found work in the beauty parlor of the Amsterdam Hotel and Lucy got her old job back at Hattie Carnegie's. The charm of New York eventually wore off for Gert and, homesick, she returned to Jamestown. Lucy stayed on, determined as ever to have a successful career.

Hattie Carnegie had suggested she become a blonde and she did. Finally a break came when Liggett and Myers chose her as the Chesterfield poster girl, and Lucy was on twenty-four-sheet billboard posters for the cigarette company.

Concerning her love life during these days: "Love? I was

always falling in love." Her small-town upbringing and feelings of responsibility to her family's "good name" determined Lucy's attitudes. Unlike many New York models, Lucy was discreet about her romances.

There is a story about a bullet that ricocheted into the bathtub in her hotel room, which over the years has given rise to the rumor that Lucy was "a gangland moll." Lucy's explanation: "A gang war was going on around the corner. I didn't hear the bullet whang into the tub, but the water suddenly began to disappear. I got out and tried to mop the floor. That's all there is to the story."

Although she was relatively successful at Carnegie's, she still dreamed about a show business career. It was the summer of 1933 when she wandered over to Broadway one sweltering day and stood in front of the Palace Theatre, hoping to see some actors. Then, "Sylvia Hollow, a New York woman agent I knew, said 'How'd you like to leave this heat?' I said, 'I'd love to' and she asked, 'How about California? I've just come from Jim Mulvey's office upstairs. He had twelve girls leaving to be poster girls in the next Goldwyn movie and one of them can't go. You're a poster girl, aren't you?' "

Her Chesterfield poster qualified her.

She met Mulvey and he said, "All right." Lucy made a long-distance call to her mother and went back to say goodbye to Hattie Carnegie. "She gave me a coat, a hat and a dress," Lucy remembered, "and said, 'God bless you. It'll be good experience, and, if you don't like it, you can come back to work.' "

Even though these seven years had been rough, two decades later, at the peak of her TV fame, Lucille Ball obviously decided that the "tough struggle" image need not be continued, "People keep saying that success came to me the hard way, after a long struggle. This myth is ridiculous. The truth

16

is just the opposite: I have *never* been out of a job. In my early days in New York, I was hardly starving. I was making good money as a model. Then I went to Hollywood and Sam Goldwyn immediately placed me under contract. Some struggle!"

2

THAT SAME summer, when Lucille Ball migrated from the heat of New York City to the lush climate of Los Angeles to start a new life, a revolution was raging in far-off Cuba.

A sixteen-year-old boy, Desi Arnaz, who up until then had lived in the pampered world of Cuban aristocrats, was also embarking on a new life.

Desiderio Alberto Arnaz y de Acha III had been born on March 2, 1917, in Santiago, Cuba. His father, Desiderio Arnaz II, was a Cuban senator and mayor of Santiago. A wealthy landowner, his property included three ranches, a townhouse, an island in Santiago Bay, a racing stable and several cars and speedboats.

Dolores, Desi's mother, was considered one of the ten loveliest women in Latin America. Desi was their only child.

Desi's memories of his youth are vivid, "The world was my oyster. What I wanted I only needed to take. Ambition, incentive, opportunity, self-reliance, appreciation of what I had meant little to me. At sixteen I had my own speedboat, motor car, ringside tables at cafés and a fast-swelling case of what, in a language I couldn't speak at all then, is called a fathead."

Desi has said that from his birth to his teens he couldn't recall ever having faced a worry or a strain. His future was blueprinted and assured: he would be sent to the United States to attend the University of Notre Dame, he would study law, and then, as the offspring of one of Cuba's number one politicians, he would return to a ready-made practice.

But in August, 1933, the hopes and aspirations of the aristocratic Arnaz family were shattered.

Desi explained, "One morning, I heard gunfire in the distance. Down the road I saw a mob of several hundred advancing on our house. Rumbles of revolution against the Machado government had gripped Cuba for some time. But this was it! My father was miles away in Havana. I was sixteen and alone in the house with my mother. Outside, screaming junta forces were slaughtering our cattle, burning our buildings."

Desi dashed for the garage. Luckily, they had $500 in cash in the house. His mother took that and their Chihuahua and met Desi at the rear of the house. They hopped into a car and drove out the back road across the fields. When they stopped to look back, their glorious ranch house, containing all their cherished possessions, was ablaze. They watched as it disintegrated and crashed to the ground.

"God help us!" His mother moaned. "We'll never reach Havana."

"In Havana we had relatives," Desi remembered, "but the trip was a nightmare. I fixed a junta flag to the radiator of our car. Whenever we encountered troops out to kill every patrician they could find, I turned the wheel over to my mother and, standing on the running board, I yelled 'Viva la revolucion!' at the top of my lungs. In this way we reached the capital, where an aunt living on the outskirts took us into hiding. What had happened to father in Havana we could not find out at first—he had disappeared.

"In one stroke, all of the life we had known was shot out from under us. All Cuba was in chaos. In Havana, two hundred to three hundred bombs were exploding every day. I saw men dragged to their death behind horses, machine-gunned for simply daring to walk past terrorist police."

At his aunt's house, Desi and his mother finally learned that his father, a supporter of deposed President Machado, had been arrested and thrown into Morro Castle with the rest of the Cuban Senate. He remained there for six months and, according to Desi, he was released only because he had remained neutral and the United States was demanding an end to the bloodshed.

The Arnazes had spent the $500 and when Señor Arnaz was released from prison, haggard and worn, he told his wife and son that all their property had been confiscated.

They had no choice—they had to leave the country. But there wasn't enough money for all of them to go. Señor Arnaz, as a political undesirable, was in the greatest danger, therefore he left first for Florida; Desi was to join him as soon as possible and Señora Arnaz would stay hidden in Cuba.

Señor Arnaz was able to send for Desi within a few months. But the outlook for life in Miami was dismal. At first, they lived in a dingy rooming house on the outskirts of town. Arnaz had no job and he and his son ate canned beans warmed on a hotplate in an attic cubicle.

"We are refugees," Arnaz told his son, "worse off than the poorest peon at home. There are no jobs for refugees here."

Desi remembered, "To save the five dollars rent, we moved into an unheated warehouse filled with rats. We found sticks and rushed around, trying to kill the rats. The spectacle of my father, a highly-educated and honored man, doing this was such a shock that I wept. I couldn't see how we could survive in America—seemingly so big, so cold and cruelly competitive."

America was a far cry from the Cuba Arnaz had known. Years later, Desi recalled that he was surprised most of all by the absence of dividing lines between the upper and lower classes. "Here there were millions of average people who owned nice homes, cars, expensive appliances. Each man was equal to his neighbor."

Desperately looking for work, one morning Desi noticed a man building something in his back yard. It was a birdcage. Young Arnaz was hungry, but he couldn't speak English, so he tried to explain, in Spanish and with gestures, that he needed a job.

"Can't savvy you, kid," the man said. "Now run along."

Desi was about to leave when the man's wife came out of the house. She was Cuban. Through this couple Desi got a job cleaning canary cages. "I went around with my little whisk broom and droppings can, earning twenty-five cents per cage cleaned and off this the Arnazes II and III lived for some weeks."

Like most immigrants to the United States, Desi learned the language and customs of America the hard way—embarrassing experiences, being "taken," often misunderstood.

Potential disaster raised its head when the Immigration Service hauled in the Arnazes. Since they had entered the country illegally and were not permanent residents, they could not work in the United States. They were told to leave the country for six weeks and return with proper entry papers.

They were stunned. They had no money to leave and had to continue working in order to eat. But the law was clear. Young Desi offered the following solution: "It struck me that if America was as open hearted to the weak and distressed as

21

advertised, maybe the rule could be given a small bend. I told my father, who spoke English, to suggest that I be allowed to stay on and clean cages, which would finance his leaving. When he returned, I would go away for the prescribed time while he took over my job."

Luckily for the Arnazes, the Immigration official decided to look the other way. And Desi has noted, "That, I know now, was the turning point of my life. A refusal by the official—which he had every right to make—would have sent me shuffling off into the shadows.

"We skipped out of there, two glad and grateful señores. Father left for Puerto Rico, where he had friends, with the few dollars we had, to stay for six weeks and get his entry papers. I went back to the canaries. When his time was up he returned, and I worked my way to Cuba by boat, assured my mother we were well, stayed out my time and returned with my papers."

Nineteen thirty-four and nineteen thirty-five were rough years for the Arnaz men, living hand to mouth. Señor Arnaz had pooled some funds of other Cuban refugees and formed the Pan-American Export-Import Company, Inc. The firm had one truck, which Desi drove, and one product, bananas. They sold one load to pay for the next and operated the entire company on a shoestring. When one shipment of fruit was completely spoiled, the company went broke.

Desperate for work, Desi decided to get a job in a band. "I walked into a jai-alai fronton in Miami and boldly asked for a job with the band. In Cuba, where everybody is musical, I had amateurishly sung a bit and played the guitar.

" 'Can you handle the drums?' the manager asked.

"I lied that I could.

"That night, I whacked vigorously away as the fronton band played the march that brought the players onto the court. Musically, it was low as you could get, but I was delighted. From there, I talked myself into a singing job in a

22

tough waterfront café. I got one dollar a night, plus tips, but not for long. When I did a soprano version of 'Moon Over Miami' once too often in fractured English, the customers began throwing salt shakers."

"Kid, you're dead until you learn the lingo," Desi's boss told him. "Why don't you go to school?" he suggested.

Desi hadn't realized that higher public education in the United States was free. He had been thinking of the expensive private schools in Cuba, which only the upper classes could afford to attend. Realizing the need for some sort of education, and especially the need to speak English well, the young Cuban enrolled in a Miami high school. The best-liked boy in the school was Sonny Capone, whose father was Al Capone, the notorious racketeer. Sonny and Desi had an immediate rapport. Desi has recalled, "Nobody judged Sonny for what he couldn't help, only for himself. For school graduation, the custom was to pick your closest buddy to accompany you to the stage when you received your diploma. When I was graduated, I picked Sonny Capone, my best pal."

Desi was voted "most courteous" in his class, but the greatest reward from his education was that, after a fashion, he could pronounce words in English up to five syllables.

Before his twentieth birthday in 1937, he wangled a job in a big-time rhumba band at the swank Roney Plaza Hotel in Miami Beach. They needed a singing guitarist, so he borrowed a tux and went for a one-night tryout. He sang what has become his most famous number, "Babalu."

"Before I even finished, the crowd was cheering, beating hands as if Bing Crosby had suddenly materialized. I stood stupefied until, looking into the audience, I spotted all my classmates. They'd all turned out, bringing their parents, to raise the roof in support of me."

The management, thinking that Desi was a hit, kept him on. Soon he was making fifty dollars a week, a huge sum for

1937. Mrs. Arnaz was sent for, and when she arrived from Havana the family rented a pretty cottage near the hotel.

When Lucille Ball arrived in Hollywood in 1933, the top box-office stars in the country were Greta Garbo, Norma Shearer, Wallace Beery, Marie Dressler, Joan Crawford, Gary Cooper, Clark Gable and Mae West.

The Depression was at its peak, but Lucille was, for the time being at least, riding high with a contract—with options —for $150 a week as a Goldwyn Girl.

She almost hadn't gotten the job. At that time director Busby Berkeley was instrumental in selecting the Goldwyn Girls. Later Berkeley would move to Warner Bros. and cinema immortality via *42nd Street* and other film musicals.

Berkeley recalls: "Goldwyn called me in one day and said, 'I want you to come up to the projection room. I've made some tests of girls from New York and I want you to see whether you like them.' We ran them and there were two girls that I liked very much. But Goldwyn didn't like them. The next morning I went by his office and asked his secretary, 'Mary, did he send for the two girls that he didn't like but I did?' She smiled and said, 'Yes, he did, Mr. Berkeley.' The two girls I had picked were Barbara Pepper and Lucille Ball."

"Lucy never was the Hollywood type," remembers Berkeley. "She worked very hard to get her breaks. . . . She was very much a positive thinker. I used to tell her, 'Why don't you get an agent? You can go far in this business.' "

Twenty-two-year-old Lucy appreciated such words of encouragement, which were few. "She sweated out every goddamn break she got," recalls an ex-Goldwyn executive. "Opportunities never 'fell into her lap.' She was one of dozens of girls at the studio watching and waiting for *the* opportunity. The difference between Lucy and the others was that she was a *worker*. That, and Jesus, what energy! If I

24

had to use one word to describe Lucille Ball then it would be *energy*."

She was, as always, eager to learn and her industriousness didn't go unnoticed. She accepted any kind of role available: extra, walk-on, bits. She never lost hope that her attitude, hard work and learning from mistakes would pay off. "Meanwhile, she was earning a living in the business she wanted to be in," observes an ex-Goldwyn Girl. "Things could have been a lot worse for her."

Lucy appeared in ten films while under contract to Goldwyn in 1933 and 1934. They can all be characterized as junk, albeit commercial junk of the day. Four were Goldwyn films —*Roman Scandals*, with Eddie Cantor; *Nana* (Goldwyn's ultra-expensive Anna Sten vehicle which bombed); *Kid Millions*—another Eddie Cantor vehicle in which Lucille, as a blonde, was an unsmiling Goldwyn Girl; and *Bulldog Drummond Strikes Back*, starring Ronald Colman and Loretta Young. She was unbilled in all these productions and unbilled in parts she had in *Broadway Through a Keyhole*, *Blood Money*, *Moulin Rouge* and *The Affairs of Cellini*. These were 20th Century pictures released through United Artists. She also did extra work in *Bottoms Up* and *Hold That Girl* for Fox.

One of the people who befriended Lucy in her early days was George Raft. "He loaned me money for my rent once, and it took me years before I could pay it back," Lucy remembered. "I've never forgotten him for it. He gave away a fortune in the early days in Hollywood."

Although Lucille was never out of work, she wasn't progressing very far. "It galled her that schleps with no talent were getting billing while she wasn't," recalls a friend. "But she didn't let it get her down. She didn't scatter her energies by hating this one and that. She knew she wouldn't benefit by doing that."

The time had come to make a decision. "I was with Mr.

Goldwyn a year and a half. Then I asked him if I could go, for by that time I was a last-year's-Goldwyn Girl and I'd been relegated to the back row. Mr. Goldwyn was very nice. 'You can do better,' he said, 'and I'm sorry we don't have more for you to do here.' So I moved over to Columbia, where my principal work was being chased before a camera by Ted Healey and his Stooges."

Lucy signed with Columbia Pictures in the fall of 1934 and became a seventy-five-dollar-a-week contract player, a substantial salary drop from Goldwyn. But it was, she hoped, an opportunity to become something more than a permanent show girl.

In those days Columbia was strictly a B-picture studio. There, in addition to being cast without billing in comedy shorts starring The Three Stooges, she was given extra and bit work in Frank Capra's *Broadway Bill, Jealousy, Men of the Night, The Fugitive Lady* and *Carnival*. The last film, in which Lucy had a small role as a nurse, was the fifteenth in which she appeared, but it was the first picture in which she received screen billing. It was released in 1935.

On the strength of her Columbia contract, Lucille sent for her mother (who had divorced Ed Peterson), brother and grandfather. She rented a small, white-frame bungalow for the family to live in, in a modest neighborhood on a tree-lined street. Thirteen forty-four North Ogden Drive.

In the 1930s this little house would provide Lucille and her family with a secure, happy home base. But in the 1950s that address would plague Lucille Ball because of certain political activities supposedly carried on there.

Lucy was intent on making it in the movies. But the family had no sooner settled into their new home when Columbia dropped Lucy's option. The studio had decided to disband its stock company, which also included Gene Raymond and a pretty young blonde actress, Harriet Lake, whom Columbia boss Harry Cohn had renamed Ann Sothern. Lucy and Ann became friends and have remained so to the present.

Not one to waste time brooding, Lucy hustled over to the RKO studios and was lucky enough to land a job there, although she took another salary cut to fifty dollars a week. Lucy recalled, "I had a call from a friend, Dick Green. He said, 'RKO is looking for ex-Bergdorf girls.'" That was supposed to be a slightly higher caste of model. "Anyhow," Lucy went on, "I had worked a fashion show at Bergdorf's, so RKO tagged me."

Lucille's first film there was *Roberta*. She was typecast as a clotheshorse, complete with ostrich feathers, and she descended a staircase in a fashion show sequence. She herself has called the part "halfway between an extra and a bit." As usual, no billing.

After *Roberta*, RKO put Lucy under contract and into their talent school. She studied under studio drama coach Lela Rogers, mother of Ginger Rogers, who was coming into her own as one of RKO's top stars. Lucy later recalled, "When I was a beginner at RKO it was wonderful having Lela Rogers give us a stage, scripts to get our teeth into and an audience. That constitutes acting experience . . ."

She worked with Lela a couple of years and did several plays. "Lucy was a shrewd politician," notes a studio executive from that era. "Lela never at any time had any fears that Lucille would try to take over Ginger's top spot at the studio. Lela guarded Ginger like a drone watching over the queen bee. Of course, you can't blame her. She *is* Ginger's mother."

Lucy "ground 'em out." She was unbilled in *Old Man Rhythm*, played a florist's clerk (she had one line of dialogue) in the Ginger Rogers–Fred Astaire classic *Top Hat* and bits in *The Three Musketeers* and *Winterset*.

About these RKO days, Fred Astaire remembers, "Everyone liked Lucille very much. She was a lady very determined to make good, I could see that. And she had talent. She was

27

just doing small bits in my pictures, but you knew somehow or other there was a lot of something going on there."

Lucy began speaking up. She marched into her studio bosses and complained about being an extra. Her determination must have been evident, since they began giving her small speaking roles. Her first RKO screen billing came with a small role in *I Dream Too Much*, a film starring opera singer Lily Pons and upcoming actor Henry Fonda. Lucy and Fonda later became friends and sometimes double-dated with Fonda's roommate, James Stewart.

"Lucy usually didn't date guys her own age, though," recalls a friend. "She preferred older men. Men who knew their way around."

One actual incident that could have been straight out of "I Love Lucy" occurred during these early RKO contract years. One day Lucy was supposed to have publicity portraits taken. It was to be the most important photo-sitting she had had up to that time, the kind of expensive session that wasn't scheduled very often.

Excitedly, she went to make-up. The make-up man was brusque and told her he couldn't work on her because Katharine Hepburn (RKO's top star) was due any minute. Lucy implored him to help, explaining how important the photo session was. Reluctantly he agreed.

Lucy had with her a box containing some caps for her teeth. (Her smile was marred by a couple of chipped teeth and one missing tooth on the side, and she had had expensive caps made.) As she got into the make-up chair, she placed the box containing her caps on the counter. Barely ten minutes later, an assistant came dashing in: "Hepburn's coming! She's on her way!"

Lucy was practically thrown out of her chair. A few moments later Hepburn breezed in, businesslike as always. "Hallo," she said to Lucy as she went over to the make-up chair, concentrating on her script. The make-up man hustled Lucy out, and, in the anteroom, Lucy realized she had left her "teeth" on the table. And she couldn't have portraits taken without those caps!

She went next door and explained her predicament to a friendly wardrobe lady, who told her to go to a small window connecting wardrobe and make-up, through which she could talk to the make-up man. Lucy slid up the window and tried to catch the man's attention, but he pretended not to see her. She became angrier by the minute as he continued to ignore her.

A tray of coffee was resting on the window ledge. Absolutely frantic and totally frustrated, Lucille picked up a container of coffee and hurled it at him. It missed him but splattered all over Katharine Hepburn, drenching her.

Hepburn didn't utter a word. She sat motionless for a moment, then got up and went home, leaving word that she would be unable to work that day. She was filming an expensive costume picture, *Mary of Scotland*, and the day's production loss cost the studio thousands. Lucy was careful to avoid her for the next few weeks, but Hepburn didn't hold a grudge.

RKO cast Lucy in another small role, this time as a member of a summer stock company, in a turkey called *Chatterbox*. She made four other films in 1936: *Follow the Fleet*, another Astaire-Rogers blockbuster, in which Lucy played one of Ginger's sailor-minded girl friends; she played a script girl in *Farmer in the Dell*, a B-movie with Jean Parker and Esther Dale; and had a bit in the less-than-memorable *Bunker Bean*.

Finally she was assigned a good second lead, playing the blonde dancer-fiancée of Gene Raymond in another Lily Pons picture, *That Girl From Paris*. But the film was only a routine programmer and didn't get any major attention.

Lucille was still frustrated. Her progress was painfully slow, but at least her salary provided her family with a stability they hadn't enjoyed in years.

At home, Grandpa was active in socialist causes and was regarded by neighbors as he had been in Jamestown—"a real character."

Cleo, now seventeen, came to live with the family. Lucy had gotten Grandpa a job in the RKO woodworking department, but it was short lived. So Grandpa Hunt, or "Daddy," as Lucy, Cleo and Freddie called him, took to fooling around in the garden and making objects of wood in the garage. He also "took to nipping."

"He was forever fighting the establishment," recalls a neighbor. Once when the city of Los Angeles refused to allow him to cut down a tree in front of their North Ogden Drive house ("it blocked his view of the world going by") Grandpa Hunt secretly hacked away at the tree's roots, carefully replacing the sod after each session. One day during a rainstorm, as he planned, the tree fell over—unfortunately, right onto Lucille's new yellow convertible.

In his later years, Grandpa retired to his "corner." It was a place behind the front door where he read the *People's World* editorials and copies of *National Geographic*. And like most old people he tried to get any one he could to listen to his views on life and politics.

Lucy had taken over as the family organizer by now. It was she who got the family together for picnics in Griffith Park and led all the parades Grandpa used to lead. She has admitted that these early years in Hollywood were her "hey hey" period socially. She had a new beau every night, went to all the clubs, loved to dance and have a good time.

Though RKO had graduated her to speaking parts, Lucy was still dissatisfied. She decided to try the stage again and it looked as if her "big break" had finally arrived when she landed the lead in a musical comedy headed for Broadway called *Hey Diddle Diddle*, starring celebrity-of-the-day Conway Tearle. But the play opened at the McCarter Theatre in Princeton, New Jersey, on January 21, 1937, and closed in Philadelphia the following month.

Lucy later said, "If Conway Tearle hadn't died during the tour, *Hey Diddle Diddle* would have made Broadway."

She went back to Hollywood and RKO where they didn't exactly pull out all the stops in honor of her return. She was assigned a small supporting role in the Guy Kibbee comedy, *Don't Tell the Wife.*

While in San Francisco publicizing the picture, she saw a young dancer, Ann Miller, in a night club. Lucy was responsible for helping Ann secure a contract at RKO.

Ann remembers it vividly, "They had sent Lucy up to appear at the premiere. After the film opened, she and Benny Rubin, who had been a comedian and was at this point a talent scout, did a couple of the nightspots together. I was appearing at the Beau Tamerin and they saw me. Lucy told Rubin, 'Better call up Sam Briskin [he was head of RKO] and tell him we've seen this girl and she's great and they ought to give her a test.'

"Lucy Ball is, to me, of all the people I've met in this town, the most down-to-earth person. She has a great sense of humor and a good heart which a lot of these people don't have."

Ann was only thirteen when she was signed by RKO. There was some problem about her working in films because of her youth and she had to secure a fake birth certificate. "Lucille and Ginger Rogers stuck by me and upheld my fake age and fake birth certificate so the studio would keep me under contract."

Miss Miller says she herself mentioned to a wardrobe lady that she was only thirteen. "That's how it got around, and somebody threatened to turn my mother, and producer Pandro Berman, into the child labor union because I wasn't being schooled on the set. Lucy came forward and said, 'Look, I was there when she signed and her mother said she was eighteen years old. Why don't you just drop it and let it go at that?' "

Lucille Ball finally got *her* "big break" when director Gregory La Cava cast her as a wise-cracking would-be actress in RKO's prestige picture for 1937, *Stage Door*, which starred the studio's two biggest female stars: Katharine Hepburn and Ginger Rogers. Ann Miller and Eve Arden were also in the cast.

Discussing *Stage Door*, Ann Miller remembers, "It was like dog eat dog on that picture—even though everyone was very friendly. They were writing the script on the set and I remember there was quite a lot of tension between Ginger Rogers and Katharine Hepburn. Lucy helped relieve a lot of the strain because she would always laugh and joke and kid. Eve Arden was the same way, and thank God for them."

Ann also recalls that Ginger and Lucy were very close friends, really chums.

About Eve Arden, Lucy later noted: "She and I competed for years—one of us would be the lady executive and the other would be 'the other woman.' They were the same roles, for we'd walk through a room, drop a smart remark and exit. I called us 'the drop-gag girls.' I didn't dig it at all, for in such parts you lose your femininity."

Lucille scored a hit in *Stage Door* and RKO renegotiated her contract. She got a substantial raise and was cast as Irene Dunne's sister in *The Joy of Living*. She also got a role in *Having a Wonderful Time* as one of Ginger Rogers' roommates at a recreational camp. Lucy wangled a small role for her cousin Cleo in that film. And off set, she played camp counselor, organizing "fun and games" for the cast and crew.

At last Lucy's career was gaining momentum. She got another break when radio star Phil Baker, broadcasting from

Hollywood early in 1938, signed her as featured comedienne with his show. She was an instant hit. Then CBS radio comedian Joe Penner requested Lucy as his leading lady in his RKO film, *Go Chase Yourself*. Though *Having a Wonderful Time* was produced first, it was released after the Penner picture.

The public was starting to appreciate Lucille Ball. As was typical of Hollywood, the studio began glamorizing Lucille's past with official and almost totally fabricated biographies that read like this: "She's flown over South American jungles to shoot crocodiles from the sky; once she took an open-cockpit plane up in weather twenty degrees below freezing to effect the rescue of a schoolboy; she plays a fast game of polo; has a hobby of woodcarving; owns a profitable flower shop; and is one of Hollywood's best-dressed actresses. Such is a portrait of Lucille Ball, RKO Radio contract player who is fast climbing the ladder of cinema success."

They identified her birthplace as Butte, Montana, and her father was incorrectly labeled an electrical engineer with the Anaconda copper company. Her mother was described as a concert pianist. To account for the seven years Lucy struggled in New York, RKO summed it up as follows: "After a year and a half in New York, Miss Ball joined a stock company and traveled with them throughout the east."

The fanciful accounts continued: "Finally back in New York City, she was seen by Florenz Ziegfeld. Because of her height, build and ability to wear clothes, Miss Ball was given a job in the chorus of Ziegfeld's *Rio Rita*, and after a tour with the company she left it to become a mannequin with Hattie Carnegie."

To humanize and at the same time glamorize their contract player, RKO released the fictional, fantastic information that "In Jamestown, Miss Ball had her own plane, and during one winter's weekend visit with her family, her ability to fly saved the life of a schoolboy. It seems that two boys had gone out on Lake Chautauqua, sailing an iceboat. The weather was twenty degrees below freezing. Suddenly word came that the iceboat had upset and the boys were missing. Without waiting to hear further details, Lucille hopped into her plane, soared into the sky and began searching the lake for the boys.

"Within an hour she had located the boys. With a daring more experienced aviators would have shuddered at, Miss Ball landed the plane on the ice and effected the rescue of one of the lads. It was too late to help the other.

"Another daring experience came while visiting friends in Colombia, South America. 'We went for a long trip into the interior,' says Miss Ball, 'just because I wanted to see the jungle. When we stopped for the night, the natives told us we had better move on. For some unexplained reason the river had swelled and was overrun with great crocodiles. We drove back to a town where there was a wireless station and ordered an airplane to be delivered as soon as possible. Within two days the plane, a rickety old two-winger, arrived. The pilot and I went up and for nearly half a day we sent slugs of lead into those huge green beasts. The natives hailed us as their saviors and we all nearly died from eating, of all things, crocodile steak!'

"Miss Ball's flying days are over, however; that is, temporarily. When RKO officials learned of her daring once she gets behind the controls of an airplane, they felt something had to be done about this young lady's aerial exploits. So, not wanting to lose the services of the vivacious Miss Ball, even though Lady Luck has guided her so far, the studio ordered her grounded."

Studio biographies such as these were not unusual and the misinformation they contained would be repeated and believed through the years.

In 1938, since she had been such a hit on Phil Baker's show, Lucy was signed for weekly appearances on Jack Haley's CBS radio program, "Wonder Show."

Lucy had gotten her wish. She was working as hard as any woman could. In 1938 she appeared in seven films. One of them—*The Affairs of Annabel*—was important for her.

In *Annabel* she played a fading actress with an over-enthusiastic press agent, Jack Oakie, who gets her involved in publicity capers that land her in jail. The film did so well that RKO quickly threw together a sequel, *Annabel Takes a Tour*, released the same year.

Then came a featured part in *Room Service*, but even Lucy couldn't overshadow Harpo, Chico and Groucho Marx as they romped through the film version of the successful play. Lucy's other film released in 1938 was a "B" production, *The Next Time I Marry*, a comedy with James Ellison and Lee Bowman.

"Lucille would have become just as big without having appeared in all that crap," notes a friend today. "But it didn't hurt. She observed directors, how they worked, how they treated the various actors and got performances out of them. And don't forget, there was a caste system in Hollywood. The $500-a-week contract players looked down on the $250-a-week group, and so on down the line. And at the start Lucille was right at the bottom of that ladder.

"It was no picnic, like it was, for instance, for someone like Hedy Lamarr. Hedy had a big studio looking out for her interests all the time. Lucille had no such luck. She had to look out for her own interests."

It had been a busy five years. Lucy herself has candidly summed it up, "I came out to Hollywood to do an Eddie Cantor picture with twelve to fourteen show girls, right? They had more experience, more money, knew their way around. Yet I made it and they didn't. Why? Maybe because they turned down more working jobs for social opportunities and I did just the opposite. As a result, I've never been out of work in this town except for two hours once between contracts."

Lucy did have time for some social life, however. In 1938

35

she was dating Broderick Crawford and they became engaged for a brief period. One of her other beaux was a sexy Cuban named Mario who had quite a reputation as an uninhibited lover. She also dated Brian Donlevy and, a bit later, "wonder boy" Orson Welles.

At this time, David O. Selznick was screen-testing every actress in Hollywood under forty for the most coveted role of them all: Scarlett O'Hara in *Gone With the Wind*. Lucille realized she wasn't exactly perfect for the part, but Selznick had asked studios to submit their contract actresses for auditions.

RKO casting chief Ben Piazza summoned several of his studio's actresses, including, of course, Lucille. Piazza explained that the studio wanted the girls to try out for the role of Scarlett and gave them script pages with three scenes from the film. He told them to study the pages and be ready to audition in three weeks.

Filing out of the casting office, Lucille was bewildered. "This is ridiculous!" she exclaimed. "Me play Scarlett O'Hara? Impossible!"

However, Lucille had no choice but to comply with her studio's wishes. She worked on the early scene in which Scarlett tries to charm Ashley, "I do declare, Ashley Wilkes, I don't for the life of me understand what you see in that skinny little Melanie . . ."

Lucy practiced in front of a mirror, but felt she couldn't make herself sound like Scarlett. The accent was giving her trouble.

She made an appointment with Will Price, the southern scholar who had been hired by Selznick as an adviser on the film. As always she was an eager pupil and Price helped Lucy to approximate a Georgia accent. She returned for more lessons and became friendly with Marcella Rabwin, Selznick's executive secretary. Miss Rabwin was sympathetic to Lucy, who appeared scared.

Actually Lucy was more terrified than scared! It rained in Los Angeles on the day of her audition, and her drenched Studebaker just about made it to the Culver City studio.

She was dripping wet when she arrived at Marcella Rabwin's office, and out of breath, she panted: "I just dropped by to say I can't make the audition today."

"But you're here, aren't you?" queried Marcella. "You might as well stay. Mr. Selznick is looking forward to meeting you."

Lucille was terrified. "Mr. Selznick! You mean I'm supposed to see *him* today? But I can't!"

Marcella assured her she could. "You'll feel better after I get you an aspirin."

"But I don't need an aspirin."

"Then I'll pour you some brandy."

"I don't drink brandy."

"Then I'll make you some nice hot tea."

Marcella took Lucy into Selznick's office and helped her out of her wet boots. She brought the tea and suggested that Lucille practice her lines before Selznick returned from lunch. Lucy dropped down on a couch and spread the script pages in front of her. She drank the tea and went over the lines. She fell to her knees.

"Ah do declah, Ashley Wilkes, ah don' foh the lahf of me understand what yo see in that skinny little Melanie," she read.

"That was a very good reading, Miss Ball."

Lucille jumped at the sound of the voice behind her. She turned and saw Selznick's burly form. Her blue eyes widened.

"I . . . I was just practicing," she said.

"Yes, and it was very good indeed. Please go on." He went to his seat behind his desk.

"Go on?"

"Yes, I'd like to hear you do all three scenes."

37

Lucille attacked the scenes with all the energy she could muster.

The last was the film's final scene where Scarlett utters the famous lines: "I'll think about it tomorrow, at Tara. Tomorrow, I'll think of some way to get him back. After all, tomorrow is another day."

As she finished, tears rolled down Lucille's cheeks. Selznick seemed genuinely moved. "Very good, Miss Ball."

"Did you really think so?" She was hopeful.

"Yes. We'll let you know our decision. Thank you for coming."

"Then I can go now?"

"Yes. Here, let me help you."

As he came from around his desk to assist her, Lucy suddenly realized that she had played all three scenes on her knees!

Nineteen thirty-nine was another hectic year. Lucy was steady-dating Columbia director Alexander Hall, ex-husband of actress Lola Lane. Columnists hinted that Lucille would be the next Mrs. Hall.

Lloyd Nolan remembers, "I first met Lucy on location of a movie I was doing with Fred MacMurray, *Exclusive*. The film was being directed by Al Hall. It was almost childlike, Lucy's interest and enthusiasm in everything and everybody. Everything was an adventure. Eveything was a great burst of joy to her and it was infectious."

Lucy's career was rolling. As a result of her *Annabel* films she was being touted as one of the "luminaries in the 1939 Galaxy of New Stars." But instead of building her into an "A" picture star, RKO cast her in five potboilers: *Beauty for the Asking*; *Twelve Crowded Hours*; *Panama Lady*; *That's Right You're Wrong*, a film version of Kay Kyser's radio show; and *Five Came Back*, which presented Lucy in her first "heavy" dramatic role. She believably played a hard-boiled tramp stranded with eleven other passengers in a South American jungle after an airline crash. (The film was remade seventeen years later as *Back From Eternity* with Anita Ekberg playing Lucy's role.)

By now, Lucille Ball was established as "Queen of the B-movies" at RKO. She was making big money—about $1,500 a week—and had certainly succeeded in making a name for herself. However, she had no illusions about her status in films and no intention of letting up the hard work.

"With the crap they gave her, it's amazing she lasted as long as she did at RKO. Greta Garbo couldn't have raised the level of those scripts," says an ex-RKO executive. "But the kid was dependable, likeable and worked hard. Maybe if Ginger Rogers had left the studio sooner, Lucille would have gotten better scripts. But the thinking was that Ginger was the 'A' picture star and Lucy was a moneymaker in 'Bs'. And that was that."

In 1940, RKO starred Lucy in four more forgettable films (including *The Marines Fly High*, with Richard Dix and Chester Morris; *You Can't Fool Your Wife*, with James Ellison; *Dance, Girl, Dance*, with Maureen O'Hara and Ralph Bellamy). Lucy played a gold-digging chorus girl in *Dance, Girl, Dance*, directed by Dorothy Arzner. In one sequence she did a modified striptease while singing "My Mother Taught Me" (her voice was dubbed).

Lucille was "almost box office." Producer Erich Pommer hailed her, somewhat belatedly, as "a new find."

It was on the set of *Dance, Girl, Dance* that twenty-nine-year-old Lucille met the handsome, sexy twenty-three-year-old Latin bandleader-singer just signed by RKO: **Desi Arnaz.**

3

Desɪ's ʀɪsᴇ from a bongo-beating performer at the Roney Plaza to stardom on Broadway had been relatively fast.

While appearing in Miami, he was spotted by Xavier Cugat, superstar of Latin band impresarios. He was signed as Cugat's headline singer, but his salary was only thirty-five dollars a week. For a while Desi was "afraid to quit for a better job," but Cugat's band manager, Nick Niccolette, urged him: "Go out on your own. If you're good enough you can go to the top."

So, after eight months with Cugat, swelled by success and the desire to make it alone, Desi left the band and returned to Miami with Niccolette, who had also quit.

"We had only twenty dollars between us," Desi said, "but by the time we were down to our last five bucks we had made a connection with a man who was opening a nightspot. Nick and I accepted a job for 'our five-piece Cuban band.' Except for me, the leader, there wasn't a Cuban in the bunch.

"Three Brooklyn boys handled the piano, saxophone and violin. There was a Spaniard on the drums, an Italian boy on the bass. We sounded terrible."

According to Desi, the band had only played one set when they were given two weeks' notice. Luckily, radio personality Ted Husing was there and suggested the club owner reconsider. "The band isn't much but the young lead singer has something. If you'll keep him, I'll broadcast his music free every night on my radio program."

It was a big break for Desi. The band stayed, too, but Desi knew the score. "They were so lousy I had to figure something to drown them out. That's why I started the first conga line in the U.S."

Desi contends that the conga rhythm originated in his hometown, Santiago, during carnival time, and that he was the first to bring it to the United States.

The La Conga night club, on 52nd Street in New York, signed Desi and he played there for a year. The young, eligible bachelor was the hit of New York and Long Island café society; everyone important in town caught his act. And then Rodgers and Hart offered him a part in their musical *Too Many Girls*. Desi decided to take the plunge and try Broadway.

It was the right choice. Desi received good notices.

RKO bought the screen rights and cast their Queen of the B's, Lucille Ball, in the leading role. Desi was signed to recreate his conga-playing Cuban playboy role.

Lucy was filming *Dance, Girl, Dance* while George Abbott was conducting production meetings on *Too Many Girls*. The group at the studio had given Lucille a fantastic build-up to Desi.

Desi remembered, "The first time I saw Lucy was in a Hollywood studio lunchroom. Lovely, dazzling Lucille Ball was to be one of the stars of *Too Many Girls*. I was eager to meet her. Then she walked in. She had a black eye, frowzy hair and was wearing a too-tight black dress with a rip in it. She

41

had been playing a dance-hall floozy in a free-for-all fight scene. I groaned, 'Oh, no!' That afternoon, when she showed up on the set where I was working, I said, 'Oh, yes!' She had fixed her hair and make-up and put on a sweater and skirt. She was a dream. I took one look and fell in love."

"He asked me for a date that very night," Lucy recalled. While she had heard reports of Desi's sex appeal, she had dismissed them as press-agentry. "But when I saw him, I realized what they were all talking about."

Ann Miller confirms this. "I was in the room when Desi and Lucy first met, and it was like love at first sight. When he first was introduced to her, her eyes just lit up. He was the cutest thing around. God, was he attractive."

That night Desi took Lucille to a club, ostensibly to teach her how to rhumba. The electricity between them was undeniable.

Ann Miller (back at RKO for *Too Many Girls*) double-dated with Lucy and Desi. "I used to date Desi. But after he met Lucy I started dating George Abbott. The four of us would go to The Serape, which was a night club up above an old market, way down on Sunset Boulevard. It was an all-Cuban place. Both of us gals really learned how to do a mean, mad rhumba."

Ann recalls that Desi "got around pretty good. He was always like a big, big kid. He was a great guy. I don't think anybody could play drums like Desi Arnaz. He would work hard all day long and yet he would be dressed and ready to go out to live it up at night—play his drums and dance up a storm, sing, whatever. And he was very nice. At night clubs if people wanted him to get up and sing and dance, he would do it—he would even lead the conga line."

To cynical Hollywoodites, the Ball-Arnaz dating at first seemed like just another studio courtship.

They loved to argue, constantly contradicting each other. An observer on the set of *Too Many Girls* recalls, "It was like a running vaudeville gag. Lucille and Desi would get into an argument, both insisting they were right and yelling 'I'll betcha! I'll betcha!' Then they'd bring out dictionaries, encyclopedias or they'd call the newspapers and libraries to settle their arguments."

About these early days and all the arguing, Lucy has said: "We couldn't have learned more if we'd been in college. His department was facts and figures and sports, especially horse racing. Mine was women—I taught Desi a lot about women."

Naturally, Desi was introduced to Lucy's family. Of Grandpa Hunt, Desi said: "Grandpa! A beautiful man. I loved him! Couldn't get in the door without his reading all those *People's World* editorials. I told him to cut it out or I'd teach him how to rhumba."

After *Too Many Girls* completed production, Desi organized his Latin band and with the money he earned from the film bought two busses and hit the road. It was the first of many separations Lucy and Desi would have to endure.

The studio put Lucy into *A Girl, a Guy and a Gob*, the first movie Harold Lloyd produced in which he didn't star.

"Practically every morning," Lucy recalled, "Harold would hand us new pages of script. George Murphy and I would read them over and start arguing. To us it seemed no good at all. But Harold would say, 'Please trust me and give it a try.' At the end of the picture I said to George, 'Too bad. We might have had a fairly good picture if things had been different.'

"You could have knocked me over with a feather at the preview. The audience just howled. It was a smash hit. That taught me not to argue too much with producers, which was probably the wrong psychology."

Dance, Girl, Dance was released in August 1940 and *Too Many Girls* in October. *Gob* was scheduled to be released the following year. RKO sent Lucy on a cross-country publicity tour, and when she arrived in New York late in 1940

43

her courtship with Desi resumed. He was winding up his tour with an engagement at New York's Roxy Theatre.

Lucy wasn't the only leading lady in Hollywood who succumbed to Desi's charms. His other dates included Betty Grable and Ginger Rogers. Ginger was very interested in the studio's new "hot-blooded Latin," and as a far more important star than Lucille, she could have advanced Desi's film career. However, the chemistry between Lucy and Desi was obviously overwhelming. "And aside from being in love with Lucy, Desi is a man with strong personal integrity who wouldn't then—or at any time—use any woman that way," notes a close friend of his.

Lucy was crazy about Desi "in spite of the way he drove a car. The first time I drove with him," she recalled, "although he slowed to eighty miles per hour at corners, I thought he was a maniac. When I said, 'Mother wouldn't like this,' he slowed down. On another date he hit a low spot in the paving on a side street. Desi merely said, 'We dropped something,' and kept on going. I'll say we dropped something— only a fender and a bumper."

Their affair was in constant turmoil. "There was more than an undeniable physical attraction," notes a friend. "They were emotional dynamite to each other. Heated arguments all the time, their explosive temperaments clashing. And then there would be intense reconciliations."

Sheilah Graham, a Lucy-Desi observer, recounted: "Scott Fitzgerald and I watched them from the balcony of his apartment on Laurel Drive while Lucille, who lived in the same building as Scott, courted Desi Arnaz. She always seemed to be asking him not to drive away, to stay. We couldn't understand his reluctance and sometimes made bets on the outcome. No matter which of us lost, we were both pleased when Lucille won."

Lucy and Desi had courted in night clubs in Hollywood

44

and now continued in New York's clubs. One night at El Morocco, he demanded: "Why wait around like this? Let's do it and get it over with."

The story goes that Lucille reacted unfavorably to this proposition and Desi quickly apologized, adding: "Honey, I don't know your language so good. I mean I can't wait any longer to get married."

On the evening of November 30, 1940, Lucille Ball and Desi Arnaz eloped to Greenwich, Connecticut, to be married by a justice of the peace. The ceremony was supposed to be in the judge's house but instead took place at the Byram River Beagle Club.

"Maybe it doesn't sound very romantic," Lucy said, "but actually it was. The judge took us there because he said all young people who were going to spend a lifetime together should start off in as romantic a setting as possible. He drove us out himself."

It appeared to many to be an unlikely match, doomed to quick failure. He was typically Latin: temperamental, hot blooded and at the same time rigidly conventional, with a double-standard attitude about women. He also was fun loving and his career only meant making enough money to live lavishly.

Lucy was career-oriented, and, though not a major star in Hollywood, she enjoyed a certain status which she had worked hard to achieve and had no intention of giving up. Desi was a bold man who "lived dangerously and appealed to women." Did the danger appeal to Lucille? "No," she said. "He frightened me. Marrying Desi was the boldest thing I ever did."

The Arnazes have always been accused of being press-conscious. A day after their marriage a magazine writer came to interview them in their hotel suite in New York. Lucille was alone. Almost immediately Lucy told the writer, "I'd love to let you copy the love telegrams we sent each other, but I'm afraid Desi would be mad if I made them public." But she couldn't resist displaying them.

Then there was the sound of a key at the door and Lucille swept the telegrams under a cushion as Desi walked in.

His first suggestion to the interviewer was, "Let's use those love telegrams for the article." The telegrams were promptly brought out of their hiding place.

During another interview, Desi turned to Lucille and said: "Darling, I love you more than Antony loved Cleopatra, more than . . ." Abruptly, he turned back to the reporter and asked: "Did you get that down? I'll repeat it. Darling, I love . . ."

Soon after the wedding Lucy resumed her cross-country tour for RKO.

By movie colony standards of the day, Lucy and Desi were two fairly unimportant people. In fact, there were no movie roles at all for Desi. He had been typed as a Latin with a heavy accent who could dance, sing and play the drums.

Desi's shrewd business acumen was evident even in 1940. The newlyweds bought a five-acre ranch in Northridge, twenty miles from Hollywood in the San Fernando Valley. It was one of the best deals Desi could have transacted—complete with swimming pool, stables and a rambling ranch house. He got it for $18,000.

If Desi had been content to stay home and be Mr. Lucille Ball, he could have remained in Hollywood. If he wanted to work and be independent, he had no choice but to travel with his band.

RKO announced plans for a film with Lucy and Desi and radio superstars Edgar Bergen and Charlie McCarthy and Fibber McGee and Molly. But Desi was dropped from the cast. The film, *Look Who's Laughing*, was made and released in 1941.

Lucy was appearing as a regular on Edgar Bergen's radio program. Desi was traveling, and he and Lucy spent a great deal of time on the telephone. (They later estimated they spent over $29,000 on long-distance calls during the years they were separated.) There was always an excuse to call— usually just to hear each other's voice.

"We spent a lot of money on the word 'what', " Lucy recalled. "When Desi was calling me or I was calling him from little towns, the connection was always so bad we couldn't hear each other. That's why 'what' was so expensive."

When asked if she and Desi ever got jealous of each other, she answered, "Yes, we certainly do. That's all, sister—don't ask for particulars—we just do."

Desi was breaking box-office records all over the country. He was climbing towards the status of Dorsey, Shaw and Cugat as an in-person attraction. But Hollywood producers saw him only as "a Latin type."

While she was between pictures for RKO, Lucy managed to work with Desi and his band early in 1942, appearing with him in his stage revue at Loew's State in New York City. Critics noted, "Miss Ball and Mr. Arnaz have created an act made up of singing, dancing, and amusing dialogue, and their presentation is entertaining. They sing 'South American Way,' 'You and I,' and 'Cuban Pete'; they dance the rhumba and conga, and Arnaz beats the conga drum and sings 'Babalu.' "

Lucy was in vaudeville at last. But she and Desi weren't able to tour together indefinitely, and Desi recalled feeling during this period that, "marriage is no good on a long-distance-telephone basis, and I thought if I got into another musical play it would help. So I hung around New York, eating at '21.' In a letter Lucy told me, 'The trouble with the "21" is if you eat there it means people think you're so successful you're not looking for a job. Eat at Sardi's.'

" 'Everybody is always reading his own reviews at Sardi's,'

I argued, but Lucy insisted, so I went to Sardi's every night for a month. Nobody even said hello, and I went back to '21.' "

RKO cast Lucy in a western potboiler, *Valley of the Sun*, with James Craig. After this assignment Lucy went on suspension from salary for refusing to play the second feminine lead in *Strictly Dynamite*, to star her ex-RKO chum Betty Grable and Victor Mature at 20th Century-Fox on a loan-out deal.

"This shows you how her career was being handled," remarks a leading agent of the day. "Her studio wasn't interested in building her into a long-range star. They were content to make a quick buck on a loan-out, even though it would have been bad for her career."

One of Lucy's Hollywood friends was Carole Lombard, who introduced her to Damon Runyon. Runyon realized Lucille would be perfect as the "heroine" of his story, "Little Pinks," which was going to be made into a film by RKO.

Runyon insisted the studio cast her in the lead—a hard, bitchy, supremely egotistical night-club singer crippled by her gangster boyfriend and befriended by a mild-mannered busboy who falls in love with her.

The role of the busboy went to Henry Fonda. It was finally a major RKO film for Lucy. The cast also included Barton MacLane, Agnes Moorehead, Ozzie Nelson and his orchestra. Lucy's singing voice was dubbed by Martha Nears.

Charles Laughton had once told Lucy, "If you ever play a bitch, play the bitchiest bitch who ever breathed." Gloria Lyons, the leading character in *The Big Street* (the film title of "Little Pinks"), filled the bill: "A girl with a foolish, unhealthy obsession which made her more ruthless than Scarlett O'Hara. It was anything but a sympathetic part," Lucy noted, "but it was exciting because it was so meaty—so rich in humor, pathos and tragedy.

"I don't feel *The Big Street* was as fine a picture as it

deserved to be. To some extent it was jinxed. The moment shooting was finished, Damon Runyon left the studio, the director joined the Army, and the editor dropped dead while he was cutting the picture. Thus, before an important phase of the work was finished, the three men who knew most about the picture were gone."

While *The Big Street* may not have turned out as well as Lucy felt it should have, it was still excellent and received good reviews. It was her best performance to date (many feel it still is her best dramatic performance). *Life* said, "The girl can really act." Respected critic James Agee wrote: "Pretty Lucille Ball, who was born for the parts Ginger Rogers sweats over, tackles her 'emotional' role as if it were sirloin and she didn't care who was looking."

The Big Street brought Lucy a contract offer from MGM. Lucy recalled, "During my time at RKO my pay went to $3,500 a week but I was only Queen of the B's. So I asked for my release and went to MGM."

Years later, though, Lucy admitted: "Charlie Koerner, who was general manager at RKO, said, 'Lucy, you should be doing better things.' And he sold half my contract to MGM. I almost had to be pushed out. I didn't care whether they were 'B' or 'D' pictures, as long as I was working."

While the move to MGM seemed to be a great opportunity—the biggest studio of them all, big salary, security—Lucy was, in effect, putting herself in direct competition with the leading young glamour girls of the day—Lana Turner (who was then twenty-two) and Hedy Lamarr. And she had unbeatable competition for straight dramatic roles at the studio: Katharine Hepburn, Greer Garson, Margaret Sullavan, Irene Dunne. While Lucy was capable of a wide range of roles, the studio initially saw her as a glamour girl and proceeded to give her that kind of build-up. Younger girls were also getting the glamour build-up—Kathryn Grayson, Donna Reed, Esther Williams.

However, Metro was pleased to get Lucy. With a studio

49

full of problem children, Lucille Ball was a dependable, ambitious, steady, talented worker and Louis B. Mayer respected her. She was given the dressing room that once belonged to Norma Shearer. The studio's best make-up people were assigned to her and then came a "momentous" change in her appearance.

When they were color-testing Lucille for her first MGM picture, Sydney Guilaroff, Metro's chief hair stylist, had an inspiration. "The hair is brown," he said, "but the soul is on fire." They dyed Lucy's hair a bright henna. The wild carrot-pink shade became her trademark. When people protest that nobody ever had that shade of hair, she firmly says: "*I do.*"

"When I chose this shade, things began to break for me," Lucy explained. "It gave me just the right finishing touch before the cameras. Maybe I didn't look so good in person but I wasn't worrying about that."

Her initial MGM vehicle, *DuBarry Was a Lady*, co-starred her friend Red Skelton. The film was regarded as Lucille's "first real opportunity to become a big-time star." The thirty-nine films that had come before were described by *Life* as "honky-tonk" pictures.

Ironically, throughout most of *DuBarry* Lucy wore a huge powdered white wig covering her new hair color. The film was a typical Technicolor extravaganza of the day, and enjoyed good—but not spectacular—box office.

During these war years Lucy was one of a bevy of stars who went on bond-selling tours. Although Fred Astaire did not work with Lucy while they were both at MGM, he did make a six-week bond tour with her. "She had a lot of spunk, a lot of pep and she wasn't afraid of telling people what she thought," he remembers. "She was one of the busy workers. I know she resented being a leading lady in B films. That bored her to death. She wanted to be queen."

Astaire remembers that Lucy liked things her own way

50

and would get angry if they weren't. "She likes to run things —period. That's it. And she doesn't care who she tells how to act or how to move or how to do anything. She's never done that with me, of course. I never worked with her like that."

Other friends describe Lucy during these years as "down to earth and refreshingly non-Hollywood." Once, at a celebrity-studded party, one MGM glamour girl was coming on "like she believed her own publicity." Lucy smiled at the girl's posing, sauntered over and said to her, "Aw, why don't you be yourself!"

During the war Lucy also worked some camp shows with Bob Hope. "It wasn't easy at first. He'd always offer to rehearse, but he never found time for it. He'd get off the plane, be swallowed by all the brass, then I'd wait for him to get back, but he never would. He'd turn up next on stage, and there I'd be, waiting in the wings, not knowing the answer to *one* joke!"

Although Lana Turner was originally cast in *Best Foot Forward*, she became pregnant, so the studio gave Lucy the starring role—a movie star who accepts an invitation to a college prom. It was in some respects a comedy part, and in every way an "A" production, produced by Arthur Freed and directed by Edward Buzzell. It also served as June Allyson's film debut.

Next came a cameo in MGM's star-filled wartime musical, *Thousands Cheer*. Lucy, old friend Ann Sothern (who was now Queen of the B's at Metro) and Marsha Hunt were in an amusing sequence in which, as prospective Waves, they were medically examined by Frank Morgan.

While Lucy's status and salary had increased, there were still no Hollywood roles for Desi. He stayed on the road much of the time. The relationship between the two volatile personalities became strained. Hollywood wags had predicted the marriage's demise from the beginning. "How could it last if she was a big star and Desi just a bandleader?" they asked. In Hollywood, an entertainer was nothing unless he was in pictures.

World War II held off the marital disaster temporarily. After refusing a commission in the Cuban Army, Desi was drafted by Uncle Sam into the infantry in February, 1943. He was later transferred to Special Services.

Before going on a USO tour in the Caribbean, Desi called Lucille from Washington to tell her he would be incommunicado for three weeks. A few days later MGM told Lucy they wanted her husband for a big part in their major war epic, *Bataan*. It was a role tailor-made for Desi and he had been dying to play it. Of course they needed him immediately—if they need you at all in Hollywood, they need you immediately.

Lucy got on the phone and several hours, many Pentagon colonels and hundreds of dollars later, she got through to the airport on Bluebeard Island in the Caribbean. As Desi's plane landed, he heard himself being paged and rushed to the phone, sure that Lucy was dead or at least badly injured. He was elated by the good news and arranged to get a leave to return to Hollywood to make the film.

Desi delivered a brilliant performance in *Bataan*, and at last he and Lucy felt his movie career was launched.

Lloyd Nolan worked with Desi in *Bataan*. "He was a lot of fun," he remembers. "He had a death scene he was really counting on. He was to get to say the Lord's Prayer when he died. He was terribly disappointed, however, to learn he would have to say it in Spanish and nobody understood what he was saying. But he was good in the film."

But, after *Bataan*, nothing. So it was back to Special Services for Desi, and the long separation from Lucille resumed as he shepherded USO troops from base to base.

Then Desi was assigned to the Special Services office at the Army's Birmingham General Hospital near Van Nuys, outside of Hollywood. It was there he arranged to get a "hot" car. At that time it was almost impossible to get a new car because industry was totally geared to the war effort.

Lucy remembered the incident. "Our car was falling apart. Desi was away, and I was home one afternoon when a stranger rounded the corner. He asked, 'Is Deesee here?' I said, 'Do you mean Desi?' and he said, 'Yes, Deesee.' I said, 'He's in Chicago,' and he said, 'I've got his car here. He ordered it eight weeks ago. You'd better make up your mind, sister. A lot of people want this crate.'

"I looked at it. It was fire-engine red; it screamed when it saw my pink hair. I said, 'I'm sorry, but we won't be able to take it. You'll have to get another color, maybe blue.' He went away mumbling, and when Desi called me that night I said, airily, 'Your car came today, but I sent it back.' He practically climbed through the phone, and after a few husbandly remarks, I called the man back at midnight and said, 'I hope you haven't done anything with that car. I've just had hell bawled out of me.' So we got it, and I kept my hair covered when I was in it."

During the war years Grandpa Hunt died. As he had gotten older, he had become harder to manage. His socialist views and moralistic attitudes had created many problems for DeDe and the family. One of his pastimes was to go down to the corner where the "hookers" hung out, lecture them on the evils of the oldest profession and offer them five dollars to "take the night off."

During the war Grandpa had been an air raid warden, but, since he had a hernia, by the time the family helped him into his truss the all-clear had usually been sounded.

Cleo was now engaged to Ken Morgan, a press agent who later became Lucy's press agent.

When Grandpa Hunt died the entire family—Desi, Lucy, Ken, Cleo, DeDe and Freddie—piled into a Cadillac and rode to the cemetery to bury him.

"It was wild," Morgan has recalled. "We kept topping each other's Grandpa stories, and before long we were laughing instead of crying."

Lucy was not pleased with her next film, a routine comedy, *Meet the People,* co-starring Dick Powell and bandleader Spike Jones. It was hardly an "A" effort and was indicative of the studio's less-than-enthusiastic approach to her career.

An ex-MGM employee notes, "Hollywood in the Forties was like a huge clubhouse. Studios were the protective mothers to their star-children, taking care of absolutely everything in their lives—any problems, go to the studio, they'll solve 'em.

"However, it wasn't all judy-poo wonderful. It's absolutely true that plenty went on between actresses and producers, directors, casting directors. You name it and there were plenty of broads who would do it just for the chance to be in films.

"It sure as hell would have been easy for a broad like Lucy, who was big and impressive looking, to have used that route. But she wouldn't and didn't and that's probably why she never had the kind of build-up that some of her contemporaries had. Lucille wouldn't sleep with a producer for a role, and consequently the roles often went to other far less capable, but far more accommodating, gals.

"Now Lucy wasn't alone in this attitude, of course. There were a handful of others—but believe me, buddy, they were in the minority."

And by now, the fiery, on-again, off-again, constantly-arguing-and-making-up Arnaz marriage had reached the breaking point.

Lucy was an old-fashioned girl who believed in fidelity and "one man." Desi was an old-fashioned Latin who had the classic double standard. His wife was his wife and he knew he could depend on her and trust her and was secure in that knowledge. Like most Latins, he would "fool around" and this would in no way affect his love for his wife. That relationship was sacred and had nothing to do with his indiscretions with women who threw themselves at him and who, in his eyes, were nothing more than tramps not worth more than casual intimacy.

However, this "arrangement" wasn't regarded too highly by Lucy. Friends asked Desi to be more discreet but as one former pal explained, "He tried being careful but it just wasn't in his nature to sneak around."

Desi's extramarital interests, coupled with pressures created by their careers, made life a rather tense existence for the Arnazes. But they had something special going for them, emotionally and sexually, that somehow welded them together and enabled them to weather all the heavy personal storms.

Up to this point, Lucy and Desi had always enjoyed a "love in the limelight" romance. Their courtship and wedding were as private as a movie premiere. They obviously considered themselves in the public domain and apparently made every attempt to remain there. However, during this period of problems and separation they shunned publicity and would give out no statements.

Suddenly, in September, 1944, Lucille filed for divorce charging "extreme mental cruelty." "I couldn't believe it," said a friend. "I had a dinner date with them for that very night!"

No community property was involved in the divorce action and Lucille's attorney said, "We expect Sergeant Arnaz to waive his right to postpone trial of the suit until after he leaves the service."

Desi complied, and on October 15, Lucille was awarded

an interlocutory decree. She testified at the trial, "He was spending too much money. When we argued about it, he became angry and went away. I never saw him for a week.

"That was a habit of his—going away whenever we had an argument. He always ran out on me rather than stay and talk the matter out. It left me a nervous wreck. I got no rest at night at all."

During the previous summer, when an interviewer had registered surprise that the marriage had lasted for almost four years, Lucy replied: "Me? I gave it a week."

4

THE ON-AGAIN, off-again relationship was on again within a month. Lucille and Desi decided to call off their divorce a week before their fourth wedding anniversary.

Years later, Lucy revealed, "I paid $2,000 for that divorce. I can show you the receipts." Desi added, "But it was never finalized, was it, baby? I could only stand to be away from her for a few weeks."

Lucy also later disclosed, "The day I got the interlocutory decree I went home and there he was."

Desi moved back into the couple's ranch house and was given a leave from the Army. Though he and Lucy were reconciled, their relationship didn't change much.

One day a friend ran into Desi sleeping in a big lounge chair in the lobby of the Beverly Hills Hotel. Rooms were very hard to get during wartime.

"Why don't you go home to sleep?" she asked Desi.

"I did," he said, "but Lucy had me locked out."

Lucy's career at MGM had definitely passed its peak. She hadn't quite caught on as a leading lady, so the studio cast her in a drop-gag role as the smart-aleck career girl opposite Keenan Wynn in the Spencer Tracy-Katharine Hepburn vehicle, *Without Love*. Lucy was billed below the title.

Then she appeared as a "glamorous siren" in a lavish, ridiculous production number of *Ziegfeld Follies of 1946*, which comes off as strictly camp by today's standards. "I was tall and long legged. I couldn't sing and I couldn't dance," Lucy said, "so MGM starred me as a costume horse in *Ziegfeld Follies*, cracking a whip over eight chorus-girl panthers."

Behind-the-scenes people at Metro remember Lucille as the court jester, "a good egg," not pretentious, always down to earth, always friendly with the crew.

A friend laughingly recalls a time when an interviewer, a bosom-conscious columnist, seldom bothered to glance above Lucy's chin level while firing questions at her. Lucille chatted away and, at the end of the interview, totally unruffled by the columnist's steady stare at her breasts, casually reached into her bodice, plucked out the padding and elaborately wielded it as a powder puff, without missing a beat of conversation. "That writer damn near keeled over backwards."

Clowning is part of Lucy's nature. Another time MGM dance director Jack Donahue, a hard taskmaster, was assigned to work with Lucy on a number for a film. Jack put her through the paces the first day. The next day Buster Keaton pushed Lucy to the rehearsal hall in a wheelchair. She had one arm in a sling, blacked-out teeth, tousled hair and a bruised cheek—all done courtesy of the studio make-up expert. In her "good' hand she carried a sign: "I am not working for Donahue. Period." She had fun parading her fake injuries all over the lot before she suffered a sudden misgiving that the gag had embarrassed Donahue. Concerned, she asked him, "You don't think anybody took me seriously, do you, Jack?"

On tour with the Goldwyn Girls. Lucille is on the far right, back row.

Twenty-two-year-old Lucille Ball, Goldwyn Girl on far left. The 1933 film *Roman Scandals* starred Eddie Cantor.

The red hair came later. This is blonde Lucy in 1934.

Lucy was briefly engaged to actor Broderick Crawford, 1937.

Lucille's penchant for props was evident even in the mid '30s.

Newlyweds Lucille Ball and Desi Arnaz, 1940.

A trio of rising RKO players:
Edmond O'Brien, Lucille
Ball, George Murphy.

Lucille steady-dated director
Alexander Hall, an "older man."

On a visit to New York, Lucille met
Mayor Fiorello H. La Guardia.

Lucille Ball had graduated to bit parts by 1935.

Sergeant Desi Arnaz dancing with his wife at The Trocadero. Their marital problems were already making news.

Lucille's best dramatic performance, *The Big Street*, 1942. With Agnes Moorehead, Eugene Pallette, Henry Fonda.

Lucille and Desi in Desi's habitat—the night club.

At the Stork Club.

With orchestra leader Darryl Harpa

On a war bond tour. With Judy
Canova and Dennis Morgan.

Lucille Ball, glamour girl, circa 1939.

Mrs. Eleanor Roosevelt with Hollywood friends Red Skelton, Lucille Ball and John Garfield.

With pal William Holden, who starred with Lucy in *Miss Grant Takes Richmond*.

Lucille at the height of her "glamour" period, 1946. She was thirty-five.

With co-star Richard Denning on CBS's hit radio show, "My Favorite Husband."

The Famous Foursome: Vivian Vance, Lucille Ball, William Frawley, Desi Arnaz.

Lucy made such an impact as a clown on the radio show, CBS executives wanted her for a comedy TV series.

Though typed as a glamour girl, her flair for comedy surfaced off-camera.

Signing the historic eight-million-dollar contract.

The Arnazes celebrating their tenth wedding anniversary, 1950.

Buster Keaton, under contract to MGM at this time, was bored. The studio felt he had "had it" and didn't assign him any films. Eddie Sedgwick, a director under contract to the studio, was considered "incurably old fashioned" and was idle too. Keaton, Sedgwick and Lucy, who by then was considered relatively "washed up" by studio bigwigs, became friends.

The comedian and the director recognized Lucy's genius for comedy, slapstick comedy in particular, and comedy utilizing props—outrageous costumes, putty noses, mustaches, wigs, tooth work. They worked with her on developing her art, working with props.

In Lucy's own words: "I always wanted to do comedy. Buster spotted something in me when I was doing *DuBarry* and kept nagging the moguls about what I could do. Now a great forte of mine is props. He taught me all about 'em. Attention to detail, that's all it is."

With little to do at MGM, Lucy, Keaton and Sedgwick met in the latter's office and, according to one source, began inventing machines. Three engineers from Consolidated Aircraft came to see the results and called them "mechanical wizardry." *Popular Mechanics* even ran articles about them.

One machine was the "cigarette lighter"; the second was the "nutcracker," a contraption which filled half the office; the third, the "Venetian blind-raiser"—the blinds flew up, a shot went off, an Edison phonograph played "Hail to the Chief" and up popped a photograph of Louis B. Mayer. Mayer eventually came to see this machine. His reaction went unrecorded but, shortly after his visit, it was dismantled by studio order.

Sedgwick and Keaton had no status at the studio. They weren't in a position to say to L.B. Mayer, "Look, this girl is a comedy genius. Give her the right kind of picture and she'll be a gold mine."

MGM cast Lucy with Keenan Wynn again in *Easy to Wed*, an Esther Williams-Van Johnson starrer. It was a remake of an old William Powell-Myrna Loy film, *Libeled Lady*, and Lucy had the role originally played by Jean Harlow, that of a dumb redhead. It was a far cry from *The Big Street* and, although it was a good comedy part, again it was a second lead with billing below the title.

Lucy was frustrated, unhappy and determined to increase her following. During her yearly layoff period at Metro, she went to New York and told the MGM publicity boys to book her on all the radio shows that couldn't afford to pay her any salary. If she didn't collect money for the appearances, the studio had no right to object.

"When word got out that I was available for free, Tom got calls from people and radio stations of which he'd never heard," Lucy recalled. "He'd tell me, 'I know you won't do this show, but I want to let you know about it.' I'd answer, 'Sure. That's exactly the type of show I want to appear on. Then I won't have to spend the next four years saying no when I'm asked to go on them.' Tom was confused. But I knew what I was doing. I wanted to reach all the people I possibly could in a short space of time."

When the war ended, Desi was quickly back on the night club circuit and the inevitable separations from Lucy continued. They were apart even when they were in Hollywood together. Lucy worked all day and Desi worked all night.

At the time, she explained the schedule. Work ended for her at six P.M. "Then I rushed for my car to make the twenty-mile trek to our ranch. I drove along Ventura Boulevard, and pretty soon Desi came along, driving the other way. We waved to each other as we passed. Then I had dinner and went to bed early, to be bright and rested for the next day's work, and he would stay up all night, playing."

Lucy said it was the same way in New York when she took a three-month vacation to be with Desi, "so we could be like married people." But she was busy all day, making personal appearances, "and he was up all night, playing. I had to get my sleep at night, and he had to get his sleep in the daytime. That's a married life?"

Desi's reputation as a lady's man hadn't dwindled, and this was the cause of many of their arguments.

Earl Wilson later wrote that Desi's pals advised him, "You should be more discreet. Stay away from girls that are known and recognized." According to Earl, Desi tried to heed this advice, but the next girl he had an affair with, although an unknown, rushed to a magazine editor and sold him her story. "I can't win," lamented Desi.

However, many times when Desi was playing in the Hollywood area, Lucy, despite her work schedule, made a point to spend her evenings with him. "That way," a friend recalls, "she made sure *she* was the girl at ringside."

Desi landed a recording contract with RCA Victor which stipulated his band would be the only one recording Latin-American music for the company.

In 1946 he starred in a "B" vehicle for Universal, *Cuban Pete*. Up to this time, Desi's movie career had included such unmemorable films as *Father Takes a Wife, Four Jacks and a Jill* and *The Navy Comes Through*.

Around this period, when he was touring with his band, money was tight. Desi remembered, "Several musicians fell ill and had to drop out. Should I pay them off and forget it? Instead, I dug deep to pay their hospital bills until they could rejoin me. Then, outside Madison, Wisconsin, disaster hit. Our bus crashed, injuring all but six of the troupe. Facing a costly cancellation in Akron, I got the surprise of my life. From competing bands there came hurrying to our rescue a pianist, a whole trumpet section, drummers and maraca players. Half a dozen rival leaders made sure that we didn't miss the date."

Things continued strained between Lucy and Desi. Back in Hollywood, she had to maintain some semblance of social life, but it was difficult. In the first place, she found little

69

pleasure going to parties or premieres without Desi. Secondly, Desi, despite being in show business, always believed that a woman should never be seen with any man except her husband. He had never become *that* Americanized.

When Lucy had to make a public appearance, Ken Morgan, Cleo's husband, would accompany her. Usually the columns would begin to buzz: "Trouble between Lucille Ball and Desi? Desi's away—Lucille was out with a handsome man . . ."

Desi's "friends" would call him to report Lucille's "dating." More arguments.

"In those days," Desi has recalled, "we had plenty of battles. And every time we quarreled, I'd throw my clothes in a suitcase and move into a hotel room. The first thing I'd do was to send my clothes out to the cleaners, but by the time they were returned Lucy and I would be made up again. That was an expensive proposition, what with the hotel and pressing bills! So I decided to build a guesthouse in our back yard. Lucy's mother, who has a great sense of humor, wanted to know why. I said, 'When that daughter of yours and I fight, I'll move out here. I can't afford to move to town every time we get mad.' But the idea cost money. From the day that guesthouse was finished, Lucy and I never had a serious fight."

Though stormy, these were financially successful years for the Arnazes although the money was being spent as fast as it was being earned. Lucy was earning her MGM stipend, and Desi's earnings ranged from $75,000 to $100,000 a year. But Lucy later complained about these days. "They were getting us. Driving home alone after work, coming into an empty house—that's no fun. And always wondering, 'Is it going to be like this forever?' That sort of existence is all right when you're kids, when you're still working for that big break."

Lucy and Desi were no longer "kids." She was thirty-five; he was twenty-nine.

70

Lucy was understandably discontented at MGM. Her unhappy personal life only compounded the frustration of being stuck with acting roles that didn't begin to exploit her talents.

Lloyd Nolan, who starred with Lucy in MGM's *Two Smart People*, says, "At this time, she was thought of as nothing but a beautiful leading woman. Well, at MGM there were a lot of beautiful women, most of them with a lot of power. They were well established and she was just batting her head against a brick wall. And she needed the comedy to release her talents."

Lucy finally asked for her release from MGM. She finished off the contract with *Two Smart People* and began free-lancing. She starred opposite George Brent in Universal's *Lover Come Back*. The film opened in New York in July, when Desi was playing the Copa. Lucy came to town and they were together, in their usual he's sleeping-while-she's awake manner.

Lucy and Danny Kaye were voted King and Queen of Comedy of 1946 by the Associated Drama Guild of America at their New York convention. The convention theme that year—"The emergence of sophisticated comedy on the American scene."

As a gag, at one of Desi's RCA sessions, Lucy made a recording, not intended for release. But RCA put it out and Lucy sued for $100,000. The disc, "Carnival in Rio," featured her singing in the background a falsetto version of the nursery ditty, "Peter Piper." The label on the record read: "Vocals by Lucille Ball." The suit was immediately settled out of court for an undisclosed sum.

Lucy and Desi wanted children. When Desi was appearing at Ciro's in Hollywood, in 1946, his car was broken into. Desi had bought an anniversary gift for Lucy, a gold lapel pin in the shape of a key, set with nine rubies—"a $300

71

novelty." On the front of the pin Lucille's name was engraved and on the back was a significant inscription: "Nursery Key." When Desi reported the loss, he was asked if the engraving meant that happy news was forthcoming. He answered, "Just hoping."

Lucy persuaded Desi to stay in Hollywood and he accepted the lucrative job of musical director on Bob Hope's radio program.

Lucy continued free-lancing. After *Lover Come Back* she signed with ex-MGM producer Hunt Stromberg to star in *Personal Column* (renamed *Lured*) for United Artists. It had a topnotch cast: George Sanders, Sir Cedric Hardwicke, Charles Coburn and Boris Karloff. Directed by Douglas Sirk, it was a drama, with Lucy as a threatened beauty who offered herself to Scotland Yard as bait to trap a sex killer. Lucy was, as always, believable, and, at thirty-six, still youthful. However, *Variety's* critic commented: "Miss Ball registers best in comic bits as a wisecracking show girl and less effectively in the emotionally distraught scenes."

Lucy was earning good money free-lancing—about $75,000 a picture ($150-200,000 was the top price paid for free-lancing stars in those days), but her career was merely "treading water."

Nineteen forty-seven was a bad year to be free-lancing. The bottom had suddenly dropped out of Hollywood's annual box-office returns because of a new gimmick that "couldn't possibly last": television.

When Columbia Pictures, at the urging of producer Sylvan Simon, offered Lucy a long-term contract, she accepted, pleased with the studio's plans to star her in a comedy. *Her Husband's Affairs* had a screenplay by top movie writers Ben Hecht and Charles Lederer. Franchot Tone was her co-star and Edward Everett Horton was featured in this story of a husband-wife advertising team. Horton said of Lucy, "She's got more talent than these people realize. I loved working with her."

72

Critics liked the picture and began likening Lucille to Carole Lombard, but the film wasn't exactly a blockbuster and Columbia didn't have another good script for her ready for production. Lucy, never one to enjoy being idle, decided to give the legitimate stage another go.

Lloyd Nolan observes, "Lucille was always a puzzle during her Hollywood career. Her career never went really big and people couldn't figure out why. You'd never think of her then as being a slapstick comedienne. It was her main forte, but she never got a crack at it, and something was wrong. She was beautiful, she could act. I guess the biggest break for her was when she went on the stage in *Dream Girl* and suddenly people realized she was a comedienne."

Lucy toured in Elmer Rice's *Dream Girl* for twenty-two weeks at $2,000 a week. It had been June Havoc, one of the stars of the play when it was in New York, who suggested to Lucy she take the role. Author Rice later praised Lucille for giving the role just the right emphasis on comedy.

It was another tough experience, however. After the tour, Lucy explained, "You haven't been in show business until you've been on the stage, and even then you have to tour with a play to know what it's all about.

"I know what it is now to do one-night stands, and to act before audiences that aren't show-wise, as well as those who are. I know what it is to experience poor houses in remote sections and big audiences in major centers. And I've learned how you have to modify and key everything that you do to the public you're playing for."

Dream Girl reinforced in the trade's mind Lucille's ability with comedy. CBS signed her to star in a situation comedy—"My Favorite Husband," co-starring Richard Denning—for their radio network. It was a portent of things to come, with Lucille portraying a scatterbrained wife unendingly involving her poor husband in ridiculous situations. The show was an immediate hit and ran for almost four years.

Meanwhile, Desi was still night-club king, but he was

73

losing interest in that way of life. "One night, feeling lazy and self-important, I staged a poor show in a small club which wasn't paying the money I expected. Sloughing through the dance numbers, I quit early. Backstage, an angry man jabbed a finger into my vest and laced me up and down. 'Who do you think you are?' he demanded. 'In this business you never give less than the best of yourself. Just remember those people out there made you!' I took another look at him. It was Harry Richman. I humbly apologized to the veteran showman. And never again have I sloughed off a performance. There have been times when I have not been in tiptop shape, but I have tried to do my best."

An actress, Yvette Taylor, sued Desi for $75,000, claiming she was struck over the head with a portable mike during one of Desi's engagements at Ciro's. Later, she dropped the suit, but the publicity reinforced the image of Desi as a hot-headed Latin. Desi's lawyer said, "We preferred to fight out the case as a matter of principle. We received offers to settle for $200."

In January, 1948, Lucy opened with her production of *Dream Girl* at the Biltmore Theatre in Los Angeles.

She had been determined to have *Dream Girl* play the Los Angeles area so that film producers could see for themselves the kind of comedy role she could handle. Naturally the other members of the cast wanted the Los Angeles engagement since it would be a showcase for talent scouts to see them as well. However, after twelve weeks in the east and a string of one-night stands on the road, bad luck struck.

Lucy recalled, "Our producer ran out of money. Some of the players got sick. I had to pay some salaries and hospital bills from my own pocket. It looked like curtains. But I promised the cast I'd get them into the Biltmore Theatre, come hell or high water, if they'd cooperate. I threatened to conk anybody on the head who failed to get the proper rest."

Lucy got the show opened in Los Angeles—and then collapsed herself. "I was delirious during one whole matinee and by the time I got out of the hospital, the play had had it. We folded shortly afterwards."

The critics, however, raved. Edwin Schallert in the *Los Angeles Times* prophetically wrote: "She is, in a sense, wasting her talents in pictures . . . Miss Ball is a striking presence in the footlight world. She has efficiency as a comedienne. She can tinge a scene delicately with pathos. She has special facility in dealing with sharp-edged repartee. She apparently never overdoes the sentimental side of a role."

Since Columbia still had nothing for her to do, they lent her to Paramount for a Bob Hope picture, *Sorrowful Jones*, a remake of Shirley Temple's *Little Miss Marker*. Lucy had worked with Hope on radio and camp tours, and in films they proved to be an extremely potent duo.

Director Melville Shavelson, then a screenwriter, worked on *Sorrowful Jones*. He remembers, "Most of the more serious moments were edited out, at least out of scenes detailing the relationship between the characters Bob and Lucy played. Lucy gave her role a whole new flavor. In those days she was very young, very pretty, very attractive. Her style was somewhat different than it is now."

Shavelson makes a very interesting point: "*Sorrowful Jones* rocked the whole boat in Hollywood for a while. At that time, production was a machine—you made three or four Bob Hope pictures a year and you knew how much money they were going to make. It meant you didn't have to pay much attention as long as you got a script the star was willing to do. And normally he didn't have much choice about that. If he didn't do it, he didn't get paid. And if he still insisted about not doing it, he would be put on suspension and couldn't work for anybody else. It was a real grinder operation.

"Well, Bob Hope pictures made a certain amount of money. *Sorrowful Jones* made *twice* as much money as any

75

Hope picture that had been made before and it upset the whole thing. Obviously, there might be a difference in the quality of what was in the picture or who was in the picture, like Lucy, that determined this. And the producers had to stop and think."

There was a renewed demand for Lucy's services. But though she was work oriented, Lucy was also more determined than ever to keep her marriage going. She and Desi hadn't been able to have children and didn't want to adopt. Friends said it was Desi who wouldn't consider it, but when asked, "I heard you were going to adopt a baby" Lucille replied: "Now *wouldn't* that be silly when I can have one of my own?"

When queried how she and Desi had made their stormy marriage work out, she answered, "You know we were separated once, and when we realized we were really in love with each other we went back and have never separated again. I have never regretted the separation because it taught me a very important thing.

"You know, that people in Hollywood who divorce and take on new mates make better wives and husbands the second time because they have had experience and know how to handle their marriage. I figure with Desi and me it was as if we had new mates. We learned our lesson and we gained experience. I treated him as I would a new husband, and he gave me the attention he would give a new wife."

Lucy returned to alma mater RKO to finish off an old commitment, and was lucky the commitment didn't finish her off. She played fourth lead—a secretary—in a story about pro-football, *Easy Living*, which starred Victor Mature, Lizabeth Scott and Sonny Tufts. The talk was Lucy had been offered the lead but turned it down, preferring not to work that hard, just wanting to finish off the commitment.

For Columbia, she finally made a comedy which took some advantage of her zany quality and reinforced her radio show image. In *Miss Grant Takes Richmond* she played a dim-witted secretary who discovers the real estate agency run by her boss, William Holden, is a cover-up for a bookmaking parlor.

She and Holden hit it off, and in a couple of scenes in the finished film it was evident that he was stifling the urge to guffaw at some of Lucy's hijinks.

That year, 1949, Desi also made a movie for Columbia, *Holiday in Havana*. The film included two songs he wrote—the title song and "The Arnaz Jam." They were both percussive Latin-type numbers and the critic for the *New York Herald Tribune* wrote, "Arnaz is boyishly enthusiastic about all this. His performance in front of the band has color and authority. This is not quite enough to redeem a mediocre Cuban-accented show."

At thirty-eight, after more than eight years of marriage, Lucille Ball became a June bride. Desi and his parents were devout Catholics although Lucy wasn't, and Desi's mother in particular had always been unhappy that her son hadn't been married in the Church.

A friend speculates, "Lucy and Desi hadn't been able to have kids and perhaps there was a psychological guilt because, according to the Catholic Church, they had been 'living in sin.' "

The Arnazes were remarried in a religious ceremony by Father John J. Hurley in Our Lady of the Valley Church in Canoga Park. Only their relatives and a few friends attended. Lucy was given away by Eddie Sedgwick and her mother-in-law was matron of honor. Ken Morgan was best man. Groucho Marx sent a telegram: "What's new?"

There was no second honeymoon for Lucy and Desi, since he was playing at a local night club and she had professional commitments which couldn't be postponed.

Lucy went back to Paramount on loan-out from Columbia to star again with Bob Hope, this time in a remake of *Rug-*

77

gles of Red Gap, titled *Where Men Are Men.* The movie received yet another title change, ending up as *Fancy Pants,* which proved to be another Hope-Ball hit.

In *Fancy Pants,* as in *Sorrowful Jones,* Lucy was used as a foil for Hope, and he got the laughs. "Lucille Ball . . . knows her small place and keeps it," wrote one critic. Another said, "Lucille Ball, handicapped by lack of comic lines, gives what help her pert presence can afford." Another critic noted, "She is a fine foil for the star, building up bits of business to a point where they are comically consequential even though they have next to nothing to do with the original plot."

Bob and Lucy were close friends and would work together often in the future. They had a lot in common. He appreciated her ability to deliver a gag or a wisecrack offscreen as well as on.

It was announced that Lucy was going to Broadway to take over Judy Holliday's role in *Born Yesterday.* Lucy later admitted that she wanted to do *Born Yesterday,* but only after the star had been chosen for Columbia's film version, because "I wouldn't want them to think I was auditioning." When asked if there was a possibility she might get the coveted role in the picture, she quipped: "Only if nobody else wants it."

Lucy gave some candid, insightful comments on the workings of Hollywood studio politics. "You can't start at the bottom of this business and rise without running into trouble. I know the various steps of the ladder so well. At one studio you're expected to be a social butterfly and make command appearances at the boss's parties; at another you run smack into a political situation where your troubles never get to the head man, who could settle them with one word. At still another studio they leave your private life strictly alone provided your pictures make money.

"Well, I used to be the sensitive type. These things bothered me and I worried. Now I leave my worrying to my agent."

78

It was no secret that Lucille had methodically fashioned her career to achieve her position. She pointed out that one of the aspects of her career she was proudest of had been the fact that she worked up to four figures a week from $50 at RKO. Seeming to forget the number of studios she worked at, Lucille noted, "Usually young actresses have to bounce around from studio to studio before they accomplish this. Of course I was at RKO for so long that I did everything, including sweeping up. If someone said, 'Ball, be there at four A.M.,' I was there. Or if someone said, 'For gosh sakes, Lucy, go home,' I would go home. Dutiful Ball I was, in those days."

Nineteen fifty was a harried year for Lucille. She was having her battles with Harry Cohn, tyrannical head of Columbia Pictures. She had even appeared in a cameo role, unbilled, in the studio's Rosalind Russell starrer, *A Woman of Distinction.*

The studio had lent her out a number of times, but seemed to find it difficult to come up with scripts that she wanted to do. Lloyd Bacon, who had directed *Miss Grant Takes Richmond*, put Lucy in another comedy, *The Fuller Brush Girl*, co-starring Eddie Albert. Lucy's friend Red Skelton agreed to do a cameo appearance in the film. This was probably the only one of Lucille Ball's movies, up to this point, that took generous advantage of her slapstick abilities. She played a cosmetics salesgirl who discovers a murder, uncovers a smuggling ring and dodges the police, despite the interference of her dim-witted boyfriend.

It was a strenuous picture and Lucy suffered some injuries during filming. She sprained both wrists while wrestling; displaced six vertebrae when she fell from a fence onto a clothesline; and pulled a muscle in her legs while walking with ankles bent, imitating a drunk.

Lucy told of one near-disaster. "I was a switchboard operator, and one of the gags was a wind machine hooked up to the board which squirted talcum powder out of the holes. One blast got me right in the eye. I didn't work again until every speck was out, four days later."

On the last day of shooting, she was suffering from a bad cold because of being drenched in several scenes. She had agreed to stop for a publicity shot to demonstrate a free-to-the-public X-ray machine. While she was posing, the X-ray technician gasped. "My God, Miss Ball! This shows you have pneumonia. Did you know?"

She didn't. But she went straight to the hospital.

Friends remember that things were still not peaceful in the Arnaz household. When columnist Sheilah Graham got wind of the dissension, she mentioned their "battles" on her radio program. Lucy, according to Sheilah, called in a rage. "I'm going to get you for this," she screamed, "and who told you?" Miss Graham replied that she could not reveal her source (but later admitted the source had been Lucille's own press agent).

Lucy became hysterical over the phone, according to the columnist, and said, crying, "You've got two children and you don't care. You say things like that about me and I will never have children."

Lucy told a friend, "I knew there was never anyone in the world for me but Desi and that we might have our ups and downs just as many people have. But I'd rather quarrel and make up with him than anyone else in the world." The friend noted that since the Arnazes had almost divorced, Desi *had* changed. "In fact, I don't think I've ever seen a boy change as much as he has in the last few years. When I first knew him he was a playboy—an overenthusiastic young Cuban, too excitable, too emotional. Now a lot of that has worn down."

Lucy admitted that the marriage's real problem then wasn't Desi's Latin temperament, but their conflicting careers.

Desi was almost constantly on the road with his orchestra.

80

"Of course," Lucy noted, "we had dates. He'd fly to me when he could, and I'd fly to him, but our dream is to both be able to have our jobs in the same town at the same time."

At their ranch, Lucy and Desi often entertained friends like Eve Arden, Farley Granger, the Bob Crosbys, Francis and Marion Lederer, Joe Howard and his wife Priscilla Lane.

Lucille was up to $85,000 a picture at Columbia. CBS was considering transferring "My Favorite Husband" from radio to TV and, naturally, the role was Lucille's if she wanted it. However, Lucy and Desi had decided that to make their marriage work, he would have to stop traveling and remain in Hollywood. Obviously, the only solution was for them to work together.

Desi was still big box office for night clubs. When he next appeared with his orchestra at Ciro's, a typical review described his "pulse-pounding prancings with the conga and bongo drums," and commented that "Maestro's showmanship, tremendously improved over the years, is flashy, and even when he fluffs a line, which is often, he holds the ringsiders in his palm."

Lucy and Desi tried unsuccessfully to persuade producers and talent agencies to co-star them in a film or a television series. "On screen, the public won't believe you're married to Desi," she was told. "After all, what typical American girl is married to a Latin?"

Lucy replied, "American girls marry them all the time, but not, I suppose, on television."

To prove that they were right and the producers wrong, Lucy and Desi put together their own vaudeville act and took it on the road in the spring of 1950. Lucy later said of the act, "It was mostly husband-and-wife situation comedy. Mixed in with it was a little music, dancing, gags and serious stuff." They also formed Desilu Productions, giving the company the same name as their ranch.

The tour proved to be a tremendous success, but it was a

81

terrifically strenuous act. In one crazy knockabout sketch, Lucy wore a fright wig, played a cello and walked across the stage on her knees. Audiences howled, and accepted the Arnazes as a married couple. Naturally, Lucy's radio show was a big hit at the time, and in the act she was playing an extension of her nutty "My Favorite Husband" character. They did six and seven shows a day, playing such cities as Chicago and New York.

While in New York, Lucille jubilantly announced that she was going to have a baby. Friends suggested that she quit the tour and wait for the birth of the baby. But the commitments were made and the tour continued on to Buffalo and Milwaukee.

In July, Lucy and Desi returned to Hollywood, exhausted. Regarding her pregnancy, they said, "You can tell the world about it, but don't say child. We're hoping for twins." The couple displayed two baby sweaters which Lucille had knitted herself, one pink and one blue. Lucy explained that she always wanted a son and Desi hoped for a girl—hence their desire for twins.

Lucy was happy the tour was a success and thrilled about the expected baby. She planned to rest until its arrival, but the tour had taken its toll. She was rushed in a screaming ambulance to Cedars of Lebanon Hospital and for almost a week doctors tried, unsuccessfully, to save the baby. There can be little doubt that the six weeks of strenuous touring were responsible for Lucy's miscarriage.

Now Lucy was more determined than ever to have a baby and she was doing "everything the doctor prescribed."

"I've changed my whole program," she said. "I'm going to a gym to keep in good health and I'm not going to do any comedies that call for physical strain. You know, I was in bed for three weeks after I made *Fuller Brush Girl*. Now I'm going to do only two pictures a year, either very quiet comedies, or somber dramas. Nothing that will make me stand on my head or hang by my eyebrows from a chandelier."

82

Her friend Louella Parsons said that it was difficult to think of Lucille in a somber drama. "She is essentially a fun girl and gets a laugh out of people, life and most everything. She is one of the wittiest girls in our town and one of the gayest. But knowing her, I am convinced she will keep her word and get herself into perfect health and then concentrate on the hope of motherhood." Louella then scolded Lucille for having continued the tour after finding out she was pregnant.

Did Lucille agree that her strenuous tour was responsible for losing the baby? "I don't know," she said at the time. "I think sometimes things are just meant to be. Yet, I am not going to take any chances, and Desi is going to make it possible so I don't have to travel to see him. He is going to open a night club and bring his band to the Sunset Strip instead of going to the hinterlands."

Desi did not open a night club, but accepted an engagement at Ciro's. Meanwhile, Lucille still had a contract with Columbia Pictures. Since CBS would not remotely consider Desi for the lead opposite Lucy in "My Favorite Husband" if and when it ever made it to TV, the Arnazes had to come up with another idea.

The idea for their own series began to take form and shape when Lucy's arguments with Columbia Pictures about roles and money were reaching the breaking point. Lucy later admitted, "I wasn't happy at Columbia ever. Harry Cohn, who headed the studio . . . is so involved in the story of my quitting movies I can't leave him out. If he seems a heavy as far as I'm concerned, I'm not a hypocrite. He'd been asking me to do things I didn't like, which meant an impasse, because I wasn't about to do something I thought was bad for me. He was trying to break my contract, and I was all for letting him break it, but at the same time he was keeping me from doing a picture for Cecil B. DeMille on a loan-out."

De Mille wanted her for *The Greatest Show on Earth*. Lucy later claimed it was for the lead that went to Betty

Hutton, but actually De Mille wanted Lucy for the support-ing role of the wisecracking, red-headed "elephant girl," a role which eventually went to Gloria Grahame.

Lucy explained that De Mille had on the q.t. discussed the possibility of her working for him. He knew she was under contract to Cohn, and asked Lucy, "How can you?" She replied, "I have no idea, but I will."

She later said, "I had several meetings with Mr. Cohn about it. But his idea was to outfox me. He kept saying, 'You don't have time. You owe me a picture.' 'That's ridiculous,' I said. 'You have nothing for me to do, and the De Mille pic-ture is a great opportunity.'

" 'We'll see,' he said, which meant he was going to hold out on me. In the meantime, the De Mille company was ready to leave for Florida and begin shooting, and I was so excited I couldn't breathe. To me, working with De Mille was the living end. I'd had some nice directors and some good ones, no super ones.

"I was getting nowhere with Mr. Cohn, so I said to him, 'I'm asking you again. Why can't you let me make this pic-ture? You've loaned me out for dogs before when it didn't matter.' What really concerned him was trying to get out of having to pay me the eighty-five grand he would owe me if I made the one more picture for him he had contracted to have me do. If he'd asked me to let him out of that commit-ment, I would have agreed to forget the whole deal. But that was too simple. He wanted to outsmart me, so one day he sent me a script about the size of a small pamphlet, called *The Magic Carpet*."

Lucy's version of ensuing events was: "I read the script, and as I read I became hysterical with laughter. It was a Hymie Levin script. His name wasn't really Hymie Levin, but since he's a nice man and I wouldn't want to hurt his feelings, I'll call him that, because he made what were called 'the lease breakers.' If they wanted you out of your contract,

they sent you a genuine Hymie Levin script. He has made
some fine pictures since, but at that time a Levin script was a
short, hurried 'B' picture with any cast he could sling
together. When I realized what was up, I was elated,
although I didn't know what Desi would say to the idea that
had popped into my head. When he got home, I said, 'I have
a script I want you to read.' He read it, looked at me and
asked, 'Are you cra-zee or something?' I said, 'All I have to
do is appear in this picture and I not only get $85,000 but
I've worked my way out of my contract and I can accept the
De Mille role. I'm going to fool them. I'm not going to turn it
down.'

" 'You wouldn't dare,' Desi said.

" 'Why not?' I asked. 'Hymie Levin is a likeable man,
besides, it'll only take me five days to finish it.' "

Lucy never saw the finished picture. "I don't remember
much about it. As I recall, I was a harem girl, lying on a
divan in lamé pantaloons, while slaves fed me grapes. I sent
word to Columbia that I would be delighted to do the picture, then I checked in for my costume fittings. I tried on the
muslin mock-up of my body they used for fittings when I
wasn't around but I couldn't zip it. And I was puzzled. I'd
made a picture only a couple of months before. The muslin
figure had been perfect then, but now it missed closing by
two or three inches. I didn't realize I'd put on so much
weight. I must have been lying around eating too much.
Then the next day I had a strange feeling.

"But I thought, *it couldn't be*. Desi and I had made up our
minds that we couldn't have a baby. Nevertheless, the doctor
said one was on the way. After that, the trick was to let
nobody know. If Mr. Cohn had realized that I was pregnant,
he could have refused to take a chance on an expectant
mother in a film, and if I couldn't have done the Levin opus,
it would have let him out of his commitment to me."

Although Turkish harem girls' middles were supposed to

be plump, Lucy chuckled to a friend, "Not so plump as this Turkish girl's middle looked. I quickly found that pregnancy made me expand like a balloon, but, of course, I couldn't tell anybody, not even the wardrobe girl who was trying to tuck me into my lamé pants and my Turkish bra. I walked around all day trying not to breathe, and every night the wardrobe girl said, 'I simply don't know what's happening, Miss Ball. I let your things out last night myself.' And I said carelessly, 'Apparently you didn't let them out far enough. You're going to have to let them out some more.'

"I finished the picture, collected Columbia's money and, with Desi, went to see Mr. De Mille with tears streaming down my face. 'Why are you crying?' Mr. De Mille asked, and I said, 'I've always wanted to work with you, and this is the only opportunity I'll ever have, but I can't do your picture. I'm pregnant.' It was very sad. Even Mr. De Mille had tears in his eyes. He shook Desi's hand solemnly and said, 'I want to congratulate you. You're the only one who's ever crossed up Cecil B. De Mille, his wife, Paramount Pictures, and Harry Cohn all at the same time.' "

There are other versions of this story. "Lucy knew she was pregnant *before* she accepted Cohn's lease breaker," says a friend. "Eddie Sedgwick told Lucy to tell Cohn she'd do the picture. 'It'll break Katzman,' Sedgwick said. 'His whole budget is less than your salary.'

"Katzman tried to talk her out of the picture, but she would have none of it. She met the writers of the film when she bumped into them in the studio parking lot. They didn't even have an office. They were so thrilled to be working with a star of Lucille's stature they offered to write additional dialogue and scenes for her. 'Don't change a word,' she told them, 'I like it just the way it is.' "

After filming her final scene Lucille phoned Harry Cohn.

"Harry, this is Lucille Ball."

"Yeah, whaddya want?"

"I want you to be the first to know. I'm going to have a baby."

"Why you son of a bitch," Cohn screamed. "Why the hell didn't you tell me before the picture?"

"I just found out, Harry."

De Mille's reaction to Lucy's pregnancy, according to an informed source, was considerably more earthy than Lucille's recollection of it. De Mille was quoted as saying to Desi, "Congratulations. You're the only man who's ever fucked his wife, Cecil B. De Mille, Paramount Pictures and Harry Cohn all at the same time." Then the world-renowned director of Biblical spectacles was said to have suggested that the couple "do something" about the baby so that Lucy could appear in his movie.

The Arnazes were horrified. Their much-prayed-for and wanted baby was the most important thing in the world to them, and Lucy was determined to have it. After seeing De Mille, Lucy called Louella Parsons to give her the exclusive on the baby.

"This time," Lucy told Louella, "I'll rest all the time. I'm even giving up my role as the elephant girl in *The Greatest Show on Earth*. I've just told Mr. De Mille that I cannot make the picture. As you know, I was very excited over the opportunity of working for C.B. But there will be other times, at least I hope so, and the baby is more important.

"We are already building a nursery," she said. "You know this happened in answer to our prayers. We both prayed so hard for another baby."

5

NINETEEN FIFTY-ONE. Television was eager for "big" names. Top movie stars shunned the new medium. Even if they wanted to appear, their movie contracts forbade it. Besides, it was beneath their stature to appear on television. Hence, television moguls had to turn to movie names who were beyond their peak and has-beens who couldn't get jobs in films.

But despite movie studios' disdainful attitudes, television had taken over as America's leading leisure-time activity. Jerry Lester's "Broadway Open House," the precursor of "The Tonight Show," was super-popular. Lester's busty blonde sidekick, Dagmar, enjoyed national popularity. Faye Emerson's cleavage was a national topic of conversation. "Howdy Doody," "What's My Line," Ed Sullivan's "Toast of the Town" were among the most popular shows. And the King of Television was "Uncle Miltie," Milton Berle.

But Uncle Miltie's "King" days were numbered. Soon there

would be a new king and queen of television, and their success would far outlast that of any TV star that had come
before—or would come after.

In the spring, while Lucy was pregnant, the Arnazes
decided to go-for-broke in their careers. Desi summed up
their years together, and their future, when he said: "We
had been married ten years. Each successful in our respec-
tive fields, movies and music. Yet we were almost total
strangers. Our work pulled us far apart, east coast and west.
We had neither home nor children. So we quarreled and
talked of divorce. But deep down I knew that I couldn't live
without Lucy, and she could not without me. We were on
the edge of breakup when we hit upon a magnificent idea.

"We could give up our separate jobs to play a man and
wife team on television. It meant canceling all our contracts
to gamble on what might prove to be nothing. 'Will be
nothing,' one of TV's most astute tycoons assured us when
we explained our plan. 'The public won't accept a Latin-type
like you in a husband role—the old gigolo curse. And Lucy,
with that chorus-girl figure, won't be identified with many
mothers.' From all sides we were told that the idea was ridiculous and were advised to give it up.

"Here was the first really big problem Lucy and I had met
together in ten years. She didn't give me a chance to get
weak in the knees. Lucy got sore. She had been a working
gal for a long, hard period before earning her break in Hollywood, and she snorted, 'Look, I was born in Jamestown, New
York, and waited on tables in New Castle, Pa., and jerked
sodas in Cleveland. You've been kicking around this country
for seventeen years. Hell, yes, we're average Americans. And
we're going to do 'I Love Lucy' even if we go broke."

It was a gamble. Movie studios did not look kindly on
movie stars who "deserted to the enemy." If the show
flopped, she would have no place to "crawl back to." How-

ever, Lucy noted, "There used to be this attitude that if you went into television, you must be starving. I made sure everybody knew I didn't *have* to do this."

In later years, both Lucy and Desi were irked by the oft-repeated story that the only reason they went into TV was because they were washed up in their separate careers. "Desi was making $150,000 a year," said Lucy, "and I got $85,000 from Columbia Pictures for my last picture, for one week's work. You think that's 'washed up'?"

However, her $85,000-a-picture days were definitely numbered in 1951. She wasn't under contract, and it was a difficult time in the movie industry to set up profitable freelance contracts if you weren't a top box-office draw.

They filmed the pilot of "I Love Lucy" (with Lucy five-months pregnant) and brought it to CBS. It hadn't been simple. Desi remembered, "The first script wasn't about Ricky Ricardo at all. It was about a successful orchestra leader, Desi Arnaz, and his successful movie star wife, Lucille Ball, and how *Life* magazine loused up their anniversary celebration. I said nobody could care less about a successful bandleader and a successful movie star not being able to go out for their anniversary on account of they gotta shoot pictures around their swimming pool for *Life* magazine. Oh, it was funny, very, very funny, but it was lousy. It was dishonest. It was wrong. That's how we happened to invent Ricky Ricardo who was just making ends meet, and she's a housewife."

Television situation comedies initially began by converting radio situation comedies to TV. In Lucy's "My Favorite Husband" radio program, her husband was supposed to be a bank vice president. Naturally, Desi would never fit this part. So for "Lucy," they hit upon the idea of him playing a character basically like himself, a bandleader. Only they made him less successful, less hotheaded and more understanding than the real-life Desi Arnaz.

90

Lucy's character remained basically the same as the wife she played in "My Favorite Husband," only zanier, with ample opportunity for slapstick in the visual medium. The role also gave her the chance to wear a wide variety of costumes and utilize a wide range of props.

With $8,000 borrowed by Desi from his booking agency, General Artists Corporation, Lucy and he produced the pilot film themselves, under their Desilu banner. Twenty minutes of the script utilized material they had tested on their vaudeville tour. They hired writers Bob Carroll, Madeleine Pugh and Jess Oppenheimer, who had written the "My Favorite Husband" series.

To play "The Mertzes," the family next door who would serve as friends and foils for the Ricardos, Desi and Lucy hired movie character actor William Frawley and relatively unknown stage actress Vivian Vance. It was a touch of casting genius.

Lucy and Desi had spied Vivian when she played a summer stock role in *The Voice of the Turtle*. Vivian had practically given up hope of ever working at acting when Mel Ferrer ferreted her out of hiding on an Arizona ranch. He persuaded her to play the role of Olive Lashbrooke, a sarcastic bitch, in *The Voice of the Turtle*. She had played the role previously and Ferrer remembered her.

Lucy and Desi saw her at Ferrer's little theatre in La Jolla and said, "There's our Ethel Mertz."

Vivian, born in Kansas, had decided to become an actress in her early teens. Her family didn't approve. Viv studied drama anyway, and when she got to Albuquerque, New Mexico, she was ready to show off her talents. The story goes that the townspeople were so impressed with Vivian's talent that they financed her journey to New York.

There she got an audition for a chorus job in *Music in the Air*. She had a big voice and played clubs after the show.

"I just kept working at everything in every spot I could

find," recalled Vivian. "I got plenty of experience and, you know, it all comes in handy now. It seems there isn't much I can't do when it comes to working out routines on this 'I Love Lucy' show. There's nothing like a lot of experience when the big break comes."

Bill Frawley was born in Burlington, Iowa, a small railroad town. His mother was overjoyed when he learned enough shorthand and bookkeeping to land a job as a railroad clerk in Omaha. But Bill wasn't happy. He wanted to be on the stage, so he took the plunge. He played the Pacific Coast vaudeville circuit for four years and after a few film roles, moved to Broadway where he spent a number of successful years.

Vivian Vance described "I Love Lucy" at its inception, "Theoretically, our show consists of three miscasts and one case of perfect typing—Lucille. I always played sophisticated other-woman roles in musical comedy, while Bill Frawley was a vaudevillian and Desi a bandleader."

When Desi took the filmed pilot to CBS, the network, and the Philip Morris Tobacco Company, the potential sponsor, liked the show—"But." The first "but" was they insisted the show be done live from New York, then the emanating point for all first-class television programs.

Desi fought the decision. He wanted his show to be filmed and emanate from Los Angeles. One reason Lucy and Desi had wanted a television program was that they wanted to settle down in Hollywood and start raising their family.

Philip Morris and CBS finally agreed to let them do the show from Hollywood, but they stood firm on their demand that it be done live. A filmed show would cost four times as much, they pointed out, and the cigarette company wasn't prepared to go that high.

Desi noted, "I was among the first to believe that film was the answer to telecasting. If a show can't leave a studio, its action is limited by how long it takes an actor to change his clothes or to get from one spot to another. So you compromise. It's tough enough to have to write a show every week without having somebody say, 'You can't do that because it will require an exterior shot.'"

Desi compromised. He and Lucy agreed to take smaller salaries in return for producing the show on film and retaining one hundred per cent of all residual rights. This meant that Desilu would own the shows after they had been televised once.

Within two days the deal was consummated, with Desilu to be paid $30,000 a week to produce each episode. Desi's long years of practical business experience with his band were invaluable during this period. Looking back, he remembered, "Innocent me. I thought all I'd have to do was act. Suddenly, because of a disagreement with the backers on where and how the show would be filmed, we became one hundred per cent owners of 'I Love Lucy,' and then thousands of shooting, casting, hiring and editing headaches rang in my ears.

"'What do we do now, honey?' I inquired.

"Lucy said sweetly, 'That's not the question, dear. What can *you* do?'

"Oh, boy, what headaches that first year! You need special mobile cameras for a fast-action, filmed show like 'Lucy.' I didn't know one from a klieg light. I had to find a studio, dicker on rent, sign contracts, buy equipment, learn to cut and edit film, study scripts, boss costumers and set designers, audition, hire and reject hundreds of actors twice as talented as I. Lucy ('I'm a big dope about business,' she kept claiming) stood back while I learned private enterprise the hard way."

About the three-camera process necessary to film the show, Desi later said, "Man, I didn't have the slightest idea what I was talking about. But I knew Karl Freund, the first man to move the camera during the shooting of a scene. And

93

I figured if anyone knew how to have three cameras working at once in a fully-lit studio and still have good close-ups of Lucy, he would.

"All I could pay him," Desi noted, "and remember, he had photographed Garbo and Dietrich, was scale. But he was intrigued by the idea, so he worked it out."

Desi leased a sound stage from an independent Los Angeles studio and decided not only should the show be on film, but it should be filmed in front of a live audience.

"Everybody thought I was out of my mind," said Desi. "Bill Paley, president of CBS, thought okay, he'll do six weeks of film and lose every cent and be doing it live in six weeks."

When a project is successful many people take credit, but it is generally agreed that the people most directly responsible for the original idea for "I Love Lucy" were Harry Ackerman, CBS vice president in charge of programming for the west coast, and Hubbell Robinson, another CBS vice president. The two men used to watch Lucille rehearse for her radio program and they saw that she was a natural-born clown with a perfect sense of timing. Neither could understand why the movies hadn't made better use of her talents and they suggested a TV show along the lines of her radio program.

With the show sold, Lucy could eagerly await the birth of her baby. She had taken care of herself and was in such good physical shape that the strenuous filming of the pilot episode had no adverse effect. Lucy later said, "Looking back on that pregnancy, I can't remember that I was ever as difficult as women are supposed to be. Desi was an angel. He waited on me hand and foot, and I felt fine all the time. The only thing I remember, I had an aversion to smoke. I'd been puffing away on two packs a day, and, all of a sudden, I couldn't stand the smell of tobacco. I made everybody around me ditch their smokes, even Desi." (This aversion apparently lasted only as long as the pregnancy. Over the years the heavy smoking had taken its toll on her voice, which has become deep and gravelly.)

On July 17, 1951, a month before her fortieth birthday, Lucille Ball gave birth to her first child, Lucie Desiree Arnaz, who weighed in at seven pounds, six ounces.

When the nurse brought the baby to her, Lucy was so overcome with emotion that she could hardly breathe. The baby was wrapped, cone-like, in a blanket. Lucy took her but when she looked down into the blanket she couldn't see the baby's face. She tried to wriggle her up higher in the blanket but tried too hard. Little Lucie popped out of the comforter and over her mother's shoulder. Shocked, Lucy whipped her head around to see where the baby had landed. Unperturbed, little Lucie was gurgling happily atop pillows behind Lucy.

Despite the warnings of friends and business associates that they were "gambling everything away" by entering TV, 1951 was a banner year for Lucille Ball and Desi Arnaz. In addition to the birth of little Lucie, their program, "I Love Lucy," which would become the most popular TV show of all time, was launched in October.

Along with the trio of top writers hired for the show and Oscar-winning cameraman Karl Freund, Desi hired director Marc Daniels and later Bill Asher. The Los Angeles studio was remodeled to allow for an audience of three hundred people, whose reactions would be registered on the soundtrack.

Director Melville Shavelson credits Desi with being one of the pioneers in television film production by building a studio with concrete rather than wooden floors, enabling the cameras to roll noiselessly anywhere.

By shooting in sequence and before a live audience, the "I Love Lucy" show had a spontaneity and sparkle heretofore

95

unknown in filmed television. In the 1951-52 production schedule, there was a total of ninety-three actors, technicians and other personnel employed for each "Lucy" show. The production costs were between $23,000 and $25,000 a week, leaving an average profit of from $5,000 to $7,000 a week for Desilu.

The show utilized four permanent sets—two were the Ricardos's apartment, the third was the night club where Ricky worked, and a fourth was used for any other scenes the show might require. Desi noted, "We had real furniture, real plumbing and a real kitchen where we served real food. Even the plants were really growing."

He also said at the time, "Our 'I Love Lucy' program is a stage show on film. We don't stop the cameras every time somebody makes a mistake, but keep going and try to find a way out. Often this helps the comedy, particularly if Lucy is carrying the ball. I've never found her at a loss at such times. For instance, when her foot got stuck in a ballet practice bar, in a scene in which the fictional Lucy was learning to dance, Lucy made a big thing out of it."

Desi described Lucy as "the female Chaplin! She walks like Chaplin. There's nobody else that can do what she does with her face, with her walk, with her action. No other comedienne in the whole world. 'I Love Lucy' was designed for her, built for her. All the rest of us were just props—Bill, Vivian, me. Darn good props, but props. In a 'Lucy' show everything starts with Lucy and works backwards. The writer might decide it will be funny if Lucy gets in a wine vat with two or three fat Italian girls and starts a fight while stomping grapes in the third act. So the whole idea is how to get the world's greatest female clown in that predicament."

Desilu's biggest asset was its ownership of the "I Love Lucy" films. Thus, the initial $5,000 to $7,000 weekly profit was only the first payment. The films would, as television history has recorded, prove to be a fantastic annuity.

Why did "I Love Lucy" find such an immediate, vast audience? It dealt essentially with the most universal situation: the battle of the sexes. Lucy's neighbor and friend, Ethel Mertz, represented the millions of women somewhat more disillusioned about husbands after years of marriage than the younger Lucy. Hence, Ethel magnified Lucy's occasional doubts, sowed seeds of suspicion and prodded Lucy to various misadventures.

One of the staples of the show was Lucy's crying jags. Her range of tears went from simpering sniffles to calf bawls, the now world-famous *Wahhhhh!* And not to be overlooked was the fact that the Lucy character was essentially a likeable, lovable child.

For the next few years, there was never a divorce between the private and public lives of Lucille Ball, Desi Arnaz and their TV show counterparts. The program made the most of their seemingly extravagant devotion to each other and their extraordinary ability to find humor in situations. Their friends say that Lucille and Desi liked practical jokes and that the horseplay on the TV program was not too far from their lifestyle at home. The courtship had started out with "I betcha" and it had become a household phrase at the Arnazes. They were constantly in competition and they used this as the theme for many of their television skits. For instance, Desi would say that modern women haven't the endurance and spunk of their grandmothers. Or Lucy would insist that men gossip more than women. They would inevitably bet on it and that week's program would revolve around comic situations when Lucy, allied with Ethel, and Desi, allied with Fred, would try to win.

The fact that the Arnazes hadn't been major news-grabbers in the 1940s was now an advantage. Their separations and squabbles had never been page-one news and so the public now could accept them for what they appeared to be on "I Love Lucy."

97

The show saved their relationship and marriage. At work, a new bond formed between them. The "I Love Lucy" show was their baby, their challenge, and a chance to prove that two people could be fiercely independent in big-time TV.

"At night," Desi recalled, "instead of wrangling over little things, we plotted new ideas, ways to cut costs, funnier situations—things that enabled Desilu Productions to cover four square blocks and revolutionize television production."

On another occasion Lucy noted, "I am no marital expert ... but I have been through an experience that perturbs a large number of young married women. I have had to plot, scratch and connive to hold a husband. I lost him once and got him back. Both of us have been sickened and frustrated many times by conflicting careers. And we had been married more than ten years before we finally managed to have our first child."

If Lucy's late films had been relatively dangerous in terms of stunts she performed, television was doubly so. Once she set fire to her dress with a cigarette but continued with the scene. "It was right in the middle of a good rehearsal and I was afraid to stop," she explained. Luckily, another member of the cast saw the smoldering fabric and hollered.

Another time, the script called for a running leap toward Desi. Lucy jumped, missed him and sailed about a dozen feet. Bruised, she got up and did the scene over.

One of the "Lucy" episodes cast her as a bullfighter. "We worked in front of a background showing the Tijuana bullring," she recalled, "and they mounted a bull's head on the camera and rolled straight toward me at high speed. Yep, I was gored, just as if it had been the real thing."

"I Love Lucy" was second in popularity only to Red Skelton, with an estimated viewership of thirty-five million. Milton Berle had dropped to eighth place. Lucille and Desi were household names. They were established not only as

98

the country's top new comedy team, but as America's new sweethearts, symbols of the ultimate onscreen and real-life happiness in marriage.

And, for the time being, the Arnazes were genuinely happy. They had a beautiful daughter and at last they had managed to combine their professional lives to achieve stardom and financial security in tandem.

In February 1952, when Red Skelton received an Emmy Award from the Academy of Television Arts and Sciences as the Best Television Comedian of the Year, he said: "I don't deserve this. It should go to Lucille Ball."

In May, Lucy and Desi's good fortune multiplied when Lucy became pregnant again. They were both delighted. However, no immediate announcement was made of the pregnancy.

Because of the huge success of "I Love Lucy," the Arnazes were in a position to command huge salaries for in-person appearances. They had been planning a summer tour, to include New York and Boston, which would have paid them, according to *Variety*, $57,000 for two weeks "plus overages on $100,000 weekly" at New York's Roxy Theatre.

During the year, expanding Desilu Productions not only filmed "I Love Lucy" but the commercials for Red Skelton's show, the pilot films for a Leo Durocher and Laraine Day situation comedy series and Eve Arden's "Our Miss Brooks."

As Desilu began expanding, so did Desi's headaches. CBS liked the Eve Arden show, signed Desi to produce it and so the summer tour with Lucy was "postponed indefinitely."

"All my life," said Desi, "I've worried what I'd do when I got too old, too fat, too ugly to be in front of a band. Now I don't worry. We're learning to produce television films."

Shortly before their second television season, Desi once again proved his business genius when he found an error in the network's budgeting of their show. "Desi has a mathematical mind," Lucy has noted, "but he had never used it much up to that point. Then CBS sent over this budget, and he began to study it. He said to me, 'They've made a million-dollar mistake.' I said, 'That's impossible.' 'No,' he said, 'I know there's a million dollars more in here for us to spend on production. They've got their figures wrong.' The next day he took the papers in to CBS and said, 'You've made a million-dollar mistake.'

"They said, 'That's impossible. Look, Desi, stick to your acting. We'll handle the business details.' So then he spread their papers out all over their office. He proved to them that they were wrong; there was an extra million in there for production. From then on, when he talked, they listened. That gave him a boost of self-confidence."

Producer Desi had another brainstorm. Of course they could work around Lucy's pregnancy, but why do that? Why not incorporate the baby into the "Lucy" series?

In retrospect it is incredible that this idea actually presented problems! But in 1952, the mention of pregnancy, especially on a family program, was absolutely *verboten*. It was unheard of. Desi said, "We didn't want to do anything that would upset the public. I called the heads of the Catholic, Protestant and Jewish faiths in Los Angeles and asked them to assign representatives to keep an eye on our shows. So for eight weeks a rabbi, a Protestant minister and a Catholic priest checked every foot of film we shot. There was nothing we had to throw out except the word 'pregnant.' CBS didn't like that, so we used 'expectant.' CBS thought it a nicer word."

Although Louella Parsons had broken the news of Lucy's pregnancy in June, the Arnazes continued their plan not to discuss the baby and to break the news on television when their show resumed in the fall.

In September, Desi sat down in conference with a battery of press agents, including men from the network and from the sponsor. Their problem: how to squeeze the maximum have two babies: one in real life and one on TV. Suddenly one of the experts had an inspiration. Since Lucy's first baby had been delivered by caesarean section, her second child amount of publicity from the fact that Lucy was going to would have to be delivered that way too. Therefore, the date for her second baby could be pinpointed exactly. Why not, the group decided, have the real-life baby and the fictitious Ricardo baby born on the same day?

The press agents drew up a five-part confidential memo: "Various aspects of the Ricardo baby in the 'I Love Lucy' publicity and promotional campaign."

The entire group swore "that there must be absolutely no word about the baby released out of any office before December 8." On that date, forty million televiewers would be informed of the secret—Lucy Ricardo's pregnancy. Plans were made to tie the show in with a Columbia record of "There's a Brand New Baby at Our House," and on the flip side, "I Love Lucy," both songs sung by Desi and played by his orchestra.

The memo had a special section called "The Secret Gimmick About the Baby's Sex." This too required an inviolate pledge of secrecy on the part of all concerned. The memo read: "The Ricardo baby will be a boy regardless of the sex of the actual Arnaz baby. Of course, if the Arnaz baby does happen to be a boy, then all writers and editors can assume that the producers of 'I Love Lucy' are clairvoyant and possessed of sheer genius. If it happens to be a girl, the story (and the truth) is that Desi was so set on having a boy ... that he went ahead and filmed the Ricardo baby as if it were, regardless."

Naturally, the matter of the baby's sex had to be decided right away because a number of episodes of the show would have to be filmed well in advance of the baby's birth to give real-life Lucy time to have the baby and recuperate.

Just as the public had become immediately involved with

101

Lucy and Ricky Ricardo, they now became caught up in the excitement of both Lucy Ricardo's and Lucille Ball's expected baby. The public had come to identify completely the real-life Lucille and Desi with the TV characters of Lucy and Ricky.

The entire nation eagerly awaited the birth of the decade's most famous baby. On the morning of January 19, 1953, Lucille Ball gave birth to a son: Desiderio Alberto Arnaz IV, who weighed in at eight pounds, nine ounces.

That night on television, Lucy Ricardo gave birth to Little Ricky. The show garnered the all-time high Trendex rating for a regular commercial program: 68.8. CBS researchers estimated that over fifty million people watched the show, which had actually been filmed in November. Everyone connected with the program had been praying it would be a boy. Just as the television script demanded, the Fates complied. There was even a syndicated "I Love Lucy" comic strip at the time, and the day Lucy's son was actually born, the comic strip had Lucy Ricardo giving birth to a son. The real-life Arnazes were on the cover of *Newsweek* on January 19 as well.

Lucy, conscious during the delivery under a spinal anesthesia, constantly badgered her doctor, Joseph Harris, "What is it? What is it? Is it a boy?" He had to calm her several times and reply: "Wait a minute, honey."

Desi later said, "Nobody had to tell me it was a boy. I could tell by the expressions of the doctors and nurses." A few minutes after the birth, Desi burst into the corridor outside the operating room and, waving his arms, he shouted at the top of his lungs:

"It's a boy! It's a boy! Boy, do I love Lucy!"

Lucy's self-appointed godfather, Eddie Sedgwick, had the task of holding Desi IV up for friends to see. Sedgwick described the hospital drama as "a wonderful, marvelous, emotional, hilarious thing." Both grandmothers were at the hospital and each found family resemblances in the new-born. "He has a pug nose just like Lucy," said Desiree. "And black hair just like Desi," noted Mrs. Arnaz.

"God, this makes me the greatest writer in the world!" exclaimed Jess Oppenheimer.

That night, over the CBS network, when Lucy Ricardo gave birth to a boy, Ricky collapsed into a wheelchair at the good news.

Vivian Vance recalled, "The night we filmed the show in which Lucy tells Ricky about a baby coming, everybody on the set broke up. She cried, he cried, the propmen cried. We were so awash in tears that we prepared to do retakes on the show, but the audience stood up and yelled 'No! No! No!' The whole thing had been too real."

No modern child was ever ushered into the world with such attention. Years later, young Desi noted: "I'm probably the only flesh-and-blood human being ever brought into the world by a television network. . . . I'm told by my Hollywood friends—although I still find it hard to believe—that my birth attracted as much public attention and news coverage as the presidential inauguration of Dwight D. Eisenhower, which—apparently through poor planning in Washington—took place on the next day."

Desi, Jr.,'s information is correct. The night he was born on television the "I Love Lucy" show garnered a Neilsen rating of 71.7 per cent. President Eisenhower's inauguration scored 67.6 per cent.

That January morning of 1953 Desi Arnaz summed it up: "Now we have everything."

The world agreed.

Two weeks later Lucy was named Best TV Comedienne of 1952 and "I Love Lucy" received an Emmy as the Best Situation Comedy Show. (Other Emmy winners that year were "See It Now," "Dragnet" and "Robert Montgomery Presents.")

Lucille Ball and Desi Arnaz—biggest superstars in the entertainment world! Lucille was enjoying a success she had never known. When queried if she was interested in returning to films, she said she didn't care if she never made another movie. "I don't know if I'll ever work again in a theater movie," Lucy yawned. "It doesn't interest me a bit. Though I might do one this summer. Just to see how I look in Technicolor. You know I've been in gray and black for a long time now."

The movie studios, which had shunned Desi and shuttled Lucy around for years, now sought them desperately. In an era when movie stars who were Lucy's contemporaries were tumbling or had been toppled from box-office favor, Lucille Ball returned in triumph to MGM. The studio signed the Arnazes to star in *The Long, Long Trailer*, at a salary of $250,000 for six weeks work. (Desi had tried to buy the film rights to the book, but Metro had beaten him to it.)

Pandro S. Berman was assigned to produce; Vincente Minnelli, who had worked with Lucy in *Ziegfeld Follies of 1946*, was assigned to direct.

CBS and Philip Morris were aware of how valuable Lucy and Desi had become. A new contract was immediately negotiated with Desilu Productions. The contract was for a staggering $8,000,000, the largest ever signed in TV up to that time. It covered the completion of the 1952-53 season plus an additional two years of "I Love Lucy." The agreement contained an incredible "no option" clause. "I Love Lucy" could not be canceled for the duration of the contract. The budget of the show went up from $35,000 to $50,000 weekly. Desilu now employed three hundred people. Desi and Lucy were the highest paid entertainers on television.

In April, they were on the covers of both *Life* and *Look* magazines. Discussing their new eight-million-dollar deal, Lucy said: "It couldn't happen to a nicer pair of kids—I mean our children, of course."

Though Desi's professional and home lives had changed

somewhat, he still retained his fiery Latin temper, his flair for the dramatic, an eye for women and a love of excitement.

An observer was present at a typical poker game at the lush Beverly Hills Hotel. "In the game, which was seven-card stud, were Desi; Harry Chesley, a vice president of the company sponsoring 'I Love Lucy'; Larry Berns, who produced 'Our Miss Brooks'; David Jacobson, public relations director for CBS; and Jaime Delvalle, another producer.

"In the last pot, everyone was frozen out except Desi and Harry Chesley. Desi looked at his last card and gave Chesley an opportunity to look at his. Then he leaned across the table. 'You remember that eight-million-dollar contract we signed a little while ago?' said Desi. The sponsor was startled. 'Of course I remember it,' he said, 'who can forget a thing like that?' 'Well,' said Desi, 'I bet you that contract, double or nothing.'"

The friend shudders as he tells the story. "At first," he says, "there was complete silence. Then somebody giggled nervously. But everybody could see that Desi wasn't kidding. When the sponsor realized Desi was serious, he became pale. 'Cut it out, Desi,' he said, 'be reasonable.' Desi stared at him, then shrugged his shoulders and made a bet. He won the pot, I remember. But nobody can remember just what cards he held, because the shock was too great. Desi actually would have bet that eight-million-dollar contract, I'm convinced, and if he'd lost—I can just see him going home and saying, 'For the next two-and-a-half years, Lucy, we work for nothing.'"

It seemed as if Desi and Lucy's luck was boundless. Then, in the fall, Walter Winchell, on one of his Sunday night television broadcasts, started a national furor. Winchell named no names. He revealed: "The most popular of all television stars was confronted with evidence of her Communist Party membership."

6

It is difficult to comprehend today what it was like in the early 1950s to be called a Communist, or have any hint of Communist affiliations, loyalties or tendencies. Since 1947, various Hollywood elite, including studio chiefs Louis B. Mayer and Jack Warner and director Sam Wood, had gone before the House Committee on Un-American Activities and denounced certain writers and directors who were said to be members of the Communist party.

In December of 1947 the studio heads got together and decided to blacklist the now famous Hollywood Ten: Alvah Bessie, Herbert Biberman, Lester Cole, Edward Dmytryk, Ring Lardner, Jr., John Howard Lawson, Albert Maltz, Samuel Ornitz, Adrian Scott and Dalton Trumbo. Only one of this group—Edward Dmytryk—subsequently confessed to having been a Communist and then abjuring it.

"Guilt by association" became the order of the day and it became a dangerous time to voice political opinions.

Throughout the late 1940s and early 1950s various Hollywood luminaries such as Elia Kazan, Clifford Odets, Robert Rossen, Budd Schulberg and Sterling Hayden came forward voluntarily and confessed to having had associations with the Communist party. Others did not come forth voluntarily and would not supply the committee with names of friends and associates who at any time had been connected with "The Party."

John Garfield, at the height of his career in the late 1940s, couldn't get a job in the industry by 1951 because he had been denied "a clean bill of health" after testifying before the committee.

The Red Scare was at its height in the early 1950s. Senator Joseph McCarthy had everyone quaking in their boots. In addition to the Hollywood Ten, many other actors, writers and directors were "unofficially" blacklisted, including Abraham Polonsky, Ann Revere, Gale Sondergaard, Larry Parks and Marsha Hunt.

That America's most beloved personality—zany, wildly comical Lucille Ball—would be involved in any way with even a long-past Communist taint was literally inconceivable.

September, 1953 proved to be the blackest month in the life of Lucille Ball. She had registered as a Communist voter in California back in 1936. This sensational disclosure, which startled Americans coast to coast, was not news to the House Committee on Un-American Activities. The committee had known this for several years, but withheld it for lack of evidence that Lucy had ever actually belonged to the Communist party.

When Winchell finally told the story, all hell broke loose, although it might almost have been a relief to Lucy and Desi to have the matter out in the open. Rumors had been flying in the industry for almost a year and a half. (The *Los Angeles Examiner* later reported that on August 25, 1953, because

107

of "the recurrent movie trade rumors that the biggest TV star was soon to be accused of Communist ties," Desi had cornered Senator Joseph McCarthy in the lounge at the Del Mar race track and at the time the ardent anti-Communist assured Desi he had no information to Lucille's discredit.)

Following Winchell's report, Hedda Hopper, Lucille's good friend, began hearing from people who said, "To us the top television actress is Lucille Ball. Tell us the report isn't true." Hedda called Lucille and Desi and asked them about the matter. "This is the most ridiculous thing in the world," said Desi. "Lucille has never been accused of being a Communist. She is completely in the clear. All anybody has to do is check with the un-American activities committee. If she was a Communist they would call her for investigation."

According to Hedda, "Lucille herself came on the phone and denied that she was in any way affiliated with the Party. I asked if she had ever attended any of its meetings and was told she hadn't."

Reporters swarmed around the couple's sprawling ranch home in Northridge. Lucy was in the house but reporters weren't allowed to see her. Desi told them, "Lucille registered for the first time last year with me as a Democrat and we voted for Eisenhower. I know that she never registered as a Communist. You can check with the Un-American activities committee. That will prove that she isn't a Communist."

Desi's comment was in reply to a Los Angeles reporter who told him that the newspapers possessed a photostatic copy of an affidavit showing that Lucille had registered in 1936 as a voter "intending to affiliate at the ensuing primary election with the Communist party." The journalists had done their homework and with the clue from Winchell they had ferreted out information.

Desi, however, still flatly denied it. "What are you gonna do—spread it all over the country?" he snapped.

However, a few days later, Desi called Hedda Hopper to

confirm the report that Lucy had indeed been questioned by an investigator from the committee. He explained she had been approached first by the investigator in April. Lucy told Hedda, "They found a registration card in the 1936 primaries. They asked me about it. They refreshed my memory. I didn't recall anything about it. . . ."

Lucille's voice broke. "The reason we didn't tell you the other day was that the committee had asked us not to," Lucy tearfully explained.

"Did you register as a Communist or a Socialist in the election?" asked Hedda.

"I don't know what they called the Party then," she replied, crying as she continued, "The committee was satisfied twice. The second time they said they had to clear themselves for sure for they had heard that some magazine was coming out with the story. So they reopened the investigation privately.

"I was told there was an ex-Communist woman who was writing a book and she had information that we couldn't verify. We had never heard of anything like that and we had to get some answers on it. That is why they opened the case up again. I never had anything to cover up or be frightened about but they now have a sworn statement testifying . . ."

At this point Lucille could not continue and Desi came on the phone. "It's terrible, Hedda, that something the poor kid did in 1936 to please her grandfather can kick back in her face now. She has never in her life done wrong to anybody; has never had any sympathy for these Commies. You know, the girl has never even been connected with these pinks out here; she has never gone to meetings, never been a member of their party—this is terrible, Hedda. It was reported she was confronted with a Communist party card. That is a lie. She never had a card."

"But why didn't you tell me this when I asked the other morning?" Hedda asked. "If you had told me the committee didn't want this known you should have said, 'no comment, in a few days you'll understand.' And I would have understood."

"If I did something wrong to you the other day, please forgive me," replied Desi. "When you get in a spot like this, you don't know what the hell you're doing."

The storm broke just as Lucy and Desi were preparing to film a "Lucy" show for the new fall season. The year-long rumors burst into fact around frenzied network officials, sponsor executives and, of course, Lucille and Desi.

The din and confusion in the Desilu production offices were now for real and not caused by any script. Desi hopped around the room and loudly denied Lucille had ever been a member of the Communist party.

"She was never a Party member or held a card," said Desi. "She never belonged to any front organization or any committees. You know Lucy. She doesn't even know who the hell was governor last year."

Lucy, understandably distraught, was having her hair dyed, toning it down from its orangey-red to a softer shade. ("I just took some of the circus out of it.")

She finally appeared, with her eyes red as well as her hair. She admitted to the press that she had testified before the House committee and had registered as a Communist in 1936 "to please my grandfather."

It had been on September 4, 1953, that Lucille, her mother and brother Fred all testified before committee investigator William Wheeler. Wheeler had been the first to go to her home in April, 1952 to question Lucy. Desi said, "I even had *him* investigated before I let him come to the house. I called the FBI. I said, 'Who is this Wheeler?' They told me there was a man named Wheeler, all right, but I should ask to see his credentials."

Lucy said, "He asked only a few questions, there was no sworn testimony. Then he said, 'I'm satisfied there's nothing wrong here. Thank you very much. You'll probably never

110

hear of this again.'" Lucy continued that when Wheeler came back, "I was glad to see him. If he had any questions he wanted to ask, I wanted to answer them."

Desi interjected, "Anytime there are rumors of any kind it's their duty to investigate so it doesn't happen here what happened in Cuba."

Lucy and Desi reaffirmed that neither had made any public statement during the year and a half that her political past was under investigation because "they told us not to talk to people. They said there was no reason to talk to anybody."

At first there was an unrecorded interrogation in which Lucy promptly denied that she had ever joined the Communist party. But later Lucy was called in to give sworn testimony:

MR. WHEELER: Are you under subpoena or are you appearing voluntarily?

LUCILLE: I am appearing voluntarily.

MR. WHEELER: Did you ever reside at 1344 North Ogden Drive?

LUCILLE: Yes.

MR. WHEELER: Who owned that residence?

LUCILLE: We rented it. I don't remember who owned it.

MR. WHEELER: When did you first register to vote?

LUCILLE: I guess the first time I ever did was in 1936.

MR. WHEELER: I would like to hand you a photostatic copy of a voter's registration and ask you if that is your signature.

LUCILLE: That looks like my handwriting.

MR. WHEELER: You will note that the party that you intended to affiliate with at that time was the Communist party.

LUCILLE: In 1936?

MR. WHEELER: Yes.

LUCILLE: I guess so.

MR. WHEELER: You did register to vote then as a Communist or intending to vote the Communist party ticket?

LUCILLE: Yes.

111

MR. WHEELER: Would you go into detail and explain the background, the reason you voted or registered to vote as a Communist or person who intended to affiliate with the Communist party?

LUCILLE: It was our grandfather, Fred Hunt. He just wanted us to and we just did something to please him. I did not intend to vote that way, As I recall, I didn't. My grandfather started years ago—he was a Socialist as long as I can remember. He is the only father we ever knew, my grandfather. My father died when I was tiny, before my brother was born. He [grandfather] was my brother's only father.

All through his life he had been a Socialist, as far back as Eugene V. Debs, and he was in sympathy with the working man as long as I have known and he took the *Daily Worker*.

It never meant much to us, because he was so radical on the subject that he pressed his point a little too much, actually, probably, during our childhood, because he finally got over our heads and we didn't do anything but consider it a nuisance, but as a dad, and he got into his seventies, it became so vital to him that the world must be right twenty-four hours a day, all over it, and he was trying his damnedest to do the best he could for everybody and especially the working man, that is, from the garbage man, the maid in the kitchen, the studio worker, the factory worker. He never lost a chance to do what he considered bettering their positions.

That was fine, and we went along with it, wherever we could. Sometimes it got a little ridiculous because my position in the so-called capitalist world was pretty good and it was a little hard to reconcile the two. We didn't argue with him very much because he had had a couple of strokes and if he got overly excited, why, he would have another one.

So finally there came a point where my brother was twenty-one and he was going to see that Freddie registered to help the working man, which was, in his idea then, the Communist party. At that time it wasn't a thing to hide behind doors, to be a member of that party.

As I recall, because of this he influenced us. We thought we wanted to do him a favor. We thought we could make

112

him happy. I at no time intended to vote that way. And I remember discussing it with my mother, how I could register and make him happy. When I go behind a curtain to vote, nobody knows who I vote for.

He also considered it a personal victory at the time that he had gotten the entire family to register. He didn't influence us enough at any time to vote; at least, he didn't influence me.

He influenced us to give a great deal of thought to whether he was right or wrong, and we always decided he was wrong, because the things he was shouting about didn't seem to be practical for this country. He admired the working man and the peasants all over the world, the five-year plan and anything that was great for the working man.

MR. WHEELER: He considered the Communist party as a working man's party?

LUCILLE: That is all I ever heard. I never heard my grandfather use the word "Communist." He never said that he read the *Daily Worker*. He always talked about the working man.

He got very confused in his latter years, when Russia and—who got together?—Russia and Germany got together and he got so he couldn't answer our questions at all then. And he would get mad and change the subject. He never quite could find out what happened to the working man after that, I guess.

We were never able to keep a maid, although we paid the highest prices we could afford or they were getting at the time. My grandfather would walk out into the kitchen and see a maid and would say, "Well, what is your name? How much are you getting?"

"Oh, $20 or $25 a week," or whatever they were being paid.

And he would say: "That is not a working wage. What are you doing here?"

And after a few weeks of that, you know, they would leave. That is just one instance.

He was always talking to the garbage man early in the morning, or anybody doing any kind of menial task, he would say, "Why are you doing that? Why aren't you doing something else?"

113

He was just a fanatic on bettering the world. That is as far as we knew, and that is why we could endorse it at all.

MR. WHEELER: Have you ever been a member of the Communist party?

LUCILLE: No, not to my knowledge.

MR. WHEELER: Have you ever been asked to become a member of the Communist party?

LUCILLE: No.

MR. WHEELER: Did you ever attend any meetings that you later discovered were Communist party meetings?

LUCILLE: No.

MR. WHEELER: Do you know whether or not any meetings were ever held in your home at 1344 North Ogden Drive?

LUCILLE: No, I know nothing of that. I don't believe it is true.

MR. WHEELER: How old were you in 1936?

LUCILLE: I am forty-two now, twenty-four.

Wheeler went on to question Lucy about several petitions she had signed in the Thirties supporting communist candidates and causes. More startling, however, was the accusation by former Communist Rena M. Vale who said her party indoctrination meeting had been held in Lucy's Ogden Drive residence. Lucy had no explanation and denied any knowledge of her house being so used. Neither did she have an explanation for being listed as a delegate to the Communist party's state central committee one year.

The Committee was also concerned with a few of Lucy's activities during the 1940s.

MR. WHEELER: Are you acquainted with the Committee of the First Amendment?

LUCILLE: Am I acquainted with it?

MR. WHEELER: Yes.

LUCILLE: Not to my knowledge.

MR. WHEELER: Or were you a member of the Committee of the First Amendment?

LUCILLE: Not to my knowledge.

MR. WHEELER: Well, your name is mentioned in the Daily People's World, the issue of October 28, 1947, page one, columns five and six, as one of the high personalities who

114

were sponsoring or a member of the Committee of the First Amendment.

That committee was formed here in Hollywood to oppose the Congressional hearings in 1947.

LUCILLE: Refresh my memory on it. I can't imagine ever signing that. Did I sign that, too? Was it under an assumed name?

MR. WHEELER: That I don't know. There was a reference to it.

LUCILLE: What is the People's World? Is that like the Daily Worker?

MR. WHEELER: Yes, a Communist publication of the western states.

LUCILLE: In 1947? That certainly was not for Grandpa. Grandpa was gone by then. I can't imagine doing anything for these people. If I was hoodwinked into it, with one of those long democratic souped-up names, that is something else. Could I see that?

MR. WHEELER: I don't have a copy of the People's World for that date.

LUCILLE: Am I supposed to have signed something in sympathy?

MR. WHEELER: Your name was used as in—

LUCILLE: Was it used or did I sign something?

MR. WHEELER: I have no knowledge of your signing.

LUCILLE: Fine. Then I have no knowledge of signing it. However, I do recall I was at a studio, and I was working on a picture and I got a call in the afternoon. I don't know who called me. I assume now—I did then—it was the Screen Actors Guild, but I can be wrong. I don't know who called me now. It was something that was through a union or the studio wouldn't have felt compelled to send me off a set and hold up production until I got back. It had nothing to do with me.

·I got the call to go to a radio station. As I remember, it was MGM—it may not have been. I remember an executive excused me and sent me to this broadcast.

I got down there and said, "What am I supposed to do?"

She said, "Dorothy Petersen"—whoever she is—"she is ill. We have to go on the air."

She said, "Will you read this?"

115

It was a long petition, or whatever you call them, as I recall. As I recall—I am not sure of this—it was about the Okies in upstate California, Fresno or someplace, about admitting the Okies. I read it. They thanked me and they sent me back to work.

I don't know how long after that it was that I was called downtown in an FBI office and asked why I did it. Apparently, it was wrong. It was my first knowledge it was wrong.

I had no answer at all, because I hadn't done it of my own volition. I had been sent there. It didn't seem wrong to go some place the studio had sent you.

I tried to explain why I had done it. I had no reason except I had been called.

MR. WHEELER: How long ago did you go to the FBI?

LUCILLE: I have no idea. I have no idea when I did this broadcast. I have no idea how long after that they called me. But that is the first time I ever—

MR. WHEELER: It was three or four years ago?

LUCILLE: It is more than that.

MR. WHEELER: Did they discuss with you at that time —

LUCILLE: Must have been six, eight, nine years ago, maybe ten. There were two broadcasts. I don't know who sent me on the first one and I don't know what the second one was about. It was something that everybody was doing. You just got asked to do these things. I again was called in at the last minute.

I had nothing to do with whatever it was. I didn't know what I was doing, but you assumed at the time, when you are called by a union or one of your—I don't know who called me. I know both times I was called to replace someone.

MR. WHEELER: Did you discuss this material today with the FBI or did they question you regarding your voter's registration?

LUCILLE: No. That was apparently just something I had read on the radio I shouldn't have. I don't know.

She concluded the interrogation with the following:

LUCILLE: I am very happy to have this opportunity to dis-

116

cuss all the things that have cropped up, that apparently I have done wrong.

I am aware of only one thing I did that was wrong, and that at the time wasn't wrong, but apparently now it is, and that was registering because my grandfather wanted us to. I at no time thought it was the thing to do, nor did I ever intend to vote in the presidential election, I guess it was at that time, I don't know. To my knowledge, I didn't vote, but I did register. Since then I have never done anything knowingly against the United States.

I have never done anything for Communists, to my knowledge, at any time. I have never contributed money or attended a meeting or ever had anything to do with people connected with it, if to my knowledge they were.

I am not a Communist now. I have never been. I never wanted to be. Nothing in the world could ever change my mind. At no time in my life have I ever been in sympathy with anything that even faintly resembled it.

I was always opposed to how my grandfather felt about any other way this country should be run. I thought things were just fine the way they were.

It sounds a little weak and silly and corny now, but at the time it was very important because we knew we weren't going to have daddy with us very long. If it made him happy, it was important at the time. But I was always conscious of the fact I could go just so far to make him happy. I tried not to go any farther.

In those days that was not a big, terrible thing to do. It was almost as terrible to be a Republican in those days. I have never been too civic minded and certainly never political minded in my life.

. . . We went maybe a little strongly Democratic one year and we got into trouble doing that. That is when Roosevelt was still active. We were always very much for Roosevelt and did everything that Mr. and Mrs. Roosevelt asked us to do, as all of Hollywood, or as most of Hollywood, was doing.

He was the only President I had ever known. It was a wonderful thing to get out and help him with his March of Dimes or bond tours during the war and we were very

117

busy. Never in my life have I had any other feeling than the Communists were wrong, that anybody in this town would dare to think of changing any of it or complaining about what they had is just the most ridiculous thing I have ever heard of.

I certainly was never in sympathy with the Dmytryks, I can't remember any of the other names.

How we got to signing a few things or going among some people that thought differently, that has happened to all of us out here in the last ten or twelve years and it is unfortunate, but I certainly will do anything in the world to prove that we made a bad mistake by, for one week or a couple of weeks, trying to appease an old man. But there has never been any thought of belonging or wanting to belong to the Communist party.

MR. WHEELER: I have no further questions. Thank you for your cooperation.

Lucille's mother and brother also testified. They too explained they did it to please and pacify Grandpa Hunt.

Mrs. Ball said she registered to vote as a Communist because "my daddy wanted us to. My father was an old man, and that was the one thing that he thought was all right . . . we did it to please him."

When asked about purported meetings in their Ogden Drive home, she testified, "Never, never." She explained she had engaged a nurse for her father in 1936.

"We never left the house," she testified, "because daddy had these heart attacks and things. In fact, he was bedridden a good share of the time and she was supposed to be there, you know and give him a shot if necessary . . .

"I asked her if there ever was a meeting, or anything, when I wasn't there, that I might have been out. I was going to Hollywood High at the time, evening classes.

"She said to her knowledge she had never known of it because daddy always went to bed early."

Mrs. Ball identified the nurse as Elaine E. Stewart, who was still with her.

118

"We didn't question daddy because, I mean, he was so firm in his beliefs and everything, that if he thought it was all right, we did it."

DeDe also said she didn't know whether her father had actually belonged to the Communist party. But when he died she had gone through his wallet and hadn't found any party membership card.

Fred Ball told the committee much the same information but noted he had been discharged from the employ of Vega Aircraft after signing one petition.

Ball said he tried to get character letters from friends to get the job back because he didn't feel he had done anything wrong and was being accused of not being a good American.

He worked at other defense plants later without trouble, he said, and served fifteen months in the Army, getting an honorable discharge.

"Grandpa," he said, "died with the phrase on his lips, 'working man,' and that is all. That is all there ever was to it, in any sense of the word. All he cared about was the poor guy next door. That is why we went along with him. It is merely a matter of our loving Grandpa, helping him bide his time."

"Loving Grandpa" back in 1936 was causing for Lucille Ball, her brother and mother, the biggest problem they had yet faced. Not to mention the problems it was causing for Desi, who had to deal with the army of hysterical network and sponsor brass who had visions of their golden goose being roasted.

Obviously the only thing to do was to reveal everything and pray that the public would understand and continue to love Lucy.

Lucy issued a statement through CBS Vice President Harry Ackerman saying, "It is true I have talked to a representative of the House Un-American Activities Committee and have given full and truthful answers to their questions. I am very happy to have had this opportunity to reply to unfounded rumors and hope very much the committee will see fit to release a complete transcript of the information I gave."

Ackerman said Lucille was perfectly willing to stand on the statement she gave to the committee investigator. When reporters questioned Ackerman about Desi's statement that reports of Lucy's being a Communist were "ridiculous," Ackerman replied: "I think that the committee's report on Miss Ball will prove him to be absolutely right."

At Lucille's request, the House committee, through its member Donald L. Jackson, a Republican from California, released for publication the transcript of her testimony to "present Miss Ball's status factually and officially."

Jackson hastily summoned a press conference at which he declared that the committee had no evidence that Lucille Ball had ever joined the Communist party. The following day, with a degree of haste unmatched in the thousands of other cases investigated by the committee, the entire transcript of Lucille Ball's examination was made public.

Some members of the press felt that pressure to release the testimony had been brought from high sources. It was obvious that CBS, Philip Morris and MGM all had enormous investments in the careers of Lucille Ball and Desi Arnaz.

Representative Jackson said, in releasing the transcript, "The House Committee on Un-American Activities is not unaware of the tremendous responsibility resting upon it to insure that those guilty of participation in the Communist conspiracy be exposed, whenever and wherever possible. By the same token, there rests upon the committee an obligation to insure that distortion of available facts be not permitted and that rumor not be substituted for the truth in any case. The prominence of Miss Ball as an outstanding moving picture and television artist is secondary to the committee's determination to be fair and just in all instances.

"In light of the fact that irreparable damage may result to

120

Miss Ball unless the full extent of the committee's information is disclosed, the committee has decided to release to the press and radio a sworn affidavit given to a committee investigator by Miss Ball . . ."

Jackson's statement went on to stress that Lucy had cooperated with the committee investigator "in all respects."

On Friday night, on schedule, Lucille and Desi prepared to film "I Love Lucy." Representative Jackson's statement had already appeared in the press. It was Lucy and Desi's first public appearance since the story broke. The studio audience, as always, was SRO—three hundred people. Before the show got under way, Desi addressed them: "I want to talk to you about something serious. Lucy has never been a Communist, not now and never will be." The audience let loose with a burst of applause that lasted a full minute. "I was kicked out of Cuba," Desi continued, "because of Communism. We despise everything about it. Lucy is as American as Bernie Baruch and Ike Eisenhower.

"By the way, we both voted for Eisenhower—so ladies and gentlemen, don't judge too soon—read for yourselves. Read her story. Don't believe every piece of bunk you read in some papers."

When Desi introduced his wife, he called her "My favorite redhead, and that's the only thing red about Lucy and even that is not legitimate."

The studio audience cheered Lucy as she appeared and both Lucy and Desi were teary-eyed as they acknowledged the applause and acceptance. An observer that night remembers that as the show progressed, Lucy cavorted as always. Her comedy showed no signs of the stress of that day. A doctor, however, was in attendance for fear she might collapse under the strain. But he was not needed, and when the show concluded, Lucy addressed the studio audience with a simple: "God bless you for being so kind."

The next morning, Saturday, a day when newspapers have

121

their lowest circulation, the transcript of Lucy's testimony was printed.

"The investigation of the committee will of course continue with respect to this case," Representative Jackson said in one story. He hastened to explain: "No case is ever closed. There are a couple of points we want to check."

Jackson said, however, that there was "no present plan to call Miss Ball as a witness" and that the committee had received no information to contradict her own flat declaration that she "is not and never was a Communist party member, or that she never attended a Communist meeting."

Jackson's unprecedented disclosure of committee information "at the investigation level" came after a telephone poll of other committee members around the nation, giving him approval to go ahead.

Lucy and Desi held a press conference that Saturday, after the testimony had been released. She wore a white blouse with an embroidered "Lucille" on it, a pink hair ribbon and pink linen toreador pants. Desi wore an air of relief that it was all over.

Lucille remarked that she had never seen Congressman Jackson, but from his picture in the paper she concluded, "He's a pretty good-looking guy."

Despite her reiteration that her conscience had always been clear, Lucille expressed gratitude to the House committee for releasing all her statement promptly, as she had requested. She admitted she had been in the dark as to what public reaction would be, but said she took the attitude in the past two days, "If anyone is making more of this than they should, why—let 'em!"

Desi added happily that their TV sponsor, involved in their eight million dollars' worth of immediate future, already had telephoned its support.

Grandpa Hunt came in for considerable discussion. Needless to say, Lucy and Desi discussed Grandpa and Lucy's past considerably less seriously than over the past week. Desi told how part of his penance in waiting for Lucille on pre-marriage dates was to listen to the old man read editorials aloud from the *Daily Worker*.

"He'd say: 'Sit down, young man. Listen to this,'" Desi recalled, and Desi would do just that, until Lucille showed up. Then he'd urge her, "Let's get out of here!"

Desi continued, "He was just the kind of a guy who wanted everybody in the whole world to be happy and get more money—I've got lots of people like that working in Desilu Productions right now. They're in my office every day, asking for raises!"

When reporters asked Lucille about her signature on a certificate in behalf of a Communist candidate in June, 1936, her big eyes aimed an SOS at Desi.

"Now, Lucy," he said, "I wanna tell you. I have been married to you for thirteen years and in that time you have signed I don't know how many thousand papers. And you haven't read one of them yet!"

Another reporter asked: "Didn't you think then, back in 1936, that this might hurt your career?"

"Career?" quipped Lucy. "I didn't have any career. I was a stock girl at RKO. Down in the small print it said I had to sweep out the office if they wanted me to."

"How old were you then?"

"I don't even know how old I am now!"

Discussing the previous night's show and the heartwarming reception they received, Lucy said: "I was pretty numb. But I was thrilled the way the audience acted. It was sensational. Unbelievable. More than you could hope for."

Lucy insisted to the reporters that she was "glad the whole thing has come out. We asked them, begged them to bring it out."

Two or three times during the afternoon Lucy's saucer eyes watered up, but she held her tears back. Lest anyone think they took the situation lightly, Desi kissed her on the cheek from time to time and muttered, "This has been terrible, terrible."

During the press conference Lucy was only occasionally her usual saucy self. "In the last couple of days," she noted, often dabbing her perspiring forehead with an embroidered hanky, "I've realized this is nothing to laugh about."

Lucy expressed total confidence in the public's understanding of the entire incident. "Hurt me?" she said. "I have more faith in the American people than that. I feel that any time you give the American people the truth they're with you."

While Lucy visited the powder room, Desi took a dip in the pool. He climbed out smiling, dripping and cool.

"You know, Desi," remarked a reporter, "yesterday was one of the hottest days of the year."

"You're tellin' me!" he exclaimed.

After Saturday's press conference, Lucy and Desi spent a quiet day alone on Sunday. Lucy was reportedly "doing housework and tending her babies."

"We're tremendously happy and grateful to everyone all over the country for their support," Desi told the press. "We've had thousands of wires and telephone messages and they're still pouring in."

He added that he and his wife were grateful to the press for its complete handling of the facts.

However, the furor wasn't over yet.

7

THOUGH EXONERATED by her public, Lucy gave information in her testimony which angered the right wing press. They felt that some radio broadcasts she had made in the 1940s, which she claimed were at the request of her studio and about which she recalled little, obviously had nothing to do with Grandpa and were difficult to explain.

Those who criticized her did so for three reasons: first, they contended that a twenty-four-year-old woman certainly *was* responsible for her actions; secondly, they implied that she had registered as a Communist because it would further her career, since in the 1930s many Communist sympathizers were in positions of power in the movie industry and people who did not sympathize suddenly found that they couldn't get jobs at the studios; thirdly, Lucy was criticized because she hadn't come forward voluntarily "to confess her past actions" but had waited until she had been "ferreted out" before "baring her soul to the public."

Columnist Ed Sullivan made some pertinent comments about the affair. He expressed the views of many when he wrote: "It's a singularly fortunate thing for Lucille Ball that she's been a weekly visitor to millions of American living rooms. In those Monday night visits, people have come to know her well. TV cameras being as revealing as they are, so the jury of Public Opinion is an informed jury as it renders a verdict on a silly thing she did seventeen years ago. 'Never be stupid enough to believe that people have the mentality of twelve-year-olds,' George Arliss warned actors and playwrights. 'Assemble them in a theatre, or any place else, tell them your story and you'll find that their mass instinct is perilously close to intelligence.'"

In Lucy's defense, Sullivan tried to re-create for his readers what the year 1936 had been like, showing how few people were concerned with "the Communist threat":

"I checked back through the papers of March, 1936, to reconstruct the era. The great menace then was Hitler, who had sent his goose-stepping troops into the Rhineland to test British and French reaction. . . . Soviet Russia then was talking in low tones. 'For the third time in the eighteen months since my country joined the League of Nations,' said Maxim Litvinoff, 'I must speak again on a breach of international relations and ask the League to secure guarantees from Germany.' In Frankfurt thousands cheered defiant Hitler as he ridiculed the Versailles and Locarno pacts.

"The March, 1936, papers were telling of Dr. Hugo Eckener's *Graf Zeppelin*, which would cross the ocean in sixty-five hours! Five major airlines in this country had just commissioned Donald Douglas to build a forty-passenger plane with a range of 900 miles, visioning a coast-to-coast trip in thirteen hours! The first color picture, *Becky Sharp*, was to be followed by another, *Dancing Pirate*. At St. Petersburg, Yankee manager Joe McCarthy told Col. Jake Ruppert that Coast League youngster Joe DiMaggio would start the A.L.

126

season in left field. Radio headliners, on March 19, 1936, were Rosa Ponselle and John Charles Thomas. Sonja Henie, Olympic champ, told New York newsmen she was turning pro, wanted to get a picture contract. In Trenton, New Jersey, Bruno Hauptmann was less than a month away from death.

"*The 1936 Ziegfeld Follies* starred Bob Hope, Gertrude Niessen, Harriet Hoctor, Josephine Baker . . . George White, in a backstage scrap at the New Amsterdam Theatre, belted Rudy Vallee out of *Scandals* . . . Undergrads at Princeton and eighteen other colleges organized 'Pay Before Death Clubs,' representing themselves as future war veterans seeking bonuses in advance."

In Ed Sullivan's opinion, "About the only one alert to, and articulate about, communism, in March, 1936, was the stage manager of the Biltmore Theatre, on West 47th Street, an unsung hero, Willie Browne.

"After the first rehearsal of the WPA drama, *Triple A Plowed Under*, stage manager Browne rushed a wire to Al Smith, chief speaker of the Friendly Sons of St. Patrick Holiday Ball, calling attention to Browne's belief that 'the play carries Communist propaganda.' The Federal Theatre project regional director, Yale's Philip W. Barber, denied this. Barber had succeeded Elmer Rice, who had resigned in protest against Washington censorship of the 'Living Newspaper' treatment of *Ethiopia*.

"So," concluded Sullivan, "I believe Lucille Ball when she says she didn't know much about Communism in 1936. Stage manager Willie Browne was one of the few showfolk who was on the ball."

But not all columnists defended Lucille. Right-wing columnist Westbrook Pegler became infuriated with the "kind" treatment of her in the press. He devoted his entire syndicated column to "the Lucille Ball Case" soon after her committee appearance. Pegler wrote: "In some published com-

ments on the affair of Lucille Ball . . . I detected a threat that
any loyal American who does not forgive this woman will be
punished. I do not react favorably to threats and I would not
forgive her anyway, because she did not come clean but had
to be tracked down and exposed. The propositions that she
was 'only twenty-four years old' and that her grandfather
was a family tyrant, a Socialist who made her do this, have
no value at all with me."

To read Pegler today presents a penetrating view of how
vociferous anti-Communists thought and wrote in 1953.
Pegler went on to say: "I hate Communists. I wish it were
possible to round up all those who are reasonably known to
be Communists, including all who have invoked the Fifth
Amendment, and put them into concentration camps as aus-
tere as the Arizona State Prison, where relatively harmless
and morally stupid criminals of the common sort must dip
water from the john if they get thirsty in the dead of summer
nights in the desert . . ."

Other Hollywood stars did not escape Pegler's wrath.
"There have been a lot of nasty fakers in Hollywood. I am
thinking of Edward G. Robinson and the late John Garfield
among those who thought it was smart to sneer at the
patriotism of better men and women earning a lot less
money by much harder and more productive work. When
they were caught they whined that they had been poor
when they were young, that they were idealists, and that
they now were terribly disillusioned, so excuse it, please
. . ."

It was Pegler's opinion that "This Ball woman knew what
she was doing when she registered with the Communists,
and I can tell you that the poor devils out there in Hollywood who fought the traitors in the movie business took terrible persecution. They suddenly lost out at the studios,
never knowing why. They got threadbare. They got drunk
and despondent, and the Reds sneered at them and snubbed
them. Their friends were afraid to be seen with them.

128

"They could have done the same thing that Lucille Ball did, but they were too courageous and loyal. Some of them have died. Did Lucille Ball ever send any of these brave, lonely men a note of confidence or encouragement? Did she ever call up Jimmy McGuinness or Pat McNutt and admit that they were right and that she had been wrong?

"Socialist grandfather. That is a new variant of the whine of the crooked White Sox player who did it for the wife and kiddies."

While such attacks horrified the Arnazes, most newspapermen were in their corner. Some wrote rebuttals to Pegler. Syndicated columnist Royce Brier said:

"It appears to be high time for the American people to pause in a moment of self-questioning, relative to the case of Lucille Ball. . . . The Ball case is preposterously simple, and so the more easily examined by the people to determine if they want this public stock to be continued in its current indiscriminate use."

Brier defended Lucy as vigorously as Pegler had denounced her. "Rumors of Miss Ball's former Communist 'affiliations' have been drifting around for some years. The committee decided to look into it.

"What wrongdoing the committee expected to expose is not clear. Doubtless if it could discover she was a messenger for the transmission of atomic secrets to Soviet agents, she could be arrested. If she asserted her right not to testify against herself under the Fifth Amendment, she could be toppled from her high place in the entertainment world. If she were hauled before the committee and said it was nobody's business what she thought seventeen years ago, the committee would be furious and would issue excoriating bulletins about her."

But the columnist noted that the events that overtook many could not overtake Lucille Ball. "She said, as she must say because her registration was public, that she had registered as a Communist. She said she was not now a Communist and had never been one. The committee believed her, having no evidence beyond what she conceded and said that was all.

"That was enough, and indeed, too much. Surely every middle-aged citizen of this country (Miss Ball is forty-two) is not under moral obligation to arise publicly and confess his or her manifestations of immaturity or ignorance at twenty-five. And surely no committee of Congress is going to save the nation from subversion by operating permanent machinery for such a confessional."

Brier voiced the opinion of many liberal thinkers of the day when he concluded: "Our freedom is in peril if this pillory for the exhibition of peccadillo and casual dissent is permitted to stand indefinitely. But it is up to us. The Congress cannot filch our liberty. Only we can from ourselves filch our liberty."

Through the month of September and into early October, the attacks against and defenses of Lucy's actions dragged on. A group of war veterans in Indianapolis protested against her appearance on television. The group, which included two former American Legion post commanders, sent a petition to the Philip Morris Tobacco Company which said that the signers would "switch to another brand of cigarettes" until she was replaced. The petition also said, "we intend to use our memberships in veterans' organizations to combat the appearance on TV, stage or screen, of anyone supporting or belonging to any party supervised by the Soviets."

Isolated unpleasant cases such as this certainly didn't reflect the country's thinking, but they did crop up and create bad publicity. However, *Variety* summed it up: FANS LOVE LUCY—TAKE HER SIDE IN RED AFFAIR. Her network was satisfied, her sponsor was satisfied, and Lucy's TV ratings remained in the stratosphere.

By the end of October, the affair was forgotten, but Lucy didn't forgive Walter Winchell. When asked how she thought he had discovered her secret she replied acidly, "Walter Winchell knew I was pregnant before I did myself."

The Arnazes had weathered the greatest storm they had yet faced. Their success had been on the line. Now that it was all over, Desilu's future was brighter than ever. In ensuing years, the entire Communist episode would be completely ignored by Lucille and Desi. The matter was never again written about in a single interview over the next twenty years.

There was no doubt that America had forgiven and forgotten the whole affair. Someone who was then on the scene notes today, "You have to keep one thing in mind here. Revealing Lucille Ball to have Communist affiliations was tantamount to saying the same thing about your favorite relative.

"Lucille *was*—still is—middle America. As far as the public was concerned, she was—is—like a favorite neighbor. She was not an offbeat 'Hollywood type' or a New York 'stage type' who had been spouting social-oriented causes. She was the housewife next door. She was *loved*. The idea of her being a Communist sympathizer at any time was so preposterous in the minds of most Americans that Lucille's explanation to the committee was eagerly accepted and the entire episode was quickly dismissed."

In November, 1953, the B'nai B'rith named Lucille "Woman of the Year." It was the first time the award had gone to an actress and it was presented for her "untiring efforts for charitable causes—Community Chest, March of Dimes, Red Cross, YMCA, Cerebral Palsy, American Cancer Society, City of Hope, Sister Kenny Foundation" and many others.

The day after the awards, Lucy and Desi flew to Washington for "Dinner with the President," a special telecast honoring President Dwight D. Eisenhower.

131

8

LUCY AND DESI went back to work selling America's best-known commodity—marriage—to their millions of fans. They appeared to live the roles offscreen as well. Lucy often attributed the success of their show to their "ideal" private lives. "I always felt our show was so successful because somehow, through film and over the air, we communicated the fact that we were excited about each other. It wouldn't have been the same had we just been playing married."

Their Desilu ranch in Northridge had been turned into a wonderful working farm. Lucy and Desi admitted, however, that "we have been more successful as producers of television shows and babies than as ranchers. We tried chickens on our five-acre place. We acquired two hundred hens and named them all. Having named them and petted them—you can *so* pet a hen—we naturally couldn't eat them. Desi even refused to eat their eggs. Most of them have now died of old age.

"Desi said that a pig was the thing for Christmas. In Cuba you always have a pig for Christmas. So we bought one at Easter time. When Christmas arrived, the pig was a hog and we adored it. We wouldn't eat our friend."

Discussing their reluctance to kill animals, Lucy recalled, "We bought a calf and named her the Duchess of Devonshire. The second night we had her she developed pneumonia. I grabbed electric blankets, pads, turpentine and sat up all night. I nursed her for a month, she recovered, and she too became one of our close acquaintances. Well nurtured and pampered, she shot up to fifteen hundred pounds and became a problem cow. One morning she stuck her head through the bedroom window and walked into the house. Then we called the dairy.

" 'Beautiful,' they said. 'Wonderful cow. We'll butcher her for you.'

"I shrieked and Desi stammered. 'No,' we said, 'just board her. Give her a nice room.'

"When the bill came to fifteen hundred dollars we clenched our teeth and told the dairy people to do what was right but not to let us know."

Lucy also noted, "Desi's hobby now is boats. He has a cruiser at Balboa Island into which I creep only when shanghaied. Like Betty Bogart, whose husband Humphrey is a famous yachtsman, I believe that a woman's place is in the home or anyway in some cozy night club." (Lucy had obviously forgotten how she loathed night clubs when Desi was earning his living in them.)

The Arnaz home had undergone considerable change after the children were born . . . $22,000 worth of change! The grey and yellow nursery, housed in a separate wing from the main house, had its own workroom, patio, play area, nurse's bedroom and an intercom with a direct hookup to Lucy's and Desi's bedroom. But by Hollywood standards the ranch house remained very informal. The great financial wealth

133

that "I Love Lucy" brought them did not change the Arnazes' lifestyle a great deal. Lucy's mother lived nearby as did Desi's who by this time had divorced the senior Señor Arnaz.

The new TV season had begun. It was their third year on the air, and, as with any television show in the top spot, they began to be the object of sneers and snide forecasts: "Lucy and Desi on the Downgrade? ... Comedy Couple Finds It Hard to Maintain Terrific Ratings ..."

Some guessed long before the Communist headlines broke that Lucy was in for a slide in popularity. Not a big slide, just some sort of leveling off. After all, the show had racked up the most amazing ratings ever, and it seemed logical that it would subside.

One critic wrote: "The opening show was pretty funny. Just pretty funny. Last year's opening, as I recall, was a riot. This one wasn't ... the Lucy shows, let's face it, are beginning to sound an awful lot alike. Miss Ball is always trying to bust out of the house; Arnaz is trying to keep her in apron strings. The variations on this theme are infinite, but it's the same and I'm a mite tired of it. I don't think I'll ever get tired of Miss Ball, though; she's a joy to watch."

Though the critics were getting a mite tired of "I Love Lucy," the public wasn't. The show was one of the few comedies on TV in which husbands were not portrayed as children. While the show had no monopoly on the humor inherent in marriage—certainly the idea was as old as time—what the imitators lacked was the extraordinary discipline and intuitive understanding of farce that the "I Love Lucy" scripts provided and the four members of the cast projected.

Lucy and Desi always knew what they were doing. Every episode of "I Love Lucy" began with a logical and believable premise. The groundwork was laid for the essential situation: Lucy vs. Ricky.

"I Love Lucy" was, in other words, marriage projected in larger-than-life size. But still believable, in order to communicate with the viewer. By exaggerating marriage they helped put it in sharp focus. And, most importantly and holding it all together, was the character—and person—of Lucy, possessing wifely patience, always the regular gal and the good sport. She was *real*.

The show remained at the top of the ratings.

On November 30, Desi surprised Lucy with a thirteenth wedding anniversary party at Mocambo, a Sunset Strip night club. Lucy had expected a quiet dinner with Desi and their friend Vincente Minnelli (who had directed them in *The Long, Long Trailer*) and his date. When they arrived at Mocambo, Desi took Lucy to a back room.

"We can't go in there," said Lucy. "Someone's having a party."

She was right. It was *her* party, with more than forty guests, who sang "Happy Anniversary" to the visibly stunned star. "This is the first time in my life I've ever really been surprised," exclaimed Lucy. She kissed Desi and added, "Honey, I just love the way you did this."

Along with a special anniversary cake Mocambo owner Charley Morrison provided a television set for the party. The highlight of the evening was tuning in to the regular Monday night broadcast of "I Love Lucy."

As a matter of fact, people all over the country were pausing from 9 to 9:30 P.M. on Mondays to tune in America's favorite show. There had been nothing like it since radio's "Amos 'n' Andy," which, in the 1930s, had brought America's home life to a halt every night for fifteen minutes. Chicago's mammoth Marshall Field department store changed its evening shopping hours from Mondays to Thursdays because so few customers showed up on "Lucy" night. Even the telephone company reported that fewer calls were made during that time period.

135

The New Year brought more riches to Lucy and Desi. MGM released *The Long, Long Trailer*, which was a huge and immediate success. The Arnazes were not only king and queen of television but of the big screen as well, and they were the only television superstars who could draw at the movie box office.

Offscreen, Lucy and Desi were concerned with bringing up their children. Although Lucy had admitted "I am no expert on babies . . . ," she was adamant in telling the public that she had not had her caesarean because of fear of pain or vanity. "I believe word has gotten around that some Hollywood actresses have their babies by caesarean because they are afraid of pain or because they fear normal delivery will do something to their figures," said Lucille. "Other girls may regard this method with envy, lacking the necessary cash to finance it or, bitterly, despising the actresses for cowardice. I know this: doctors do not encourage caesareans unless they are necesssary. At least one prominent pediatrician tells me that normally born babies, even when they arrive after long labor in a condition he calls 'beat up,' are usually stronger than the unexercised caesarean babies. My first baby had to be born by caesarean and so my second, weighing eight pounds nine ounces and strong as a tractor, was also delivered by caesarean, because normal delivery would not have been possible. I shouldn't like to be accused of saving my figure. Because of young Lucie and her new brother, I've hardly had a figure for the last few years."

Like most little girls, Lucie loved to imitate her mother. One day, Lucy was sounding off at home about someone or other. "Who does he think he is?" she demanded. "What a nerve! I'd like to tell him a thing or two."

Little Lucie, playing with a doll in a corner, said nothing. But a few days later, Lucille and her daughter were waiting on a Hollywood sidewalk for their car. Little Lucie chose this moment to show off. "That driver!" she shrilled. "What a nerve! Why isn't he here? Who does he think he is?"

Three or four passing mothers stopped in their tracks and looked around. Little Lucie was just warming up. "He should be waiting for us here instead of keeping us waiting like this," she declared. "What a nerve!"

"Hush, dear," said Lucille, smiling glassily at the ladies who were glaring at her.

"He oughta be fired!" bellowed little Lucie. "I'd like to tell him a thing or two!" All around, the faces grew frostier and frostier. Nothing was said but "so *this* is the way Lucille Ball brings up her children" was in every expression.

The car finally pulled up and Lucille bundled her still screeching daughter inside, followed by the cold eyes of half a dozen women.

Lucy was trying her best to raise the children as normally as possible under the difficult conditions presented by a Hollywood home life. She said, "We want our children to be liked. I think nobody, especially the child, is happy when a child is spoiled. I hope the neighbors will never have to say when they see us coming: 'My God, she's got the kids!'"

She noted, however, "Desi is the disciplinarian in our house." And she also said, "Desi and I both have a fetish about child psychology books. We want no part of them. It is our conviction—and we can and do read—that too many academic treatments are merely prescriptions for pampering children and making life tough for parents. It's tough, but life is made up of rules and don'ts."

After the release of *The Long, Long Trailer* Desi remarked, "We can make pictures any time we like. But we'll concentrate on television. But if either Lucy or I want to do a movie, we can always pile up a backlog of TV films that will tide us over."

Lucy, however, had specific thoughts on the subject. "I'm not particularly interested in going back to movies." Discussing the TV show she noted, "We work four days and rest three. You can't do that in picture making."

A touch of real-life drama occurred in February when Lucy spotted a stranger emerging from Desi's dressing room. She gave the police such a good description of the man that they located his record in the police files, circulated his photo at all the studios and eventually the burglar was apprehended.

To publicize *The Long, Long Trailer*, Lucy and Desi visited New York. Metro announced plans to shoot another Lucille Ball-Desi Arnaz film and Desilu reached an agreement with MGM, promising it would not release the theatrical film version of "I Love Lucy"—three episodes strung together for showing abroad—until *Trailer* had completed its overseas bookings.

Being a successful businessman was changing Desi. When Lucille was asked what she thought was mainly responsible for the excellence of the program, she quickly replied: "Desi does it all."

People connected with the show have said that although that statement seemed like a supremely generous admission for a wife to make, her judgment was basically correct—Desi was the producer-in-chief, and it is an axiom of television that everything rises or falls with the talent of the producer.

Others countered, "A lot of people get credit for 'I Love Lucy' being as good as it is. But just think what kind of show it would be without Lucille Ball!"

Desi contended they had good people around them, "and I let them do the work. The rest is a cinch." But he had not always felt that way. In a revealing statement he admitted, "I found that bringing 'I Love Lucy' to home screens was ninety per cent desk work, ten per cent acting. Soon I developed an eye twitch, headaches and my first grey hairs. I was worrying myself sick trying to be everywhere at once. My pal Bill Frawley remarked, 'Remember when you led a band? You just waved a stick, and the boys took it from there. Why don't you develop faith in others?' That took

138

some of the air out of me. Once I tried delegating authority, making each of five hundred workers feel pride through accomplishing a task unassisted, everything went twice as smoothly."

"I Love Lucy" rolled along, topping the ratings. However, the sponsor wasn't happy. For some unknown reason, though millions were watching "I Love Lucy," the show wasn't selling cigarettes. At the conclusion of the 1955 season, Philip Morris dropped out of the show as their eight-million-dollar contract came to an end. By this time, they were alternating sponsorship with Proctor and Gamble.

General Foods, which by this time had also been co-sponsoring the show, eagerly stepped into the spot Philip Morris was vacating. Lucy would now be selling Jell-O, as she had on "My Favorite Husband."

In November, 1955, Lucy and Desi celebrated their fifteenth wedding anniversary. Desi attributed their happiness to "a sense of humor and the ability to laugh." He told a friend, "Often when we've had words, one of us sees the absurdity of it and starts laughing. If people would laugh more, marriages would last longer."

Lucy also acknowledged the marital spats, adding that "before we know it one of us will interrupt a disagreement to say, 'What a perfect situation for the show.' That's how so many of our marital problems have been incorporated on film."

Press agents for the show claimed that a psychiatrist had written the Arnazes, saying that a half hour of watching their show on TV often solved problems that ordinarily might require weeks of treatment.

As the series progressed, Jess Oppenheimer and the writers decided to expand the Ricardos' horizons. They took them out of their usual setting via a cross-country motor trip to Los Angeles, where Ricky was to make a film; a stay in Los Angeles, enabling movie stars to make guest appearances; a trip to Europe with the Mertzes. On these various jaunts, Lucy and Ricky left little Ricky with Lucy's mother, but in real life Lucille Ball Arnaz was seldom if ever separated from her children.

Jess Oppenheimer remained with Desilu until 1956, when he became an NBC executive. He analyzed the "Lucy" character as "a childish, compulsive person. Most people are terribly inhibited. She does the things you'd secretly like to, but don't *dare* to. That Lucille! She has all the fire and temper of Lombard; like the young Ginger Rogers, she can act a common, gum-chewing working girl, yet be lady enough to move in any milieu. Watch that face! You get the feeling that a wall is missing, that you're looking right into her head!"

Desi personally ran the *Lucy* script conferences, or "note sessions," and it was largely at his insistence that the character of Ricky Ricardo displayed such husbandly dignity. Ricky never flirted seriously with other women, for example. He was firm with Lucy, but always fondly tolerant of her feminine illogic. As an actor, Desi had evolved from the rather awkward young Latin of early *Lucy* shows into a polished foil for his wife's wacky style of TV comedy.

Lucy remarked, "I believe that Desi is a better actor than he gets credit for being. I take note, and many another professional are taking note too, that against my wide, sweeping style of comedy he is doing a deft job of quiet underplaying, mighty good, I think. Even 'mushin pitchers' have finally come to look on us as a team."

Lucy and Desi's second vehicle for MGM, *Forever Darling*, was based on a script originally written in the 1940s for Lucille and William Powell. It was updated, rewritten, and the Arnazes' Zanra (Arnaz spelled backwards) Productions produced the film for MGM. It was directed by Lucy's boyfriend of two decades earlier, Alexander Hall.

The Long, Long Trailer had been a big hit and they were

hoping to hit again. Lucy pointed out that "thanks to television, we have a hold on a few million people who feel we're part of the family. That's all we are—just part of the family."

"They're just like any folks next door who earn two million dollars a year," observed a friend wryly.

To ballyhoo *Forever Darling*, released in the spring of 1956, Lucy and Desi went to her hometown, Jamestown. It was a gala "Welcome Home" for the girl who was at one time snickered at as being "one of the fastest gals in town." On this return visit, Lucy reminisced: "I get so emotional realizing this is where I learned about life."

Lucy and Desi went on to New York City where the *New York Herald Tribune* invited them to be marriage counselors at its 1956 seminar for brides. The questions at the seminar covered just about every aspect of what Desi termed "the sea of matrimony." With her famous sharp wit, Lucy parried the more personal questions. She warned the ladies not to try and change their mates: "They never change," she observed with the voice of experience. "You just get more tolerant and more tolerant," she added with a resigned grin.

Back in Hollywood the Arnazes had sold their Northridge ranch and moved into a $90,000 mansion on Roxbury Drive in Beverly Hills. Her neighbors were Jack Benny, José Ferrer and Rosemary Clooney, the Oscar Levants, Ira Gershwin. The new house was not the typical flamboyant home of a superstar. It was a dignified setting for successful business people.

One month a year Lucy and Desi would take the children to Del Mar, a wealthy resort area near San Diego. On weekends, they would go to their home in Palm Springs, where Lucille would supposedly spend her every waking moment as Desi's playmate and as camp counselor and game supervisor for Lucie and Desi, Jr., who was a bubbly replica of his father, and with a half-dozen moppets from neighboring luxurious homes. She would make homes movies and tape-

141

record mock interviews with the children. The Arnaz house stretched along the seventeenth fairway of the swank Thunderbird Golf Club.

However, Lucy later revealed that as early as this, "I noticed the change in Desi. When I felt fatigued, I could relax at home with the children. Now I could see evidence of overwork in Desi. There were weekends when he stayed home with us and seemed to enjoy it, but not enough of them to build up his physical reserve. When he found he couldn't relax, he would go out on the town. Desi had a tendency to play even harder than he worked.

"At the beginning, he would go off on long fishing trips, which were perfectly all right with me. I understood a man's need to be alone occasionally. But then it dawned on me that Desi was seeking more than solitude."

Desi was not discreet in his pursuit of other pleasures, and it was hard for Lucy to stand by silently and even harder for her to save face among friends. "It is a horrifying experience to watch someone you love, someone you think you know, turning into a stranger," she later noted. "We saw it happen. Then we hardly saw him anymore."

People on the scene observed that it wasn't that Desi couldn't relax; he simply couldn't turn off business pressure and transform himself into the homebody that Lucy wanted. Desi's idea of relaxing was playing hard; Lucy's was to stay home and "be a family." "And Lucy had no desire or intention of curbing her professional life, despite anything she said," observes an ex-colleague.

In June, 1956, Desi was hurt while filming an "I Love Lucy" episode with Bob Hope. In one scene Lucy was thrown into the air by Bob and Desi. When she came down, she leaned too heavily on Desi, tearing ligaments in his back. Desi kidded that Lucy must have been gaining weight; she retorted that maybe he wasn't as strong as he used to be.

Forever Darling was Lucy and Desi's last movie together.

142

It was not the commercial hit that *The Long, Long Trailer* had been, and though other film projects with the Arnazes might have been contemplated, they never materialized.

When queried on why "I Love Lucy" was still flourishing in its fifth year, while other situation comedies weren't, Lucy answered: "I really don't know why. We just sit back and enjoy it. The fact is that we try to give the audience a slice of life. I would suppose that the ability of the audience to identify themselves with Lucy and Ricky and the Mertzes and the things that happen to them is the key to the success of 'Lucy.' We have always tried to be honest with the public and have never tried to slough off our responsibility. A major share of our credit is due to the writers. Desi and I say a prayer for them every night."

About Desilu, Lucy said: "Desilu Productions and the many ramifications of it are all in Desi's bailiwick. I can say I read somewhere that the company produces some twelve million dollars a year of TV and theatrical films and commercials. I assume that's true because it quoted Desi."

Lucy summed up Desilu's involvements at the time. "Desilu produces 'I Love Lucy' and 'December Bride.' It films 'Our Miss Brooks,' 'Make Room for Daddy,' 'Line-up,' 'Wyatt Earp,' 'The Jimmy Durante Show,' 'The Red Skelton Show.' The new Orson Welles show is being produced by Mr. Welles with Desilu. We also produced *Forever Darling*, 'High Tor' and a new potential series, based on helicopter pilots, 'Whirlybirds.' "

Did Lucy participate in production matters? "I handle personnel relations, such as planning the annual picnic and matters of that sort. The business is handled by Desi and the capable executives with whom he has surrounded himself."

Regarding the future of "I Love Lucy": "We can't be objective at all about 'Lucy.' No other show has ever equaled its record. And there is no precedent by which to judge. We thought we'd go to an hour this year, on a once-a-month

143

basis. But Desi was told by the sponsor and the network that you can't break up a winning combo. They pointed to the fact that 'Lucy' was number one more often than any other show on TV."

Lucy noted that the show was contemplating format changes. "The principal change will be to shoot many locations. We'll go outdoors more often than in previous times, although you must remember we shot a lot of footage in Europe and across the country. There will be a shift of emphasis to our son, Ricky, who is now 'old enough' to be included in many situations. We have signed, you know, a wonderfully talented five-year-old boy, Richard Keith, to play Ricky, Jr. We'll travel some, too. Mainly, the Ricardos will continue to develop and grow. To be truthful, that's all I know. The rest is up to the writers. They tell us what to do and we take it from there."

Did Lucy enjoy acting in the series? "It's still a thrill a minute." Did she plan to make more motion pictures? "Yes. We may not make them as regularly as one a year, but we will make more movies whenever the time allows and we find a good script. I would say that our next one would be filmed next summer, but we let Desi decide that."

Did she look forward to retiring? "I don't think any actor or actress actually looks forward to retiring, any more than anybody else 'looks forward' to it. Let's face it, why should I? I spend four days a week working, but the early mornings and evenings are spent at home with my husband and children. We might someday work on a schedule that is less regular than once a week."

How would she spend her time if "Lucy" folded? "I don't even want to talk about that."

Lucy also commented on a persistent rumor. "People keep saying that I am the real power behind the Desilu throne, that I make the big decisions. No myth could be further from the truth. I don't make one bloody decision! My job is at

144

home with the kids. Desi does ask my opinion once in a while, but only on personnel problems or the very biggest matters. Even then, the decisions are always his."

By the end of 1956, Desilu Productions was a giant, grossing around fifteen million dollars a year and using up more raw film per year than MGM and 20th Century-Fox combined. Eight hundred people were on the payroll. Though Lucille was vice president, she "kept her hands off the business transactions."

President Desi was by now portly and quite grey, wore tortoise-shell spectacles and smoked a Cuban cigar. He presided with authority over Desilu.

At the conclusion of the 1956-57 television season, Desilu dropped a bombshell when it announced that "I Love Lucy," in its half-hour filmed version, would be discontinued. The decision was no last-minute maneuver. It had taken Lucy and Desi almost two seasons to persuade CBS and the sponsors to abandon the half-hour format in favor of a monthly one-hour show.

The stars were deluged by protests from an outraged public.

Lucy was candid. "Sweetie," she told a reporter patiently, "we've loved our work and we've loved being pioneers but the time has come to let somebody else 'enjoy' it. We're a little brain-weary, you know. How do you make people understand that? In letters, viewers tell us they're sad because of our plans, but I don't think they understand. As I say in the return correspondence, we're not exactly quitting. There'll actually be as much of 'Lucy' around next season as they'll want to see. Even the kids will be able to see us next season. CBS is going to show our reruns in a 7:30 P.M. time slot, so the whole family can watch to their heart's content. Then, there'll be the five one-hour shows we're going to do for Ford. Ye gads, isn't that enough?"

Lucille was slated to begin production shortly on the first

145

of her big monthly shows, each of which would have a huge budget of $350,000.

Lucy disputed the "absurd" idea that "laziness" had anything to do with the curtailed schedule. "That's not the case at all," she remarked with finality. "We might do something else besides television next year." Lucy then mentioned an idea she had which she would eventually see through to reality: "We might, for instance, do a Broadway play."

She scoffed at a remark that "All clowns yearn to play *Hamlet*." "Are you kiddin'?" she snapped. "What would I do in a dr-ah-ma? I'm strictly a clown and not a frustrated one either."

Lucille was proud of frequent comparisons between her and the late Carole Lombard. Lucille said she often dreamed about Carole, whom she idolized. "Carole usually shows up wearing chiffon," Lucy said, "with a big diamond thing at the throat. She smokes a cigarette in a long, snaky holder. Lord, what a wonderful face! What bones! Years ago, everyone warned Desi and me that we were committing career suicide to go for broke on TV. Then I dreamed about Carole. She was wearing a very smart suit, and she said, 'Honey, go ahead. Take a chance. Give it a whirl!' I later saw Clark Gable at a Hollywood do. I told him what a marvelous help Carole was to me. He stared, gulped and plowed off in a daze."

"I Love Lucy" was by now an international success. "Lucy" was the second most popular show in England. The program began running in Australia in 1957 and eventually would be shown in dozens of countries, seventy-seven in all, including Japan, Hong Kong and Kuwait.

Impresario Arnaz announced two spectacular business deals in 1957. He sold 180 "I Love Lucy" half-hour segments to CBS for five million dollars. Three months later, he used the money to purchase RKO Studios.

Desilu already owned the huge lot which was once known

as Motion Picture Center, which had seven acres and nine sound stages. Now it added the old RKO Studios in Hollywood which had fifteen sound stages and fourteen acres and RKO's Culver City facility, with eleven sound stages and a twenty-nine acre backlot.

Lucy was aware of the ramifications of the deals in her personal and professional lives with Desi. "When he decided to buy the RKO Studios for Desilu's expanding business, I knew this would mean more pressures on him than ever before," she noted. "Some columnists wrote that both of us had been fired from RKO in years past and we were now taking revenge. That was ridiculous. Neither of us was fired from RKO; our association had been peaceful. I, for one, certainly never thought of buying the studio. In fact, I never dreamed of owning anything. I never had such high aspirations.

"Desi had high aspirations, but I can't believe they included buying RKO. It just happened. We needed more space and it was available there. Someone asked, 'Why don't you buy RKO?' and he said, as usual, 'Well, why not? How much do they want for it?' He went to the bank and said, 'Can I buy a studio for $6,150,000?' and they said, 'Yes. You have excellent credit.' Neither of us decided, many years ago, 'Someday we'll own that place.'"

It was reported that Desi's purchase was a fantastic bargain. "Actually, he got the studio for a song," insiders said. Howard Hughes, who had bought the studio in the 1940s, sold it to General Tire and Rubber for twenty-five million dollars in the mid-Fifties. General Tire had planned to reestablish RKO as a major film producer but failed. The tire company then decided to retain most of the company's assets (TV and radio stations, etc.), but divest itself of the physical plant. There weren't many buyers for motion picture studios in 1957, and Desi got his bargain with the aid of a loan from the Bank of America.

147

In addition to RKO and Motion Picture Center, Desilu's holdings included a music publishing firm, a prospective record company, Desi Arnaz's Western Hills Hotel in Palm Springs and a considerable amount of real estate.

Lucy and Desi remained sole owners of Desilu, despite hints that key members of their permanent staff would be awarded percentages.

Jess Oppenheimer, who had parted company with Desi because of "certain irreconcilable differences in their thinking," later noted about Desi's business acumen, "The timing was good. He was in at the birth of television, but as television matured, Desi matured with it. He's the number one man in television film production today. The top men, the L.B. Mayers of television, come to this boy for advice." (Arthur Godfrey, on the eve of his new program of the 1959 season, wired Desi and asked him to find time to watch the show. "We'd like your opinion," said Godfrey.)

When "I Love Lucy" was first signed by CBS, the network assigned a production manager, Martin Leeds, to the program. He and Desi fought over every nickel spent and their battles became well known in the industry. Desi later hired Leeds for Desilu, where he eventually rose to the rank of executive vice president. Desi said he wanted Leeds because, "A man who would fight so hard for CBS—that's a man who I want on my side."

Leeds has offered a graphic analysis of Desilu and why he joined the company: "They had a winner in 'Lucy'—and a winner could be parlayed . . . [it is] a young organization . . . average age thirty-two . . . well paid . . . can't get more elsewhere . . . not a single resignation of the permanent staff in five years . . . it is the first television film company to pay bonuses to its permanent staff . . . has done it four consecutive years . . . [it has] twenty pilot films going on on our RKO lot, fifteen per cent of what the entire industry will do

148

in the season . . . Desi has a particular knack for hiring the right person and then letting him work."

In a time of crumbling motion picture studios, Desilu was flourishing. The first of the one-hour Lucille Ball-Desi Arnaz shows went on the air in the fall of 1957. The public responded as always—the ratings were tremendous.

The new shows utilized more guest stars—Ann Sothern, Tallulah Bankhead, Hedda Hopper, Betty Grable and Harry James, Danny Thomas, many others. Filming, as always before a live audience, utilized four cameras instead of three. The first show was seventy-five minutes long, and the network balked at running it.

"It was funny about that first film we made in the new series. In the middle of the rehearsals, everything went like this," Lucille told a friend, snapping her fingers. "Suddenly Desi slowed down. I thought, 'This man has finally forgotten a line after seven years.' But no, he had suddenly got the idea the script was so good it had to be extended another fifteen minutes!"

The network flatly refused to telecast a seventy-five-minute show. Desi was told by network head Bill Paley to either cut it down or pad it by fifteen more minutes.

"Of course I asked him why we couldn't run it like it was," recalled Desi. "I didn't want to cut anything, because that would weaken it. And I didn't want to pad it, because that would spoil the show too.

" 'Now let me tell you something, Cuban,' Paley said to me. 'We do half-hour shows, hour shows and hour-and-a-half shows. There's no such thing as an hour-and-fifteen-minute show.' "

Desi pointed out that the U.S. Steel Hour, which followed "Lucy" on CBS, had been taking a beating in ratings. Why not ask U. S. Steel to do a forty-five-minute show just that one week? Paley told Arnaz he was crazy to think anyone

149

would stand still for cutting an hour show to forty-five minutes.

"They'll love it," Desi told Paley. "They'll get a tremendous holdover audience from our show."

Paley said no.

Desi said he'd call the head of U.S. Steel on his own. He did, and, astonishingly, the time cut was agreed to.

"After I told him, Paley just smiled and said: 'You crazy son-of-a-. . . .' Well, the result of it all was that we got our fifteen minutes and U.S. Steel had the highest rating they ever got."

Although the public still loved Lucy and Desi, some of the critics were not happy with the longer format. The initial seventy-five-minute show culminated in a wonderfully funny drunk scene between Ann Sothern and Lucy. TV critic John Crosby noted, "Operating within half-an-hour, Lucy has always managed in the nick of time to get her feet out of the wet cement . . . This [drunk scene] was well worth waiting for, but I don't know why they had to add forty-five minutes to the normal running time to work it in."

In addition, Crosby noted, "Somewhat hesitantly I point out that the accumulated ages of the participants in this romp [Lucy, Desi, Cesar Romero, Ann Sothern, Hedda Hopper, Vivian Vance, Bill Frawley] would add up to a very impressive statistic indeed and I wonder if it might not be wise in the future to leaven the roster with somewhat younger actors, if only to spread the work around."

The Arnazes became the official owners of RKO in 1958. Lucy took over the dressing room formerly occupied in the studio's salad days by Ginger Rogers. Lucy had it redecorated from Ginger's pink, peach and black to white and yellow. The "dressing room" actually included a sitting room, kitchen, make-up room and full bath.

One of Lucy's initial projects at the new studio was to set

150

LUCY: *The Bittersweet Life of Lucille Ball*

up the Desilu Workshop. She hadn't forgotten the days when she had benefited from acting experience gained at Lela Rogers' RKO Little Theatre. And she had another motive for setting up the workshop: it would keep her mind off other things. She wasn't getting along with Desi.

The Arnaz children were aware of their parents' unhappiness together. Desi, Jr., years later, disclosed: "I learned pretty early to relate to 'I Love Lucy' as a television show and to my parents as actors in it. I *had* to learn that, because there wasn't much relationship between what I saw on TV and what was really going on at home. On TV, my mother was overplayed and my dad was underplayed. Those were difficult years—all those funny things happening each week on television to people who looked like my parents, then the same people agonizing through some terrible, unhappy times at home, and each of them trying to convince my sister and me separately that the other was in the wrong."

Desilu aide Maury Thompson was assigned to help Lucy with the workshop. Lucy spent six hours auditioning the first batch of sixty-two people. She not only watched them perform, but met each one personally. In all, 1700 were auditioned, from which Lucy eventually selected twenty-two.

Discussing her students, Lucy said, "We don't take any money from them. We pay them sixty dollars a week—the Actors' Equity minimum—and they're free to work anywhere they want. They're not tied to us at all."

She added, "I understand the old agency trouble these kids have. It's the same old vicious circle: you can't get a job unless you've acted, and you can't act unless you've had a job. We're just trying to give them exposure!" Lucy wasn't interested in exposing them too young, however. "We won't pluck them out of high school or college. We tell them to finish what they're doing and then to come see us."

In 1958 the *Los Angeles Times* named Lucille Ball "Woman of the Year."

The Desilu Workshop was hailed by many Hollywood observers as the only practical workshop to come out of television production.

By this time the Arnaz marriage was in serious trouble. Although Lucy was constantly denying rumors of any rift, insiders knew that things were drastically wrong.

"My concern was that Desi was overtaxing his health. I had failed to stop him from working too hard," Lucy later lamented. "The only thing I could admonish him about was that 'it's enough to overwork, but don't overplay.'

"Sometimes I went out with him on the town. But I am an eight-hours-of-sleep girl, and his hours were a little long for me. He did nothing in moderation. He never does. Naturally, I went through a long period of being positive that I was the one to blame. It was hard to keep working, to keep on being funny, when I was condemning myself. I became so depressed I couldn't go on alone. I had to get advice."

Lucy later revealed that she had even gone to psychiatrists to help save her marriage. "When it was pointed out that what was happening to Desi was not my fault, at least I could live with myself. I began to understand my situation."

People told Lucille that it was her career that was standing in the way of her happiness with Desi. If she would retire, they said, the rift would be healed. Lucille was in total disagreement. "No one who really knew me would say that," she said. "Desi never asked me to retire. It meant something to him, having me work. He always was proud of my work and still is. He respects what I do as a performer. It was he, as the guiding genius of 'I Love Lucy,' who presented me in the best possible light.

"Whatever his faults, he is not one of those men who automatically assumes that all career women are competitive. He knew me too well for that. The first lesson I learned, as an actress, was how to take direction. Only a stranger could imagine me competing with Desi."

152

On another occasion she noted, "When I married him, I knew that Latin men expect their wives to take a secondary role. I was all for it. I think one of the reasons Desi wanted to marry me was that I felt this way about him. I wanted him to be the boss. He knew I adored him. That's a hard thing for a man or woman to resist."

Desi's drinking increased as his unhappiness and pressures at the studio mounted. He began "playing" harder than ever. There were a number of separations which were never made public. Lucy always forgave him and took him back.

She set up a trip to Europe for the family in an attempt to save their marriage. Observers recall that she was determined to take the children along. A close friend advised, "Why don't you try it alone, just the two of you?" But Lucy was stubborn. "I won't go without them."

It was a gala trip. Lucy bought tons of clothes and a magnificent full-length sable coat. It would be summer in Europe, but Lucy didn't care. She told a friend, "I've bought it and I'm going to take it. Besides, Desi hasn't seen it."

When they returned, Lucy was scarcely speaking to Desi. Though he was a loving father, he had, according to a close friend, resented the presence of the children on what was to have been "a second honeymoon" for him and Lucille. Desi and Lucy had quarreled constantly and he never saw the sable coat. Lucy later said, "I used it on the ship as a blanket for the kids."

For the outside world, however, the Arnazes kept up their image of being happily married.

Desi mused that despite being committed to do thirty million dollars worth of business in 1958 he was "as broke as anybody."

"But I don't worry about it," he added. "I've been broke before, but I've never really been hungry. But we've got no trouble so far."

Lucy was concerned with the way the children were being raised. It sometimes struck her that they didn't think she was capable of normal housewife chores. "One night, the cook was sick, so I prepared dinner," remembered Lucy. "When I called, 'Dinner is ready,' Lucie called back, 'How can dinner be ready when Frances is sick?' It was frightening. Although I have always prided myself on being a good cook, my seven-year-old daughter didn't even know I could bake a potato. So I decided to do all the cooking during the first two weeks of our vacation. But I was sick with a virus during those first weeks at Del Mar, so Desi did the cooking."

The Arnazes were offbeat sandwich eaters. Lucy didn't care for them too much, but when she was in the mood it was likely to be a bean or a lyonnaise potato sandwich. Desi liked something with zip, so high on his list was the delectable combination of peanut butter and onion.

About their personal lives Lucy noted that people thought "with success, we can now sit back and relax. Not while Desi has sixteen shows in production. We're lucky to get away for a long weekend, let alone a real vacation. Desi is usually up by seven and at the studio by eight. His day doesn't end till long after the children are in bed and he's had his supper and wrapped up a few conferences he couldn't fit in at the office."

Bob Hope's old gag that Bing Crosby owned ninety per cent of the money in America was out of date by 1958. The estimate had to be revised, because Lucy and Desi were considered to have at least fifty per cent.

Lucy remarked, "I often argue with Desi because he works too hard. He brings the same drive to business that he did to golf. I remember how his hands would become sore and bloody from the blisters. But he would bandage them, grit his teeth and go back to his driver and balls, saying: 'I'll master this game if it's the last thing I do!' There's no moderation, no in-between, for Desi. He's go, go, go. He even has conferences in his car."

Although through these years Lucy contended it was

154

Desi's obsession with business which was their main problem, years later Desi, Jr. revealed that his mother's ambition was as strong if not stronger than his father's. "Even when we were young, my mother was never really able to turn off from whatever it is that drives her in her work. Ever since I can remember, she has talked about 'getting away,' and when she does, she's great—for about three weeks, then she has to get back to work."

Although Lucy and Desi's marriage was faltering, Lucy remained impressed with Desi's business acumen. Even as their marriage was disintegrating she stated, "Over the years I've watched a brilliant mind blossom. He surprises me—I think he even surprises himself. He's intuitive. He lives from minute to minute. But I call him Nostradamus, he seems to know what'll happen next. And he learned every job in our setup before he hired anybody else to do it."

Lucy always gave Desi full credit for their professional successes. "I encouraged him from the sidelines, but his own triumphs day after day encouraged him more than any person could . . . Whatever help I gave him was in the beginning. CBS knew my work from the radio show. Hollywood had seen me around. The television empire that Desi built, he did entirely by himself."

While Desilu flourished, Lucy and Desi were being driven farther and farther apart. It was an ironic situation, because their marriage had weathered years of shakiness and struggle and now, as Lucy later stated, "We came apart only when it looked as if we finally had smooth sailing ahead."

In May, 1959, Lucille Ball received the first bad publicity she had had in years. She went to Oklahoma to appear at a youth rally, but refused to perform because of what she termed "a small crowd." The Kiwanis Club Youth Rally to combat juvenile delinquency was being held in Oklahoma City's Taft Stadium, which seats 12,000. Only 2,000 showed up, and Lucy refused to leave her air-conditioned Cadillac

155

for a scheduled comedy routine and a talk on delinquency. One young boy had a dozen roses to present to her, but when she wouldn't leave her car he kept the roses, saying he would give them to his mother for Mother's Day.

The program chairman, Fred Daugherty, told the audience that Lucy was "disappointed with the crowd and declined to perform." The show went on without her and later Daugherty said, "The crowd didn't seem too disappointed."

Lucy drove to the airport to return to Hollywood. She told newsmen, "I didn't go on because of the small crowd. I believe in youth rallies, but there weren't enough there to do any good."

The following day, she told the Hollywood press that 'only 325 people appeared in a stadium built to seat 14,000' The Kiwanis apologized and everybody apologized, but somebody goofed and forgot to tell the people.

"I've played to thirteen people in a dugout. It doesn't matter to me how many there are. But when they don't care enough to publicize the affair, it's high time they stopped asking people to go thousands of miles to perform."

The publicity about Lucy leaving the stadium in a huff continued for several days. Daugherty contradicted Lucille, claiming that plenty of publicity preceded the event. He added: "I don't know what kept them away. Maybe she is too easy to see on TV."

Desilu Productions announced that its gross for the year was $20,470,361. Its profit for 1959 was almost a quarter of a million dollars, up from only $90,000 in 1958. But the company had not yet begun to move. Its real profits would be in reruns of films it was currently making. Desilu had about 560 half-hour TV shows to be rerun; by the end of the year it would have almost a thousand. The studio had three types of productions: its own shows, for which it supplied all facilities and talent; associated shows, supplying some talent and facilities in return for a percentage of the company; and shows to which it rented out its studio facilities, termed below-the-line shows.

Although Desilu was doing nicely, things hadn't always been financially smooth. It seems that in 1954 Desilu had sold twenty-four per cent of its stock equity to CBS for a million dollars. The deal included a five-year contract under which Desilu agreed to produce at least two TV series a year for the network. But in 1957, the stock was repurchased from CBS. Desi later told the Federal Communications Commission, "We only made the original sale to CBS for one reason. My wife and I needed the money."

By 1959, however, Desilu was involved in twenty-seven shows and rented studio facilities to three others. In addition to its other successful programs, "The Untouchables" was about to be launched. It would become an enormously successful series about the FBI fighting organized crime. It also proved that Walter Winchell had obviously made amends with Desi, since he was signed to narrate the series for an astronomical $25,000 a week.

"In Hollywood, business is business," notes an ex-associate of Desi's. "Winchell provided an authenticity for 'The Untouchables' that Desi considered extremely important. He was willing to let bygones be bygones."

Desilu stock had gone public, starting at ten dollars a share. It shot up to twenty-nine and leveled off at between sixteen and eighteen. At one point, before the public offering, Desi encountered Texas oil millionaire Clint Murchison at the Del Mar race track. Murchison casually, but sincerely, offered Desi $11,000,000 for Desilu. Desi, just as casually, replied, "Not enough."

An observer at the time remembers that the Desi Arnaz encountered on the Desilu lot was unrecognizable to anyone who had seen him on the screen. On TV he appeared fairly

157

short and unassuming, with slick black hair. At the studio he dressed casually, appeared burly, broad chested and had ruffled grey-white hair. (He dyed his hair for the TV show, but washed the dye out after each performance.)

Some thought he looked like a Latin-American dictator relaxing in sports clothes, and that he acted like a dictator on the lot—a hard working and determined dictator. Desi's temper tantrums grew legendary. A fifty-four-year-old character actor, David O. McCall, alleged that Desi had attacked him without provocation while "grossly intoxicated" on a day in July. He later brought suit against Desi for $100,000, claiming back injuries and numerous bruises. The suit never came to trial.

The only similarity between Desi offscreen and on was the thick Cuban accent. In real life the accent was liberally sprinkled with American epithets for emphasis. His accent was so thick that there were times when even Lucy couldn't understand him.

Desi was a dynamic force on the lot, shouting orders, constantly having conferences with propmen, lighting technicians, script girls. "His movements were almost acrobatic," says one observer.

When he had a problem that required concentration, he would drop his chin to his chest and rub his thinning hair. Or he would slouch into a director's chair and bury his face in his hands. But these periods would only last for a few seconds. Then he would jump up, throwing his arms about like a Latin windmill, shouting orders, muttering to himself. One time, throwing his arms open wide to direct something, his hand hit an electric fan, cutting his fingertips.

When he was directing actors he would hop in and out of the action, moving them physically, showing them where to walk. He was noted for planning every detail of production and he would often learn the lines of all the actors.

Milton Berle was a guest star on one of their hour-long

158

specials. Berle and Lucy had one bit of business that would only last about thirty seconds on screen. The rehearsal for it took about a half hour. Desi had them rehearse the bit numerous times. Then he said, "Now we go through it one more time." "Ah, c'mon now, Des," Berle said.

"No," Lucy said flatly. "We're not doing it again."

"C'mon," Desi said. "We do it one more time."

They did it again.

"He was manic in rehearsal, but downright frantic during shooting," recalls an observer.

He often skipped lunch. While other people were eating, he conducted business conferences. It was not unusual for him to consult with the casting director, talk to the propman, set designer, the script editor and listen to some salesman, all within a matter of ten or fifteen minutes. He handled them all with executive ability and efficiency.

"One thing about him, though," notes an ex-associate. "He always listened to your advice. You could discuss anything with him. But the final decision was always his."

Milton Berle said about Desi, "I was so struck by the way he handled everything on his own show that I asked him to direct a show for me. He's got a tremendous flair for comedy; there's almost nobody like him around. He's a driver, a perfectionist, and he usually knows ninety-five per cent of what he wants."

Another Desilu executive remembers that Desi was loyal to all his workers. "He didn't like to fire anybody."

During this period Desi was rarely away from work. He did get a chance to play golf sometimes with friends like Phil Harris and Bob Hope. He was a good golfer, with a handicap of only nine. He also loved the races and would go to Del Mar as often as he could. And he was an avid Los Angeles Dodgers and Rams fan.

But Desi had changed radically. The only apparent carry-over from his pre-mogul days was his churchgoing. He still

159

attended Mass regularly, whether in Hollywood, Del Mar or Palm Springs.

In the summer of 1959, for the first time in ten years, Lucy and Desi took separate vacations. Of this period, Lucy said, "I had three months off, but I spent most of it working with the kids in our training program in the Little Theatre, helping them put together a revue. And I spent as much time as possible with our children—I took them to Del Mar a couple of times, to Disneyland, Marineland and helped them with their French lessons."

Desi went to Europe that summer—to work. When he returned, he continued working, except for an occasional trip to Del Mar or to Dodger Stadium.

In the fall, production problems were staggering, and Desi would often take a drink or two or more at the end of his twelve-hour day. One night in September he was picked up by police "on a simple drunk charge." He was seen "weaving down Vista Street." Two plainclothesmen saw him and went over to offer assistance. According to the police, Desi denounced the officers with offensive language. Desi didn't believe they were police, but Desi's chauffeur, parked nearby, called two uniformed officers who convinced Desi that the plainclothesmen were "authentic."

The melee wound up at the police station. Desi was released on twenty-one dollars cash bail after spending half an hour in a cell. But he failed to appear in court the following week. When Desi's lawyer said, "He's out shooting," the judge misunderstood and thought Desi was hunting. It was explained that "shooting" meant making a film, but the judge still noted: "This courtroom is filled with people who had to leave work."

The lawyer asked for a week's continuance, but the judge ordered Desi to appear the following morning. Desi did not appear, forfeited bail and the episode came to an end. For some unexplained reason the judge later said that there was no necessity for Desi to appear in court.

160

Desi's drinking problems and the Arnazes' less-than-ideal marital situation could no longer be kept from the public.

Hedda Hopper was appearing on a TV show for Desilu. Lucy was making her debut as a director. The cast consisted of a dozen players from her Desilu Workshop. Hedda recalled, "Desi was back from Europe and he and Lucy were arguing." Vivian Vance, Bill Frawley and Hedda all took cover from the storms between Lucy and Desi.

Hedda warned her, "You can't insult him before the entire company. You're partly responsible for this show too, you know."

Obviously Lucy's directorial talents left something to be desired. "It seemed we were doomed to have a flop on our hands," noted Hedda.

During dress rehearsal Desi calmly asked, "Lucy, dear, will you let me see if I can pull this thing together for you?"

Lucy snapped back, "Okay. Try it!"

Hedda recalled that while Desi might not be winning medals as a husband, he was a great producer-director. In ten minutes he had whipped the program into shape.

Amid louder rumors of a marital rift, Lucy told a friend: "I believe he is going to Europe for a month." Her friend was nonplused: "She said it as though she were speaking of some casual acquaintance."

Lucy was again talking of leaving television and going to New York to star in a Broadway play, heightening rumors of the split. She shrugged when confronted with the reports. "Some people live on rumors. Desi and I have been in this whole thing long enough to be accustomed to them. We got through that kind of thing before, and we'll get through it again. Maybe it's good for some couples to be separated for a time. Maybe it can renew and refresh a relationship."

By the end of 1959, the last of the "I Love Lucy" shows, with Lucille, Desi, Vivian and Bill, had been shot. It was the end of a TV era.

Lucy had to abandon the Desilu Workshop. "Sure, I'll miss

the workshop. It's a satisfying thing," she said. "But I've given two years of my time and my heart to the kids, and you can't do everything for them. The objective of the workshop was to provide a stepping stone for young, talented performers. I think we achieved this." But she noted, "I found myself *caring* about each one. They took two years out of my life as a lay psychiatrist. That's over now, because they drained me dry. I figured if I ever wanted to work again I'd better conclude it."

When Desi sailed in October, without a bon-voyage visit from Lucy, there were more printed reports of the rift. Desi pooh-poohed the rumors: "We're working too hard. That's the only trouble. Probably someone heard we had an argument. But we have lots of arguments. When a redhead and a Cuban get together, we argue pretty good."

This time there were not only reports of a possible divorce between Lucy and Desi, but it was said that Desilu was up for sale. Lucy labeled the rumors about the divorce as "cruel and absolutely false." She also denied that Desilu was for sale. "I'm not too well informed about the business-end of Desilu, but I do know that if the studio were going to be sold I would have been told about it, and I have been told no such thing."

Reports of the Desilu sale had surfaced because the board chairman of National Theatres and Television, Inc., announced that preliminary negotiations were underway to buy controlling stock in Desilu.

Lucille countered with, "We have had many offers from many corporations in the last few years, but we haven't considered any of them. We are a going concern and everybody wants to buy in." She added, "When there is a sale, we will be the first to announce it."

About the divorce she sharply noted: "Desi is in Europe on business. When he returns to this country around December first, he will come home and live here with his family as he always has."

But Lucille was only putting on a good front, as she had so many times in the past. At Christmas time, she packed up the kids and spent the holidays in Sun Valley with Ann Sothern. Desi went to Palm Springs alone, for a different sort of vacation.

No one could ask them what was really happening. But a witness on the scene noted that their business relationship was a definite tip-off. "There was no sign of unpleasantness. At the studio they acted with deference and courtesy to each other. In the old days, their relationship had been marked by an easy give and take. They used to kid each other unmercifully. Now they were being *too* nice to each other. We all knew something was wrong."

Lucy later confirmed this. "Strangely enough during the last few months, I didn't have the same problems at work. The set was one place that was fairly good humored."

However, home life had become unbearable. Lucy subsequently observed, "When our problems began affecting our children, I had to act. With Desi away from us most of the time, I knew they felt deserted. Kind, as all children are, they never said a word.

"One night, as I stopped by little Desi's room for the nightly tuck-in, I heard him uttering whimpers of anguish. Lucie, normally a sound sleeper, was tossing and turning in her bed when I looked in there.

"Their grades in school went down, and I was called in and told that my children were showing symptoms of 'a troubled home life' in their attitudes. The experts said to tell them, so I did.

"I took Lucie aside first, because she is the older. 'Lucie,' I said, 'I have to tell you that Mommy and Daddy are not getting along and I know that the unhappiness you see is affecting you. And I want you to know that it has nothing to do with you. We love you very much. I want you also to know that we are trying to work things out.

"And she said 'You wouldn't get a divorce, would you?'

"And I said, 'What do you know about divorce? What is a divorce?'

"She stammered. 'W-well, it's—well, you wouldn't get one, would you?' She didn't quite know what it was.

"So I told her: 'I am only planning on being separated from daddy, and I just want you to know that it has nothing to do with you. We will probably see much more of daddy, actually.'

"After I confided in Lucie, she perked up. I'm sure it was because she knew what was going on and didn't worry about her own part in it any more. She relaxed and stopped having nightmares. She was safe.

"Shortly afterward, I had to tell little Desi, because he was taking daddy's absences even harder than Lucie. He adores his daddy. I said to him, 'You know how you and Lucie fight over your games or something. Well, mommies and daddies have their problems, too. They get angry with each other. It takes time to work these things out, and then everybody's happy again.' He just nodded."

Despite the insistent rumors for over a year, it was still a shock to the public when Lucille filed for divorce in early 1960. According to a close friend, it was a shock to Desi, too, who was convinced that she would never leave him.

Few marriages were more famous. Few Hollywood marriages had seemed so perfect. But though the public thought of Lucille Ball and Desi Arnaz as Lucy and Ricky Ricardo, it was strictly an illusion. Lucille Ball was not erratic, extravagant, always-inventing-wild-schemes Lucy; she was conservative, even tempered and slow to accept change.

Desi was hardly the level-headed Ricky, slow to anger, a steadying force on his scatterbrained wife Lucy; though a successful business tycoon, Desi was noted for being pleasure seeking, impulsive and hot headed.

Desi's drinking, temper tantrums and obsession with busi-

164

ness were said to be the reasons for Lucille's finally making the move. "But what irked her most of all," believes an ex-Desilu employee, "was Desi's continued interest in other women—women considerably younger than Lucille."

In later years, when discussing Desi, Lucy said: "It was romance—out of step. It was romantic and fun, occasionally. It was emotional. But our sense of values were different."

Lucy once compared success to a custard pie in the face. "I learned about success the hard way," she said. "When it came, fast and furiously, to Desi and me, I waited for happiness to follow. Although Desi's success was greater than mine, a fact that made me as proud as a red-haired peacock, it didn't satisfy him. When no laughter followed that particular custard pie, when the enjoyment and companionship went out of our marriage, it became a cold and soggy mess."

When the final break came, Lucy realized she and Desi had to tell the children. They drove to their home in Palm Springs, specifically for that purpose. Lucy asked Desi to tell them.

He did, while she sat there. In Lucy's own words, "He began by saying that mommy and daddy were not getting along. Lucie again said, 'But you won't get a divorce?'

"Desi explained that perhaps we would. They got very quiet, put their heads down and didn't want to look at us. He said a little more about how we would see each other often and that he loved them very much.

"Finally, little Desi looked up and said, 'But, Daddy, a divorce? Isn't there some way you can take it all back?' That was almost more than we could take."

The divorce affected the children more than Lucy and Desi wanted to admit. In Desi, Jr.,'s words: "They were divorced when I was seven, and I stayed home at my mother's for several days hoping the public attention would quiet down. I still remember the first day I got on the bus to go to school; the other kids couldn't wait to question me about

165

what had *really* happened. But when you're seven years old, you can roll with things like that, and I did. Those days upset me much more later when I thought back on them than when they were happening."

After she filed for divorce, Lucy, in a somewhat public-relationsy statement, explained, "I feel success had been difficult for Desi to take because he gave up the goal we shared. Security was only one of them. Prestige still another. But happiness—the mature happiness that comes from making other people happy, the laughter that follows the comedian's custard pie—this was our principal goal, and it was abandoned by Desi somewhere along the way." She added, however: "It's still my goal, without Desi."

Lucy announced she would leave Hollywood to return to New York to accomplish a long-time ambition: to star in a Broadway show.

"I assume that Desi will come to New York, so that the children will see more of him than they have during the crisis that affected all our lives," she remarked. "I know that my attitude toward him will be friendly, so that we won't disturb the children.

"I know better than most people how much the 'I Love Lucy' legend was built around the marriage of Desi and me. Now that I have to go it alone, I am not frightened. I know it will not be as satisfying to me, because I loved the legend while it lasted." Giving deep insight into what makes her tick, Lucille concluded: "But I am a performer, and when I perform, I perform with all my heart. As long as I can make people happy, that is all I want to do."

166

9

AMIDST ALL the divorce hullabaloo, the last Lucille Ball-Desi Arnaz television special was broadcast, on April 1, 1960. It was called "The Redhead Meets the Mustache," and co-starred Edie Adams and Ernie Kovacs. The plot revolved around Lucy Ricardo masquerading as a chauffeur in order to get Ricky a TV job with Kovacs.

Edie Adams recalled, "Everytime they wanted to film a funny scene, Lucy would break down and cry. Nobody could stand to watch it."

At the end of the filming, an air of unhappiness hung over Lucy, Desi, Vivian Vance, Bill Frawley and the other members of the cast and crew. The 209th "I Love Lucy" show was the last.

Though the Lucy-Desi divorce trial revealed a seamier side of Lucy and Desi's marriage than the public could have imagined possible, by Hollywood standards it was as amicable as could be expected.

Lucy arrived at the Santa Monica hearing with her cousin Cleo, her corroborating witness. Outside, Lucy clowned for photographers in her usual manner. But her composure seemed to vanish when she took the stand before Superior Court Judge Orlando H. Rhodes. When her attorney, Mickey Rudin, started questioning her, Lucy's chin began to quiver and she only nodded her answers about Desi's alleged cruelties. The judge told her to make her replies vocal.

Lucy was smartly dressed in a black and white, tweed silk suit, and she carried a jeweled black umbrella. During the hearing Lucy wiped her teary eyes several times as she told the judge:

"We could have no social life for the last three or four years . . . I couldn't bear to be at parties when he would blow up. I preferred the privacy of our home when the battles started."

She also stated, "It was a Jekyll and Hyde thing. He would frequently have fits of temper in front of everyone, including the children. It got so bad that I thought it would be better for us not to be together. These tantrums would happen everywhere. They happened at home, they happened at work. It could be anything that set him off."

As an example, Lucy told of a time when the water pipes burst in their Beverly Hills home. "He made himself sick for two days over it. He blamed everybody and everything. By count there were sixteen people he blamed. He was hysterical and screamed and raved about it. There was no discussing with him in such violence."

Lucy said it had been difficult working with Desi for the past nine years "with this sort of thing going on."

She told Judge Rhodes that because of Desi's frequent outbursts she felt "for the sake of the children it was better for us to be apart."

Rudin asked her, "Did you try to work things out?"

"There's no discussing anything with him," Lucy answered. "He doesn't discuss very well."

Cleo confirmed Desi's "completely irrational behavior."

Both Lucy and Desi gave out official statements to the press. Desi's was: "We deeply regret that after long and serious consideration we have not been able to work out our problems and have decided to separate. Our divorce will be completely amicable and there will be no contest. Lucy will pursue her career on television and I will continue my work as head of Desilu Productions."

Lucy's official statement: "I'm sure our separation will come as no surprise since every columnist in the country has hinted at it for months. I've tried so hard to be fair and solve our problems—but now I find it impossible to go on."

Lucy said she and Desi had agreed on joint custody of the children. "We both love them very much," said Lucy, "and Desi can see them as often as he likes."

The financial arrangements of the divorce were simple. Everything was split fifty-fifty, with their Palm Springs hotel being turned over to a trust fund for the children. Lucy kept the Roxbury Drive house, Desi the forty-acre ranch and stock farm in Riverdale which they had bought in 1959. They each got 282,800 shares of Desilu stock, which was worth approximately twelve dollars a share at the time. Desi would also pay $450-a-month child support for each of the children.

Lucy was asked whether there could possibly be a reconciliation, as there had been with the 1944 divorce. Her simple reply: "Nope."

If friends were saying, "Poor thing, without Desi her life will be so empty. What will she do now?" they got an immediate answer. Lucy had contended that they had been working too hard and that Desi wouldn't stop to relax and enjoy everything they had, but after the divorce Lucy continued her professional activities at the same pace.

She signed for her first film in five years, a comedy with Bob Hope called *The Facts of Life*. "She didn't even wince at that title," notes a friend.

Desi had a rough siege during the divorce. While Lucy was testifying, he was in Las Vegas brooding and having one too many Scotch-on-the-rocks. It was a tough period in his life. He was asked to leave the Desert Inn because the manager decided his language was offensive to the other guests.

But Desi's ability to bounce back from disaster was as strong if not stronger than Lucy's. Shortly after the divorce, he checked himself into a Los Angeles hospital for a ten-day "rest" and friends noted that that was apparently all he needed. He returned to work cheerful, relaxed and full of energy.

Later a friend met Desi while he was playing in a golf tournament at his Palm Springs club. "He had two eggs, ham, three pieces of toast for breakfast—the same Desi who used to start with tomato juice laced with Worcestershire sauce and a chaser of Scotch and then no food till noon. He'd been 'on the wagon' for three weeks when we met and thinks the ride will be permanent."

Although it was Lucy who had always pleaded for Desi to slow up, she was the one who now set an exhausting schedule of work for herself, while he appeared to be taking her advice for the first time and enjoying some of the results of his undeniable dynamism.

While he summered at Del Mar, combining business with two of his favorite forms of pleasure, golf and horse racing, Lucy was shooting *The Facts of Life* at Desilu. But in the film, the ending was a happy one, even though it was the story of two unhappily married people.

In it, Lucy and Bob were each married to loving spouses, but the spark had gone out of their marriages. Lucy was married to Don De Fore, who was concerned with business; Bob was married to Ruth Hussey, who was devoted to her home and children. Bob and Lucy decide to have an affair, but, needless to say, comic situations intervened "in the nick of time," preventing them from committing adultery.

170

Mel Frank, director of *Facts of Life,* said of Lucy: "She may be the single greatest talent I've ever worked with. She is one of the really superb actresses of our time. I just say 'Action!' and all the magic comes out."

An associate recalls that while Lucy was filming *Facts* she was busy negotiating for rewrites on her upcoming Broadway play. There were also phone calls about television business. During these calls, Lucy talked in terms of $50,000 and $100,000 as casually as the average woman might discuss the price of tuna fish.

"How does it feel to be Hollywood's richest woman?" a production assistant once asked her. "Nyah!" was her only reply.

Lucille Ball is not sweetness and light off-camera. She is human. An observer has recalled an occasion when Lucy received a call from a show business friend, asking if she would like to go out that night. Lucy seemed bored as the man chattered on. He apparently had made plans to attend a young night-club singer's act.

"I've seen him twice already," said Lucy into the phone, "and his press agent is now saying I've been there eight times. If I go again the kid will be saying I'm in love with him. He's two-feet-six and nine years old. I don't want any part of it." The voice on the phone pleaded with her to change her mind. Lucy held the phone away from her and looked to the sky for help. She finally hung up.

"I go out because people ask me to," commented Lucy. "I have no love for night clubs, unless there's an act I especially want to see. And I don't especially want to see this kid's again."

During filming of *The Facts of Life* she had an accident on the set and was rushed to the hospital with a bump on her head. Desi, immediately notified, rushed to the hospital to console her. Then he accompanied her to their beach house at Del Mar. The obvious question was, now that they were

171

living under the same roof again, did this mean a reconciliation? Desi wouldn't answer, but Cleo and her husband Ken Morgan did. "We see no way of their being reconciled at this time."

Romantics wanted to believe that America's sweethearts would indeed be reunited and everything would be all right. But it wasn't going to happen. Lucy and Desi had split permanently.

Under no circumstances would there be any more Lucy-Desi specials. "Even if everything were all right, we'd never work together again," Lucy said with finality. "We had six years of a pretty successful series and two years of specials. Why try to top it? That would be foolish. We always knew that when the time came to quit, we'd quit. We were lucky. We quit while we were ahead."

Years later, Lucy admitted that breaking up her marriage to Desi was "wrong." They were America's most beloved couple and Norman Vincent Peale used to remind Lucy that they were everyone's idea of the perfectly married pair and if they admitted they were fallible they would betray the faith of millions.

Dr. Peale was right. Lucy later said, "I received eight thousand letters at the time of the divorce announcement and read most of them; I couldn't answer them all, of course. They asked me not to get a divorce. They said, 'Why isn't there something you can do?' They didn't know I had been trying to do it for years.

"I was painfully aware of the feeling the American public had for Lucy and their need for Lucy and Ricky as a happy family. The awareness held up my decision for a long time, until I couldn't allow it to do so any more. Lucy solved a lot of marital problems for our viewers, and the idea of finding a laugh in a hopeless situation worked for Desi and me for a long time also."

Lucille's sense of humor sometimes helped her through the

172

bad days just after the divorce. On one occasion, when she was driving from Desilu to Paramount to confer on the Bob Hope picture, she stuck her head out of her chauffeur-driven limousine and yelled to a friend, "Hi! Remember me? I used to work at Desilu."

People thought remarks like this reflected the classic laugh-clown-laugh tradition. She was *not*, they said, truly jovial and outgoing. ("I don't *think* funny," she stated years later.) She rarely showed her devastating sense of humor, with its cutting edge, to outsiders. Others noted that she was rarely even pleasant to outsiders. When a reporter asked her if she planned to marry again, she glared at him for a few moments. Then she answered, "No."

After divorcing Desi it was, according to Lucy, "the worst period of my life." She said in retrospect, "I really hit the bottom of despair—anything from there on had to be up. Neither Desi nor I have been the same since, physically or mentally, though we're very friendly, ridiculously so. . . . I did everything I could to right that ship, trotting to psychiatrists. I hate failure and that divorce was a Number One failure in my eyes. . . . Anything in excess drives me crazy. He'd build a home any place he was and then never be around to enjoy it. I was so idealistic. I thought that with two beautiful babies, a beautiful business, what more could any man want? Freedom, he said, but he had that. People don't know what a job he did building that Desilu empire, what a great director and brilliant executive he was, yet he let it all go . . . maybe Latins have an instinct for self destruction. . . ."

Was *that* the conflict, a Latin temperament married to an old-fashioned American female? "No, the *machismo* didn't bother me. I like to play games too."

On the rare occasions when she reminisced, friends recalled Lucy would often stop to wipe her teary blue eyes. But she would always quickly change moods, preferring to look ahead.

173

A few months after the divorce, Lucy's reaction to it was beginning to set in. "I get tired too easily," she confided to a friend. "I've had pneumonia twice in a year. That's not good."

"And now it is time to start a fresh page," Lucy said characteristically. "I have always wanted to do a Broadway play, but kept putting it off because of my Hollywood commitments. Starting this fall, I will have none. My divorce had nothing to do with my decision to move to New York," she fibbed, "but I will be grateful for the change of scenery as I cross this new bridge."

It was generally agreed that Lucy was running away from Hollywood, Desi, the continual reminders of their life and careers together.

Desi still looked out for Lucy's professional interests. In fact, after their divorce their relationship improved considerably. Although Lucy supposedly wanted financing for her Broadway show handled by outsiders, Desi suggested that Desilu pick up the tab. Hence they wouldn't have to share the profits and they would also own the movie and televison rights.

Later, discussing Desilu's investment in her Broadway venture, Lucy said: "There is a twofold reason for this setup. For one thing, I just didn't like the idea, once I'd made up my mind to do this show, of having to be responsible to a number of individual backers, including many friends, who were all too willing to invest in it.

"Also, the Desilu stockholders weren't too happy about my stepping out of the TV picture after eight very profitable years. But, by making Desilu the backer of the show, there is a continuing relationship, and I am still working for them with the possibility of bringing in more profits."

Was she happy, at least? "No," she admitted frankly. "Not yet. I will be. I've been humiliated. That's not easy for a woman."

It was on to New York and Broadway. "I intend to devote my time to the stage from now on," she said. "We'll keep our home in Beverly Hills. My mother will accompany us to New York to help me get things started, then she'll return to California to live in our house. But I am selling the house in Palm Springs that Desi and I built five years ago. We've been suffering from an excess of houses for some time. Desi is building a new house for himself. He enjoys building houses; I prefer living in homes."

"Every spare moment I get, I want to concentrate on my children," she stated on another occasion, observing that "They've had too many servants, too many people hovering over them. They haven't been called upon to do all the things they could. They should be more independent than they are."

During filming of *The Facts of Life*, Lucy had also suffered a leg injury, necessitating a minor operation. Along with the gash in her leg she picked up a stubborn staphylococcus infection. Antibiotics eventually cleared it up, but the drugs lowered her resistance to virus infections—and Lucy's good health was about to undergo its severest ordeal.

After *The Facts of Life* was completed, Lucy moved east. Her New York apartment was on the twenty-third floor of Imperial House at Lexington Avenue and 69th Street—a luxury apartment with seven rooms and a terrace. Lucy took along a nurse and a maid. She furnished the apartment in a contemporary California style, with bright fabrics, light woods. She loves vivid colors.

Lucie was enrolled at the Marymount School, a branch of the same school she attended in Los Angeles. Little Desi was sent to St. David's. Both schools are Catholic.

"They are homesick for California," admitted Lucy about her kids, "but my work is in New York and I want them with me."

They wouldn't lack for reminders of home. "I brought all the terrace furniture from Palm Springs, five TV sets, a piano that was sitting out there doing nothing, the toys for my daughter Lucie, little Desi's bongo drums, all my paintings and all my books," noted Lucy. "Plus a limousine with chauffeur, and a big package of courage."

In New York, news stories turned from the divorce angle and the end of the "I Love Lucy" series to Lucy's Broadway debut. It's interesting to note, in retrospect, that all publicity about the Ball-Arnaz relationship, marriage and divorce, was told from Lucille's point of view. Why had talkative Desi kept mum? Hollywood observers offered several possible explanations, the most dramatic being that Desi was in no position to criticize Lucy since his "indiscretions" could be used against him in court and enable Lucy to gain full custody of the children. More likely was the theory that Desi's love for the children prompted him to make the divorce as amicable as possible, for their sake. Still others opined that Desi just didn't care which story was given out—if Lucy wanted to tell the story her way, it was all right with him.

Lucy never was abusive about Desi in her comments. As a matter of fact, shortly after the divorce was official she seemed to "remember more of the good times than the bad. It's so true that when some previous part of life has come to an end, it's the fun and the laughs that stick in your memory, while the bickerings and violent arguments fade away," she reflected.

However, they didn't fade away completely. And certainly not as quickly as she wanted people to believe.

At forty-nine, Lucille Ball was going to tackle the roughest physical experience of her professional career. A friend recalled, "She was so desperate to leave Hollywood she would have played *Abe Lincoln in Illinois* if it would take her to Broadway."

Lucy didn't have any illusions about herself. "I'm not beautiful, not sexy and don't have a good figure," she told Hedda Hopper. Hedda concurred. "She knew she couldn't sing, admits she was too old to dance, but for her Broadway debut she would sing, dance and have to hold the whole show together."

As a vehicle, Lucy chose *Wildcat*, a comedy with music by Richard Nash, author of *The Rainmaker*. *Wildcat* had many elements similar to *The Rainmaker*, and the lead character was described as a sort of Annie Oakley of the oil fields. The score was by Cy Coleman and Carolyn Leigh. Michael Kidd was signed to direct, co-produce (with Nash), and choreograph the show.

"Professionally, I exchanged Desi for Michael Kidd," noted Lucy. "I needed someone I could depend on. I love people who know their business. I bow down to talent."

"I'm terrified too," she admitted. "I've never really been on the stage before, except years ago on the tour with *Dream Girl*. It's a challenge. I'd gone as far as I wanted in TV. I know I'm sticking my neck out—but I stuck it out in TV, too. It won't kill me if the play flops, but I'm not anticipating failure. My contract runs eighteen months, and I've leased an apartment for five years, but I hope the play doesn't run *that* long."

Would she stay with the show beyond the eighteen-month period? "If the show is a hit, I naturally will stay with it to the end of the run." Referring to Kidd and Nash, "we three make the decisions. Right or wrong, this way it's faster. I like people who know what they want. I have no qualms—this way I don't have to check with forty people. One reason for the success of 'I Love Lucy' was that Desi didn't have to check with anyone."

Lucy began arduous singing lessons. "Why, I haven't even been in the habit of singing in the shower. Naturally, I've been taking vocal training like mad. I have a marvelous coach, Carlo Menotti, and by the way, he's not Gian Carlo Menotti, the opera composer.

"I'm not going to do any of that talking-off-a-song stuff the

177

way some nonsingers do in musical shows these days. Seems to me that that is harder than actually trying to sing. I'll just have to take my chances by rearing back and letting go. Fortunately, I'll have mostly funny or action or character-type songs. That means I'll be doing a lot of cavorting around while I'm singing, and maybe that will keep people from paying too much attention to the quality of the voice."

About a leading man, Lucy said "I want an unknown. He has to be big, husky, around forty. He has to be able to throw me around, and I'm a pretty big girl. He has to be able to sing, at least a little." (Keith Andes got the role of "Dynamite Joe.")

Discussing her role: "It's a sort of tomboy type of role," she said with relish. "I get into the oil business because my father was in it, and there is the incentive of trying to make good because I have a crippled sister to look after. The romance angle is a continual fight with the leading man. I'm the sort who always thinks and talks big without any substance to back it up. I guess you'd say I'm sort of a con woman in the oil business."

The "con woman" aspect of the character bothered Lucy. But she went along with it—for the time being.

Lucy's daily regimen was agonizing. "We rehearse all day and perform all night. I'm drenched with perspiration when the curtain goes down.

"You know, after all those years filming 'Lucy,' I couldn't believe the show wasn't taped and I'd have to go to the theater every night. I had to be talked into it," she kidded.

"Rehearsing is a seven-day, seven-night deal. Out in Hollywood, I worked four days a week and could spend the rest of the time with my two kids."

But *Wildcat* was, in concept at least, a labor of love. Lucy told an observer, "I've always wanted to be on the Broadway stage. It's a new medium for me, my first time on Broadway. Sure I'm scared and I get butterflies when I think of the

178

opening night. But I'm also excited about it. I chose *Wildcat* because it's close to the character I play in 'I Love Lucy.' It's comedy, and, while comedy is harder to do than drama, I thought I'd better do something I'm known for. Later on, if Dorothy Parker's 'Big Blonde' story is still available, I'd like to do that on the stage in New York. It's a wonderful story. But for my first Broadway appearance, it's too morose."

As rehearsals for *Wildcat* progressed, Lucy began to feel uneasy. At least there seemed to be a genuinely friendly relationship among the principals of the show. Michael Kidd called Lucy "an outstanding combination of naivete and self-consciousness," intent solely on "living the character. What she felt was real for the character became her own feelings."

Lucy had to be convinced of several things during production. "I can't do it," she told Kidd about one of the songs. "It embarrasses me." Kidd noted, "We tried to show her that she was a con woman who would say such things." The song was dropped.

She also had an altercation over costumes. When designer Alvin Colt showed her the sketches, she was horrified and insisted upon wearing her rehearsal clothes—an old denim shirt and blue jeans.

"We had a horrible time convincing her," Kidd said, "that on the stage a certain artificiality is accepted. I told her someone in real jeans and a torn shirt doesn't generally appear on a lighted stage in make-up, in front of painted scenery before an audience and sing songs accompanied by an orchestra, or strike oil that comes out of a scenic artist's oil well."

Director Kidd recalled how inadequate Lucy felt as a singer. He said he was convinced that it was this feeling of inadequacy that made her forget the lyrics midway through a song every once in a while. But he also noted that she turned these lapses to her advantage. During performances

179

she would raise her hand, stop the music, tell the audience what happened, ask the conductor to start from the top again and the song would still end up with rousing applause.

The show began its tryout in Philadelphia, where the *Wildcat* heroine was an attractive but tough, raucous, profane and two-fisted girl equally adept at bringing in oil wells and bringing down men. It didn't go over very well and thereafter bits of business and references that television viewers associated with the "Lucy" character were added. One observer noted that these "Lucy" additions "were inserted like maraschino cherries in a tuna fish salad."

Lucy was deadly calm opening night in Philadelphia, but later said, "Of course I flipped three weeks later after all the changes."

The show still wasn't going over as expected and Lucille wanted even more of the "Lucy" character written into it. Author Nash objected violently, but the public obviously was paying to see the Lucy they knew, and Nash later admitted: "We found out the audience had come to see Lucy, not Lucille Ball playing in *Wildcat*. She became increasingly unhappy. Should we run against audience demand and her increasing unhappiness, which might have kept her from opening? I had a responsibility to $400,000. I was writing against my own views as a writer, but I had to."

Director Kidd had his hands full. And Desi was a frequent visitor. "They finally got around to making the changes he suggested and they're still making them," Lucy noted while the show was in previews.

It was a trying time for all concerned. A friend recalls accompanying Lucy to a local restaurant. " 'Goddammit,' Lucy said, 'why don't they make tables so you can put your legs under them?' The proprietor quickly brought another chair. She hoisted her feet up on it, made herself comfortable and ordered a Chianti on the rocks."

About her personal life during this hectic period: "The

180

children are completely adjusted to their changed mode of living. They see their father a lot more these days and so do I. Everybody's happier." While the show was in Philadelphia, Lucy's mother brought Lucie and little Desi from New York every week to see the show and visit their mother.

Wildcat opened on Broadway at the Alvin Theatre on December 15, 1960. By this time the character had been furiously rewritten into a reasonable facsimile of Lucy's television self.

"It's fine with me," Lucy said at the time. "I love Lucy, love doing her. Love the mugging. Saying to a character on-stage, 'Say, you know a fellow named Fred Mertz?' They eat it up. I have a ball. Do what I like. . . . Little Mousie, the Yorkshire terrier we use in the show, made a, well, a mess on stage one night. I stopped the show, grabbed a mop and pail and cleaned it up. Told 'em I'd read the small print in my contract. They loved it."

Lucy's personal notices were enthusiastic, but the show was panned. Walter Kerr said: "Naturally, in the case of *Wildcat*, what you really want to know about is Lucille Ball. So do I. . . . Miss Ball is up there, all right, doing all of the spectacular and animated and energetic and deliriously accomplished things she can do. . . ."

Although Lucy's worst fears about the play were realized, she was determined to make the show a success. Other stars had carried Broadway turkeys for long runs—Ethel Merman and Sammy Davis, Jr., for example. There was no doubt that people would flock to see Lucille Ball no matter what she was in.

Her film with Bob Hope, *The Facts of Life*, released only the previous month, was a tremendous hit. Critics called it the best of the films Lucy and Bob had done together. But she couldn't really enjoy its success. *Wildcat* was wearing her down tremendously. "That role would have knocked out a girl twenty years younger than Lucille," notes a friend. "She

181

was incredible, the way she delivered her performances. But she wasn't a kid, and the ordeal took its toll."

Officially, Lucille remained optimistic. She had said, "I want to devote at least five years to the Broadway stage, now that they'll have me." After all, she had achieved one of her girlhood dreams by starring on Broadway. "When I roamed around New York as a struggling young actress, I couldn't *buy* a job on Broadway. Now here I am prancing around in my first show, and it's even more fun than I thought it would be."

But she candidly told a chum, "How long can you have a ball saying the same things and dancing the same steps?"

And her health was failing.

Bill Frawley came to see *Wildcat* one evening, and created a minor sensation. "It's Fred Mertz," the audience buzzed. Another visitor was Dr. Norman Vincent Peale. He stopped backstage one night and told Lucy, "I hear you're very ill and working too hard." "Work never hurt anybody," Lucy protested. But he reminded her she had two beautiful children to bring up. "If I was in bad shape, how could I do it?" Lucy realized. "I've learned you don't rake more leaves than you can get into the wheelbarrow. I've always been moderate, but I was too spread around, trying to please too many people. You don't become callous, but you must conserve your energies."

Lucy had become a follower of Dr. Peale and his "power of positive thinking." Dr. Peale's philosophy calls for bringing God and the teaching of Jesus Christ into one's life. Lucy also became an advocate of *The Art of Selfishness*. "I ran across the idea in a decrepit old book when I was at a very low ebb. It said don't worry about the whole world. If you do it will overwhelm you. Worry about one wave at a time. Please yourself. Do something for you and the rest will fall in line. This idea appealed to me. The theory said, pin up

182

a sign: IS THIS GOOD FOR LUCY? The point was, 'to thine own self be true.'"

Lucy's personal life seemed at a standstill. She was, in fact, dating at the time, but declined to mention any names. "The only plans I have," she said, "are to make no plans. Marriage? Who needs it? I had it."

She wasn't too happy with her New York existence. "I hibernate in New York," she observed. "Can't go out in the daytime, you get recognized. And I'm not much of a night club kid. I enjoy going to Sardi's, and at the risk of sounding corny, I enjoy being with show business people."

Lloyd Nolan's last encounter to date with Lucy was in Sardi's during the *Wildcat* run. "There had been a muck-up with Lucille's reservation," remembers Nolan, "and they didn't have a table for her and her party. I asked her to sit at my table until they got her one. She was so damned mad she could hardly speak. I don't blame her."

Also in town during *Wildcat* was Busby Berkeley. Lucy invited him over to her apartment and they talked about old times.

Despite the unenthusiastic notices, Lucy seemed to like and defend her *Wildcat* role. "Look, I'm just a slob. I have no desire to play heavy drama. I want to do things with heart in them, yes. That's as much drama as I care about. The technique of getting a laugh fascinates me. I love feeling out an audience every night. What strikes them funny? Why do they remain silent when I expect them to break up?"

And around this time she hinted that she might retire after the run of the show. "I'm signed for eighteen months and then I have a commitment to do another movie with Bob Hope. After that, what I'm going to do is take the children out of school and get a tutor for them and then go and live in different places, wherever we choose to go."

"She probably meant it when she said it," says a former

183

associate. "She was tired and the idea of retirement couldn't have been all that depressing at that time in her life. For the first time, she was working but not having fun."

The Alvin Theatre could seat a total of 11,200 a week at eight performances. Tickets were priced so that weekly capacity was a hefty $65,000. The average weekly gross for *Wildcat* usually ran above $55,000. It even surpassed that figure during one week of February snowstorms. There was no doubt that Lucy was a huge draw. But in February the show had to close for two weeks because she was suffering from a viral infection, physical exhaustion and bursitis in her right leg. She spent the two weeks recuperating in Miami.

On her return the show resumed, but Lucy's health never quite recovered. Over the next few weeks there were a couple of occasions when she fainted on stage.

It was obvious that she would not be able to continue, and her physician ordered her to take a leave of absence from the show long enough for her to recover from her "severe respiratory infection complicated by exhaustion."

It was announced that the musical would go on vacation and reopen in August. But the show closed. "It just about broke my heart," she said after the closing. "And some day— when I get time and if I can still walk—I want to do another Broadway show."

The year seemed to be a disaster for her. In addition to the show closing and her failing health, Lucy had been named one of the worst-dressed women of the year by the fashion world's flamboyant "Mr. Blackwell," who described her taste in clothes as "a sense of turmoil." Lucy was in good company, however. Blackwell also rated Brigitte Bardot, Kim Novak, Anne Baxter and other luminaries as "worst-dressed." But Lucy headed the list.

By September, Lucille had returned to California. (Her divorce from Desi became final months before.)

Years later she candidly summed up the post-divorce and New York-Broadway experience. "That was a terrible time in my life. . . . all those years as 'Lucy' and I felt like I would get out of my rut if I did a Broadway musical, so I did *Wildcat*. Ugh! You know, I learned something there, too. It was the first time in my life Lucy didn't venture an opinion. I hired the best people in the business (I *thought*) to do what they do and they didn't do. I should have shouted some and maybe it would have been a better show, but I was tired. It was the first time in years I had been free. I had my divorce and I wanted to move bag and baggage away from trouble. I backed the show with my own money, sank thirty grand in an apartment and settled down for a long run. It was never anything more than a female *Rainmaker*, but nobody told me how bad it was. Except the gypsies in the chorus. They knew everything. Finally I began to listen to them and they were right. But you know we were SRO from the time we opened and when you're a hit, the powers-that-be are inclined not to change anything. But I was fixing and changing *Wildcat* up to the night I closed. When I left the show, I was so sick they almost carried me out in a coffin. I had to give them back $165,000 outta my own pocket for ticket refunds—the most money ever refunded, they said.

"Now I don't think I'll ever do another play. The loss of the days and contact with the outer world is terrible. You don't sign up to do a flop, you sign for a long run, and I don't have that kind of time anymore. But I learned something good, even from a horrible experience like *Wildcat*. I learned the people came to the theater to see the Lucy they knew and I didn't give it to them."

A TV special had been planned, called "Lucy Goes to Broadway." It was called off because "there really was no time to do it," noted Lucy. "Desi, who was to produce it, has

not been well and I certainly wasn't in any shape to do it."
Viv Vance and Bill Frawley were also scheduled to star in
the special.

What would she do after *Wildcat*? "Who the hell knows?"
she said.

What she did do after *Wildcat* was the most surprising
thing she could have done—she got married again.

Gary Morton, who started out life as Morton Goldapper,
was a relatively successful comedian whom Lucy met in the
summer of 1960, while rehearsing for *Wildcat*. At the time,
Gary was a stand-up comic at Radio City Music Hall, working seven days a week.

They were introduced by one of Lucy's *Wildcat* co-stars,
Paula Stewart, who was then married to comedian Jack
Carter. The Carters felt that Gary and Lucy would hit it off,
and one night after the show the four went out for a pizza.

Morton was forty-two, almost ten years younger than
Lucy. A big, amiable, sexy man. He was struck with Lucille's
gaiety as they shared that first pizza. But he claims he had
no idea he would wind up marrying her (he had been married once before).

"The first thing I noticed about Lucy was her warmth,"
Morton has recalled. "The second was her carriage. I mean,
she's like a thoroughbred. When she walks into a room, you
know she's there."

Gary and Lucy had "a lot of fun" on their first date, and
they followed it up by exchanging kidding telegrams. Then,
"one date led to another, and, without realizing it, we were
going steady," Morton said.

After *Wildcat* had closed and she was about to go to
Switzerland for a vacation, she was asked if she intended to
marry Gary Morton.

"Oh, don't talk marriage to me," she said. "I've had it."

"I'll bet Gary will be in Switzerland to see you while

186

you're resting," noted a reporter. Lucille didn't say yes and she didn't say no. The reporter pressed onward: "I'd like to make a bet that you will marry Gary Morton."

"You'll lose your money," said Lucy. "Don't bet. It's nice this way."

She later explained, "I didn't intend to get married again. I didn't think I would find a mature, adult person like Gary, a really understanding guy who is wonderful to be around and uncomplicated. He has none of the worrisome characteristics I lived with. I learn from experience. I wasn't going to walk into the same trap."

Gary and Lucy had more in common than people realized. "We both came up the hard way," Gary said. "I got started in World War II, clowning for USO shows. I've been in show biz for thirty years and can appreciate what she goes through."

Professionally, Morton was noted mostly for his work in the "Borscht Belt," the famous string of Jewish hotels in the Catskill Mountains. But he had also played some top night clubs, including the Copacabana in New York. When he appeared at the Copa in the spring of 1961, Lucy was often at ringside.

Gary's background was strictly New York. He was born in the Bronx. His father, a truck driver, and mother, Rose, lived on Long Island.

When Lucy returned to California, Gary followed. He met Lucy's friends, and she noted, "He knew more people there than I did. By the time he was here for a while, everybody was saying 'Why don't you marry the guy?' "

Lucy had met Gary's mother and was especially thoughtful of her. "She often called from California to see how Rose was," said a friend. "The first time she called was to wish her a happy birthday."

Friends noted that Gary's style of comedy changed after he met Lucy. "Lucille influenced him tremendously," an

187

associate pointed out. "Once he was like all comics—throwing lines constantly—always 'on.' Then he became almost distinguished. You could say he got 'class.'"

"He's just a wonderful guy," Lucille said. "A great guy. I like to make someone happy and I guess he was a candidate since he made me and my children happy."

In California, Gary was introduced to Desi, Sr. They liked each other. "It's all set," Lucy told a friend. "He accepts Gary." She later told Earl Wilson, "Desi has been very sweet and very nice about the whole thing—he certainly has given his approval."

Lucy and Desi would, of course, retain joint custody of the children if Lucille remarried.

Lucy and Gary decided to be married in New York. They set the date for November 19. The wedding was performed by Lucille's friend, Norman Vincent Peale, at Marble Collegiate Church on Fifth Avenue. Lucille wore a gown she bought at Bergdorf Goodman's. Paula Stewart was matron of honor and Jack Carter was best man. Lucille's close friends and family, including DeDe and the children, were present. The wedding was followed by a small reception for about fifteen people at Lucille's Imperial House apartment.

"We've had a beautiful year together," said Gary, "and we want to continue having beautiful years together."

After the reception, however, Gary had to leave for Palm Springs and a night club engagement. Lucy had to remain in New York to rehearse for a TV special, "The Good Years," with Henry Fonda.

Lucy had told Earl Wilson that she wouldn't go to Gary's night club openings. "I'll frequently be busy, but even if I weren't busy, I wouldn't go. Because if you go people mistake the reason. They don't think you go because you want to be with somebody you like. They think you go to help business."

Lucille admitted that she had made some attempt to coach

188

him in his work. "Yes, I'm guilty of that. I heard him do his act one night at the Concord. One word bothered me. I didn't say anything for weeks. Then he did it again and I said, 'Guess I'll tell him about the one word he's dropping.'"

Gary said, "Criticism of that kind is like coming from the Queen. And it worked. I wasn't pronouncing one word clearly. When I corrected it, what was a snicker became a scream—"

Lucille cut him off. "It was just a set up for a joke," she noted.

It was a happy Christmas for Lucille. She was rested and in good spirits, kidding and joking on the set of "The Happy Years" with Fonda, director Franklin Schaffner and producer Leland Hayward.

Gary's marriage to Lucille didn't hurt his career. For the first time, he was booked on the "Ed Sullivan Show."

"Poor Gary," remembers a friend. "Millions of 'Lucy' fans all over the country were horrified that she had remarried. They had all preferred to believe that Lucy and Desi's divorce was nothing more than a temporary separation. But now Gary was going to appear on national television and there'd be a huge audience sitting in judgment on the new man in Lucy's life. Boy, he had better be funny *and* attractive, both at the same time."

Gary was a pro, and he came off respectably. However, in the opinion of critics, he was "nothing out of the ordinary." Unfortunately, the public concurred and his career as a television comic was short lived.

But Lucy hadn't married him for his comic talents. She found in Gary exactly the qualities she had been looking for. "I didn't make the same marriage mistake twice," she noted. "Gary digs what my life is. Why I have to work. We have tranquility. We want the same things, to take care of what we have."

About his hobbies, Lucy commented, "My husband is a

189

clothes and car nut. [His cars include a Model T Ford, a Mercedes-Benz 300SL, an Astin Martin, a Rolls convertible.] But it's a harmless vice. Better than booze or chasing women, right?" One didn't have to be an expert in psychology to conclude that Lucy had chosen Gary as the antithesis of Desi.

Gary and Lucy continued to pursue their individual careers. "We have no plans or even thoughts of working together," she said shortly after their marriage. "In the first place, he works in another area of show business—the supper clubs—and has not thought much about TV."

Even if Morton wanted to transfer to TV, it was felt by some observers that Lucy would be careful to keep their careers separate. But long-time Lucille-watchers knew that she believed in nepotism. Her family had always been closely involved in her business activities. The feeling was that Lucille had the same plans for Gary. However, Gary's move into her professional life had to be gradual so no one would be embarrassed—especially Gary.

The special with Henry Fonda was broadcast in January and Lucy was on the cover of *Life* with the caption: LUCY'S BACK ON TV.

She had a commitment for another film with Bob Hope, and the plans for the "Lucy Goes to Broadway" special were reactivated by Lucy and Desi.

Desi was still running Desilu as efficiently as ever. He wasn't as frantic and temperamental as he had been and he was on the wagon. He continued to be involved in controversies. The year before, he had had a fight with Frank Sinatra and Sinatra moved his film company off the Desilu lot, objecting to the portrayal of Italians as hoodlums on Desilu's long-running "The Untouchables."

Hedda Hopper said that Frank told Desi, "The boys don't like it." Desi didn't care what "the boys" liked or didn't like.

By the end of the year, however, Sinatra and Desi had reconciled. Frank said, "C'mon, Cuban, let's make up. I don't remember what we fought about." They contemplated several television ventures, but none materialized.

Instead of a special for Lucille, Desilu formulated a new series, "The Lucy Show," starring Lucy and Vivian Vance, even though Lucy had said she would never do another TV series.

The new show would be produced by Desi, written by the old "Lucy" writers and filmed before a live audience at Desilu.

About the new series Lucy said, "I don't think I'd be doing this if it hadn't been for Viv. The studio had the idea, and the offers were fabulous. But the thing that jelled it was Viv."

What would the series do to her new marriage? "Nothing —I hope. Gary will work and I will work. We have our own careers. And Gary is adult about it. His work is mostly out of town. But he'll be home some of the time, too."

Before production started on the "Lucy" show, Lucy completed her new film with Bob Hope, *Critic's Choice*. Then she turned all her energies to the new TV show. She loved the character she was portraying and noted, "Even when my marriage to Desi was falling apart I never got tired of 'Lucy.' "

In announcing her return, James Aubrey, Jr., president of CBS, said: "We are delighted that after her record-breaking run in 'I Love Lucy' she has decided to return to 'active duty,' and we are certain that her millions of devoted fans will welcome her back with deep affection."

Looking back now, it seems ridiculous that the question then asked in the TV industry was, "With millions of dollars riding on the answer, can Lucy come back?"

Lever Brothers and General Foods were the new sponsors. Desi announced that the show would be adapted from a book, *Life Without George,* by Irene Kampen, an account of a divorcee's life in the suburbs.

Insiders predicted, however, that Lucille Ball would never

191

be presented as a divorcee and they were right. The part was written with the Lucy character a widow with two children, a son and a daughter. Vivian Vance played a divorcee. Dick Martin, of the Rowan and Martin team (who, with "Laugh-In," would be Lucy's toughest competition in a few seasons) was cast as their bachelor neighbor.

When the series debuted in October, 1962, one critic noted: "Ever since her retirement, television comediennes have been competing for the crown of Lucille Ball. Last night, that contest was decided. Miss Ball herself is back."

Jack Gould, television critic for the *New York Times*, wrote: "Lucille Ball is back in her first weekly series since 'I Love Lucy' and she is as remarkable a gal as ever. Put her in the wildest half-hour of improbability, the sort of far-fetched doings that so regularly trip up many TV notables, and she makes it all seem not only quite likely but diverting fun in the bargain."

About the situation of Lucy and Vivian being husbandless, Gould noted that the arrangement was "entirely incidental to the show's primary purpose, which was to provide a serviceable situation in which Lucy can display her zest and craftsmanship in broad clowning."

More important than critical acclaim were the ratings. Lucy's devoted fans hadn't deserted her.

When Lucy and Gary, married a year, came to New York, Lucy expressed how happy she was with her new husband. When Gary entered the room during one of Lucy's interviews, writer Kay Gardella observed, "Almost too politely, he took a seat opposite Lucy. His manner indicated he did not want to intrude. Frequently, he had to be prompted by his wife to talk.

" 'Tell Kay about your plans,' she directed.

"Briefly and reluctantly, Morton mentioned two ventures: a plan for a golf center in California's San Fernando Valley and a production company to make offbeat short films for art theatres."

192

Gary, who had just finished an engagement at the Copacabana, told Miss Gardella that night clubs were dying. Kay noted, "He no sooner had said this then the phone rang. It was for Morton. After the conversation he turned to Lucy and said lightly: 'That was an offer for a job in Milwaukee.'

" 'Forget it,' replied the redhead with a wave of her hand. Morton did."

The new "Lucy" series was a success, but it was overshadowed the following month by a decision Lucy made. She and Desi had remained together professionally after their divorce, so many assumed that the business relationship would continue. It was a surprise when Lucille bought him out, gained control of the company and assumed a new role —business tycoon. She bought Desi's shares of Desilu stock "at a price considerably in excess of the current market." The stock was selling in November for about seven and a half. The high for the year had been twelve, the low six and a half.

It was initially reported that Lucy paid Desi two and a half million dollars for the stock, but *Variety* later reported the figure was three million.

Although three million dollars was a lot of money, many in the industry felt Desi had sold out "cheap." Westinghouse had sought to buy Desilu just a couple of years before this, and the fixed selling price was in the area of twenty million dollars.

"Desi wanted to get out," according to a former associate. "He had had enough of the pressures. He was sick of life being one continual emergency and felt that, if the time ever came when he wanted to build another empire, he would. He wanted to spend his time at other activities, like his thoroughbred breeding, golf, his Palm Springs hotel."

Another associate says that Desi had wanted out for some time, but didn't want to leave when the studio's fortunes were at a low ebb. Now that the "Lucy" show was a hit, as well as "The Untouchables," things were in good shape financially. At the stockholders meeting in August, Desi had painted a rosy picture of the company's future prospects. The studio was running at eighty-seven per cent capacity, and Desilu's first feature film, *The Scarface Mob*, which was actually the first two one-hour segments of "The Untouchables," was ready for release. Desilu Sales, Inc., the company's syndication subsidiary, had passed $1,750,000 in sales.

At the time Desi sold out, the company was producing three series and nine other shows were being filmed at the studio.

Lucy succeeded Desi as president, but all other officers of the company remained the same: Edwin E. Holly was administration and finance vice president; Jerry Thorpe, programing vice president; W. Argyle Nelson, production and studio operations vice president.

Desi had hand-picked all the executives. He had a knack for perceiving executive ability.

Desi resigned as director of the company and as executive producer of "The Lucille Ball Show." Lucy became the first woman in show business history ever to be president of a major production company. (The only other woman ever to be president of her own company was Mary Pickford.)

Although "I Love Lucy" reruns still appear throughout the world and new generations associate Lucille Ball and Desi Arnaz as husband and wife, Lucy's takeover of Desilu marked the final professional split between America's "most famous and beloved couple."

Since her days as an aspiring actress in Jamestown, Lucy had faced and overcome many problems. Now, at fifty-one, she was embarking on still another career.

10

AT FIRST almost no one outside the industry could visualize "Lucy, America's beloved scatterbrain," as a Hollywood tycoon. Supposedly, neither could she: "I never expected to be president, but Desilu was, in a way, our baby. It seemed only right that one of its parents should, after all this time, accept custody."

At this early juncture Lucy was modest about her new role. "The place was running nicely and had been for some time," she said. "I didn't have to jump in and worry. So far, I don't believe I have been allowed to make any mistakes."

Despite all her efforts to make light of her new position— "It's still all in the realm of comedy," she quipped—there was no doubt that it was no laughing matter and Lucy was firmly in charge. "She *was* the president," an associate remembers. "She ran the place."

Friends noted that when she took over the reins at Desilu there began to be a definite change in Lucille. "She has a mind as tough as any man's, but the body is still all-feminine," a friend said. "The combination can sometimes be fascinating but sometimes devastating."

She moved the president's office to her three-room dressing-room suite. Discussing the formal president's office in the administration building she noted dryly, "I've seen a total of eleven presidents in and out of that office. I wouldn't know how to behave in a place like that. I'd see a lot of ghosts. In fact I still refer to this place occasionally as RKO. I'm sure an analyst could find something Freudian there someplace."

Lucy contended that she would have been happy to continue the business relationship with Desi, and she flatly denied that her marriage to Gary had been instrumental in breaking up the business partnership. She also insisted that Gary would not become an executive at Desilu.

But some observers believed that Desi's sellout had been triggered by a number of factors, one of which was definitely the marriage situation. "Lucy now had *two* men giving her advice," stated a friend.

Others said that the "final straw" came when Lucy and Desi had a showdown over "The Untouchables." Desi had announced a week before he sold out that he was "restoring violence" to the series, which was sagging in the ratings.

"We made one mistake this year, eliminating too much violence from 'The Untouchables,'" Desi had said. "The show has suffered by it. I'm going right back to the Mafia, the gangsters, the machine guns. I'm not going to let any senator talk me out of it." He was referring to the extended Senate investigation into violence on television.

Leonard Freeman, executive producer of the series, had already left Desilu because of "differences of opinion" and Lucy was against continued violence in the series as well. However, the most talked-about reason for Desi's departure —and the one Lucille stressed—was his desire to be free from day-to-day responsibilities.

196

Her explanation of the details of buying out Desi was simple. "When we started this operation, Desi and I were in charge of it together. Our marriage was going well. . . . But we set it up so that if anything ever happened, if he wanted out or if I did, one could buy the other's stock. It was always that way. And even if we hadn't had trouble and broke up, he was planning to retire long before I was going to."

Lucille said that when she decided to go into her new TV series, Desi said, "If you're going to do that, how about buying me out now?"

Lucy said, "Fine," and claimed that that was the way it happened. "The truth is," Lucy admitted wistfully, "Desi had wanted out for a long time. He's had the business bit. I honestly believe he enjoyed launching Desilu more than the actual running of it. He now feels he's accomplished everything he wanted to, including establishing trust funds for our children—so he's finally retiring. That's really all there is to it."

A friend remembers that during this period a note of pride would creep into Lucy's voice when she spoke of Desi. She told friends she thought he would marry again soon.

When a friend remarked, "I was so sorry when you and Desi separated," Lucy retorted, "I'm sorry, too." And then, "But Desi never loved me. It took me a long time to realize this. I think he'll meet somebody one of these days, marry her and be happy. He's taken hold of himself and I'm proud of the way he's straightened out his life. Our children are a bond which will always come first."

Now that Lucy was on her own and "running things," it was inevitable that people would accuse her of "turning into a man." Lucille Ball was saddled with the "boss lady" image.

"As a matter of fact she *didn't* turn into a man," notes an ex-associate. "At first she went out of her way *not* to appear to 'walk all over people,' but she was so damn efficient and no-nonsense that her approach was misinterpreted. If a

197

reporter came to interview her for a half-hour, the impression he or she walked away with was, 'Wow, what a ballsy broad.' When, realistically speaking, she was just being efficient and not wasting time.

"It would have been easy as hell for Lucille to assume a phony attitude for interviews. Most people are in awe of her anyway; she can act any way she likes. But she lets them see the real her, and people assume that if they're seeing Lucille Ball, President of a Corporation, that's the way she is all the time. It's just not true. Just because she doesn't display her inner self to strangers doesn't mean she's 'turned into a man.' "

However, there are dissenting opinions. A top director says: "The whole purpose of Lucy's career from this point on was to show Desi she didn't need him. She had gotten herself a new husband; her new TV show was a hit; and now she was out to prove that she could run the studio as well as Desi could."

"Listen, honey," Lucy herself told Rex Reed a few years later, "if I was going to turn into a man I would've done it a long time ago. I've been in awe of most men all my life. It never occurred to me how an executive should be. I've been *told*. But when I took over this job I decided to do it my way. My ability comes from fairness and a knowledge of people. The rules were here before I took over. My job is just to keep everybody happy. I never wanted to be an executive, but when my marriage to Desi broke up after nineteen years, I couldn't just walk away from my obligations and say forget it. (We were an institution.) Life takes guts. If you don't take chances, you'll never bathe because you might get dirty again; you'll never eat because you might get sick. So I took on all of our responsibilities, but I ran my studio like I ran my home, with understanding for people."

Lucy claimed to Reed she hadn't liked being a woman executive. "I hated it," she said. "I used to cry so much—and I'm not a crier—because I had to let someone go or make

198

decisions I didn't understand. There were always two sides to every question and the trouble was I could see both sides. No one realizes how run-down Desilu was. The finks and sycophants making $70,000 a year, they were easy to clean out . . ."

About the days prior to and after her takeover she has also candidly revealed, "I wanted to go to Switzerland with the kids, anywhere to run away, but Desi wanted out. Then I found out that for five years, our empire had taken a nose dive and if I wanted to get my money back, I had to rebuild it first. For the first time in my life, I was absolutely terrified —I'd never run any show or a big studio. When I came back from doing *Wildcat* I was so sick, so beat I just sat in that back yard, numb, for a year. I'd had pneumonia, mononucleosis, staph, osteomyelitis. Lost twenty-two pounds. Friends told me the best thing I could do physically, psychologically, was go back to work."

There were many headaches to be faced as president. To begin with, Lucy was unhappy with the time slot for her new show, and there was some question whether she would renew for the upcoming 1963-64 season. As the trade was fond of noting, Lucille Ball was the only star who annually renewed the network, rather than vice versa.

This hesitation on Lucy's part to renew was the start of an annual ritual which could continue for the next ten years. "Lucy was using her own show as a wedge to try to sell some of Desilu's other products," says an ex-network executive. However while her demands for herself and her "Lucy" show were always met, she was relatively unsuccessful in persuading CBS to buy other properties.

For the 1963-64 season, Desilu did manage to sell to CBS not only the "Lucy" show, but a new situation comedy, "Glynis," starring Glynis Johns. The studio also sold a one-hour weekly dramatic circus series, "The Greatest Show on Earth," starring Jack Palance, to ABC.

But there were a number of Desilu shows that hadn't sold.

199

Lucy's greatest disappointment was the failure to sell a series starring Ethel Merman. Lucy later said that during the Aubrey regime at CBS, "I couldn't sell the new pilots. . . . I couldn't sell anything but me."

As Desilu's fiscal year ended in July 1963, the company wound up with a loss. Although income was up to over $21,-000,000, the loss exceeded $650,000, for which special write-offs in the fiscal year were deemed responsible. The stockholders were not happy.

At the annual meeting, President Ball stressed that the write-offs were in line with the firm's "hard, conservative policy."

It was interesting to observe Lucille's "hard-as-nails" attitude when she was presiding as an executive versus Lucille Ball, actress. "Eventually," an associate says, "those two attitudes meshed into one."

Lucy's professional life for the next few years was concentrated on her show and coping with Desilu's corporate problems. She did double duty as president-actress and ran "a tight ship."

Lucy's personal life, of course, concentrated on her children and her new husband. After the takeover, although she was keeping the same rigorous work schedule, starting rehearsals on Monday and working through a late Thursday night shooting, her home life was considerably different than it had been with Desi. Gary was always within easy call.

Shortly after selling out to Lucy, Desi married again. His wife was forty-five-year-old socialite Edith Mack Hirsch, who had just received a Juarez divorce from her millionaire husband, sportsman Clement Hirsch. Hirsch, who had made his fortune in dog food, and "Edie" had been Lucy and Desi's Del Mar neighbors for years. They all shared an enthusiasm for horse racing.

Edie and Desi had been dating for several months. Lucy

had even predicted to friends that marriage between them was likely, and she had described Edie as "a friend of ours for years. She's a real doll."

They were married on Desi's forty-sixth birthday at the Sands Hotel in Las Vegas. Only a few close friends were on hand, including the Jimmy Durantes and Van Johnson. Edie wore a "knockout" net lace cocktail dress. Margaret Durante was maid of honor, and Dr. Marcus Rabwin was Desi's best man. Edie was described as "a Lucy look-alike," with the same red-gold hair.

Lucy sent the couple a horseshoe-shaped floral display, with a note: "Congratulations on both of you picking a winner."

"Despite Lucy's happy façade, Desi's remarriage had its effect on her," speculates a close friend. "Sure, she had remarried first, and Lucy's relationship with Desi was a hundred per cent calmer and friendlier. But the guy had been the one big love of her life."

Though she tells friends today that she and Desi have a better relationship than they have ever had before, she also frankly reiterates that since their divorce, "Neither Desi or I have been the same."

However, Lucy's working day left no time to dwell on the past. Decisions all day long; meetings, day-to-day production emergencies and just plain problems calling for a consultation with the president. Work. Work. Work. She was working harder than ever and that's the way she wanted it.

Lucy made sure her children were leading as normal a life as possible. "They attend Catholic school in Beverly Hills, where they mingle with many other youngsters of celebrities," said Lucy at the time. "They are not singled out for preferential treatment."

Little Lucie, almost twelve, and Desi, Jr., almost ten, began making brief professional appearances. Lucy said, "This is something they have been asking about for the last

201

three years . . . since they were really very tiny. The roles aren't much but they are a start and I don't see any reason to say, 'Oh, no, you can't,' because there are thousands of 'Why nots.'

"And there is really no reason why not, and it gives us a chance to see if they are equipped, by not denying them at this point and by allowing them to see that it is hard work and that it does take concentration and it does take an awful lot of application."

"I see a good change in my children," she observed, "because they have been allowed to spread their wings a little and see what is required of them. And little Desi doesn't think he knows it all, now that he's had a chance to get in there and stack up alongside others. And Lucie never thought she knew it all, but it is bringing her out in a nice way."

Late in 1963, Lucille made her dramatic TV debut in a segment of Desilu's by-then-floundering "The Greatest Show on Earth." Titled "Lady in Limbo," it was broadcast before Christmas amidst much publicity hoopla. Lucy had finally appeared in "The Greatest Show on Earth," although it was not directed by De Mille.

She had only done it, of course, to bolster the show's failing rating. "It isn't the perfect dramatic spot for me," said Lucy honestly. "The ideal serious role will pop up sometime in the future."

The critics agreed. The show was panned. "She shouldn't have gone to the trouble," one critic noted. "She is much better at provoking yoks than putting on a long face for most of an hour, miscast as a lonely circus performer who falls for —and wins for adoption—a small, orphaned boy."

As renewal time for her own show rolled around, Lucy was supposedly entertaining notions of retirement. But this merely meant that the network had better give careful thought to Lucy's other wishes.

CBS wanted her to extend her show to an hour. Lucy repeated that she was not sure she would continue her series at all for the 1964-65 season. Associates said she felt she must devote more of her energies to Desilu, since the company hadn't sold any of its ten series pilots to the networks.

The firm had plowed a greal deal of cash into development of new properties since Lucy had taken over, and insiders said she was shocked when none of the new shows were picked up. She was especially rooting for a Dwayne Hickman series, "Mr. Hannan and the Little People," about a grammar school teacher and "The Hoofers," with Donald O'Connor and Soupy Sales as turn-of-the-century vaudevillians.

The O'Connor series had been Lucy's own idea, and she said, "Television needs a talent like Donald. For his versatile talents to be fully appreciated, he needs weekly exposure."

The networks didn't agree. And Lucy had been disappointed that "Glynis" had been dropped after its first thirteen weeks. "She's a great performer," said Lucy about Glynis Johns, "and it was a wonderful show. But if things aren't good, they start breathing down your neck and what are you going to do?"

Lucy noted that many hit series didn't start out as such and had to be given a chance to build an audience. "Listen, do you know how we all begged the sponsors to keep the 'Dick Van Dyke Show' on when it was just starting?"

Lucy wired CBS President James Aubrey that "the rigors of a weekly half-hour program combined with the added task as president of Desilu made it impossible to do justice to both jobs," and that she felt she could be of "greater service" to Desilu by concentrating on her duties as president and only doing an occasional one-hour special. Aubrey remained calm, saying he was sorry to lose her weekly show but would "look forward" to her comedy specials.

However, the matter was far from closed.

Palm Springs was Lucy's usual getaway spot. To unwind after her grueling work week, Lucy spent most weekends there with Gary and the kids.

Did the kids see much of Desi? "Their daddy has a house right down the road from ours, so they get to see him often," Lucy said. Did she visit Desi too? "Of course not—I have my own husband to look after," she told a friend, averting her eyes. "I see Desi on business only. He still directs some TV episodes."

Although the children lived with Gary and Lucy, they spent many weekends and a lot of the summer with Desi. Lucy always said, "He'll never have any trouble getting the children any time he wants them."

Naturally, when Gary married Lucy the major question was how he would get along with the children. "They didn't exactly welcome him with open arms at the beginning," notes a friend. But Gary understood and so did Lucy. "After all," Lucy later explained, "they were only seven or eight when this strange man showed up. Gary was a nice man, but he was no father figure, and my children weren't about to accept him without a battle. They'd seen *The Parent Trap*, the movie where Hayley Mills tries to get her parents back together after they separated. They thought that if they took me to see the film often enough, I'd get the idea. I must have sat through that picture five times! But I kept telling them that their daddy was happily married, and so was I. Eventually, mostly thanks to Gary's patience, it all worked out."

Later Lucy remarked, "I wouldn't even call it an adjustment. The children really dig him. Gary gives them the kind of discipline they have never had before, and they love it. I can be strict—for about sixty seconds. Then the children can wind me around their little fingers. You can depend on the person who disciplines you, because he is always the same way; he's dependable."

A friend notes that though there wasn't the romantic spark

there had been between Lucy and Desi, there was a genuine affection and understanding between Lucy and Gary. "With him, a home isn't just a place to change your clothes," Lucy observed. "He loves every room. And I'm contented because someone is doing with me the things he likes to do, and I'm doing with someone what I like to do."

"Lucy can't run a company by herself," Gary later said. "Maybe with me around, when she walks on the set, her mind is at peace. I pop in from time to time, on conferences, rehearsals. I can tell from her if things are going well, if the *laughter* is there. She's a thoroughbred, very honest with me, a friend to whom I can talk about anything. She never leaves me out of her life; that's important for a man."

Morton acted with Lucy's children in amateur theatricals in their garage theatre, and he played golf with little Desi. "In fact," recalls a friend, "he even played golf with *big* Desi, which everyone considered a fantastic display of unnecessarily civilized behavior."

The children were always referred to as "little Desi and little Lucie."

"It has always been little Lucie and big Lucy, never, God forbid, young Lucie and . . . .", a friend notes, rolling her eyes upward in mock horror.

How did big Lucy spend her rare free time? She had never been particularly sports-minded, but was mildly interested in golf and riding. "I think I might make a golfer," Lucy once said. "I want to have another go at that. Several years ago I took nine lessons. Then the instructor put me in a foursome with three other girls. On the fourth tee I hit my ball a powerful whack and it disappeared. I went home when I couldn't find it—didn't know you could use another ball. But I have a trophy from the last time I played. I'm a thirty handicap, a happy hacker. I love the game, but never had time for it.

"I'm best at riding. When I lived in the east years ago, I

used to go on hunts. They used a little worn-out fox, but I never laid eyes on him. I went along for the steak breakfast.

"There's another sport with horses I'm interested in: I play long shots. Once at Del Mar I put two dollars on the daily double and it paid $1,300. I wasn't even at the track, just sent the money in."

While Lucy might venture a couple of dollars on a long shot at the races, her career was not something she would gamble with. "At the last minute," Lucy finally signed for another season with CBS. Insiders noted that Lucy had been prompt to reevaluate her situation when ABC dropped "The Greatest Show on Earth." Without the Lucy show, Desilu would have had no shows on the air at all.

James Aubrey announced, "Lucy has exercised a woman's prerogative and will be back on the CBS Television Network this fall." Her time slot for 1964 would be changed from 8:30 to 9 P.M. It was felt that the new spot would improve her ratings, which had slipped from the top five to between ten and fifteen.

During the season Lucy reunited with pal Bob Hope for a special, "The Lucille Ball Comedy Hour." Jack Gould noted: "It was the counterpoint of Miss Ball's distinctive wackiness and Mr. Hope's handling of the throwaway lines that provided the needed stage chemistry to keep a viewer looking." He concluded, "there is nothing wrong with corn when it's professionally done."

As if Lucille's schedule wasn't already bulging, in the fall of 1964 the world's foremost tycoon-actress-wife-mother took on still another job. It was a radio interview program on CBS, with husband Gary producing and occasionally joining her on the air.

"CBS didn't have to twist my arm when it was suggested that I might want to take over the radio spot Garry Moore was vacating, along with his television program. I love radio. I did some radio work before television, but it was situation comedy stuff. I've never done this sort of thing before."

"Let's Talk to Lucy" would be a Monday-through-Friday morning talk program. "I'll find people wherever I can and we'll gab."

She would take a portable tape recorder along wherever she went—on the set or wherever she might meet celebrities to interview.

She had already taped interviews with Bing Crosby, Danny Kaye, Jack Benny, Dean Martin and his wife Jeanne, Red Skelton, Bob Hope, Agnes Moorehead and Hedda Hopper.

Describing the show's modus operandi: "It's not difficult, I have people do research. All I have to do is be near a tape recorder. It's just a matter of spending a half-hour with a friend of mine. The show will be heard ten minutes a day. My staff has to cut it down to broadcast time. I have no trouble talking. I'm usually interested in what I'm discussing. It's easy and it's fun."

Lucy enjoyed the show because, like most show people, she is starstruck. When Barbra Streisand was her guest, Lucy asked her how it felt to be only twenty-one, a big recording artist and star of the Broadway hit *Funny Girl*.

"Not much," replied Barbra.

"That cool really flustered Lucille," cousin Cleo remarked. "It violated everything she believes in. For Lucy nothing ever came easy."

About Streisand, Lucy recalled, "I didn't know one thing about her. She'd just moved into her New York apartment and I was completely in awe of her. I couldn't believe anyone twenty-one could have this feeling for songs or be so good. She came in from the kitchen with this compote with peaches in it, eating. I said, 'All right, honey, sit down. Could you get a little closer to the mike?' She didn't and I didn't dare ask her again. So finally I asked her a question and she nodded, she didn't answer. I cut and said, 'Barbra, this is radio.' She said, 'Okay.' And she moved in and there was the sound of her spooning the peaches."

By now, Oscar Katz, a former CBS program executive, had taken over "the major chores" at Desilu.

"All I have to do now is to attend directors' meetings, policy sessions and approve or disapprove potential programs," said Lucille.

Then the inevitable question: Will Lucy be back for another season with "The Lucy Show?" The inevitable answer: "I don't know. Two or three times, I didn't think I'd be back this season. I lost my long-time writers, the network suggested a one-hour weekly show, with which I'm not about to kill myself. I wanted to do a series of specials, which the network didn't want. So, here I am, back at the old stand. Who can tell about next season? All I know is that I'm not tired of working. I love it."

However, Vivian Vance *was* tired of working and announced that after three seasons on the new "Lucy" show she wanted out. Viv was weary of commuting to the coast and wanted to stay home in Connecticut with her husband, literary agent John Dodd.

At first Lucy thought she could persuade Vivian to change her mind. She even went to Connecticut to apply a little friendly pressure. But she later abandoned her efforts. "I didn't want to bother her after our initial crying spell—we cried ourselves out."

So Lucy lined up guest stars for the season, including Ann Sothern and Joan Blondell. But she noted there would be no regulars—"Nobody can replace Vivian Vance."

By now Jim Aubrey had been deposed as chief of CBS. "I know I shouldn't open my mouth, but I don't think Jim was asked to resign or that he got fired," commented Lucille. "He's too bright for that. He's smarter than anybody up there. I personally think he played his show as long as he wanted to play it and before long you'll hear he's opening someplace else."

There was talk that Aubrey would join Universal, but Lew

Wasserman, president of MCA, the studio's parent company, denied it. Aubrey remained unaffiliated for several years before assuming the presidency of MGM.

Lucy was having her continuing problems with the networks. As always, she was finding it difficult to sell Desilu's products. One of the new pilots she was excited about was "My Son, the Doctor." Lucy noted, "Naively, I believed that if you had a good series you could sell it. I guess there's more to it than that."

She was still upset over the failure to sell the Donald O'Connor series and Ethel Merman's show. Lucy appreciated Merman's approach to her work, which was similar to her own. "That Merman, she's a trouper—somebody who gets to work with no fuss, no mess," commented Lucy. "Not somebody who gets temperamental like Jack Palance, and you can quote me."

Somehow Lucy found time to engage in a few civic and educational activities during the year. She was a guest lecturer at the tenth annual Sam Goldwyn Creative Writing Awards at UCLA.

Goldwyn himself was on hand. His relationship with Lucy had remained cordial through the years. Lucy sometimes referred to him as "the man who started the Ball rolling."

Before addressing the students she was checking her notes. A reporter asked, "Dr. Ball, where did you matriculate?"

"I never did that in my life," she said tongue-in-cheek.

"But where did you get your degree?"

"Oh. Well, I graduated from the Goldwyn Girl line."

"Let's see, that was Class of 19 . . .?"

"We won't go into that."

Lucy commented to the audience, "You students are well protected here in this wonderful university where you get the best of instruction and advice. You are surrounded by love. But I know you must be worrying about what will happen to you when you go out in the world and there will be no one to guide you and look after you. I think it will help you if you will remember to recognize the small successes that you will have. Don't let the brightness of that big goal blind you to what happens on the way toward the goal. Meet one wave at a time and enjoy what progress you make. I want you please not to be taken up in the undertow of pessimism. Never lose your interest in people."

In the summer of 1964 Lucy and Gary went to New York. August 31 was declared "Lucy Day" at the World's Fair. Crowds of screaming, camera-clicking fairgoers were on hand to welcome television's most popular star.

"I've never seen anything like this in my life," noted one of the burly police captains, surveying the crowds. "We've had a lot of public figures at the Fair, but Lucy pulled more people than any ten of them put together."

She arrived at 9:45 A.M. with two busloads of newsmen invited by CBS. Gary, her mother and Hedda Hopper accompanied her. Lucy started the day by putting her handprints in concrete at the Hollywood Pavilion. Hedda also put her handprints in, but first had to remove six rings.

The day was billed as an international salute, since Lucy's show was now seen in forty-four countries. None of the foreigners working at pavilions and exhibits seemed to have any trouble recognizing "the redhead."

Fair officials noted that Gary proved to be more than just an added attraction. "He gagged his way through many embarrassing pauses at the stops along the way and he was helpful in winning over other performers by joining in their song and dance routines."

Lucy and Margaret Hickey, public affairs editor of the *Ladies' Home Journal*, were honored by the Los Angeles chapter of Theta Sigma Phi. Lucy was given the "Woman in the News" award, and Miss Hickey the "Woman Behind the News" award.

Lucy also found time to give advice to kids who wanted to

210

Lucille, baby son Desi IV and nineteen-month-old Lucie.

Lucille and her first child, Lucie.

Little Desi already had a way with girls: a kiss from sister Lucie.

Lucille and Desi face the press after the ordeal of testifying before the House Un-American Activities Committee.

Lucy clowning with Academy Award winner Ingrid Bergman.

One legendary clown impersonating another.

Three generations of Balls: Desi, Jr., Lucille and Lucille's mother, Desiree ("DeDe").

Mama and the kids, now ten and eight.

Lucie, eleven, entered show business first, via Mama's show. Desi, Jr., visited the set.

They always publicized their anniversaries.

Smiles masked behind-the-scenes problems with Lucille's Broadway debut in *Wildcat*.

The Wildcat role was super-strenuous and took its toll.

With long-time friend and co-star, Bob Hope.

Lucille wanted to play Lillian Russell to pal Jackie Gleason's Diamond Jim Brady. The project never materialized.

Lucille and Vivian Vance soloed on the new 1962 Lucy Show.

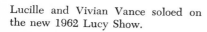

Lucy, displaying her famous legs, with guest star Danny Thomas.

The resemblance between Desi Arnaz, Jr., and his father is remarkable. Their attitudes about life are similar, too, and differ from Lucille's.

Lucille and husband number two, comedian Gary Morton. Their wedding day, November 19, 1961.

Lucie, Lucy and Desi, Jr. The kids have established careers of their own.

With husband Gary and Vivian Vance, 1969, when Lucille was named First Lady of Television.

With Don Adams, Bill Cosby, 1968.

With Don Adams, 1967.

Lucille and the TV industry's highest honor—the Emmy.

Lucie's wedding, July, 1971. Lucille, bridegroom Phil Vandervort, **Lucie**, **Desi**.

Desi, Jr., Liza Minnelli, Desi, Sr., at the premiere of *Cabaret*.

break into show business. "I get fifty to sixty letters a week
from these kids around the country, and a hundred or more
show up every week at the Desilu studio gate," Lucy said.
"Most of them have no experience, no hobbies. They don't
excel in anything, yet they all want to know how to become
a star. They never ask, 'What should I learn?'

"None of these kids would be dumb enough to sign up to
be house builders or secretaries without first getting some
experience. But they come to Hollywood with no agent, and
no chance of getting into the Screen Actors Guild, and no
idea of what they can really do. I had one tell me that she
wanted to belong to the 'Star Guild,' whatever that is.

"After they sit on a stool at Schwab's Drug Store, and
some of them grow old there while claiming to be out-of-
work actors, then they begin running with a pack in this
town. What happens to a lot of them after that I don't even
want to talk about.

"If I do get time to talk of any of these kids, I tell them
that show business in Buffalo is the same as here, and they
should stay put in their schools or workshops or little thea-
ters and learn all they can. I don't think they believe show
business is the same in Buffalo, but it's true."

She felt that the increasing number of "fame seekers" in
town was due to the quick and freaky success of teen-age
stars like The Beatles.

Oddly enough, in a short time, her own son would enjoy a
similar "freaky success."

No matter how busy Lucy became, she tried to keep communications open between her children and herself at the
same time keeping close reins on them. "We *touch* in our
house," she noted. "I come home dead-tired, and if I feel my
kids stiffen, I say, 'Honey, don't stiffen up. Momma needs
you tonight. There's so little time. Let's take advantage of
the kisses and hugs while we have them.'"

219

"I'm observing, watching to see how much of my philosophy of life has rubbed off on them," she remarked on another occasion.

"Desi, Jr., however, was a dynamo and there was no holding him back. His sister has laughingly remarked, "Desi's been thirty-four since we were kids!"

While Lucie remained an amateur actress, Desi, Jr., turned professional at twelve. With his pals Dino Martin, thirteen-year-old son of Dean Martin, and Billy Hinsche, fourteen-year-old son of a business executive, he formed a trio: Dino, Desi and Billy. It wasn't difficult to start this ball rolling. The trio gained invaluable experience performing as part of the Lucy show's warm-ups. Billy's father, Otto, handled their business affairs. Dino's father's friend, Frank Sinatra, gave the kids a recording contract and the group was on its way.

"I wanted to get Dino, Desi and Billy on my show and waited for a good script," said Lucy. "By the time it came along, I couldn't afford them. They had four big hits." Lucy said she could only afford to pay them $400; the boys had made their TV debut on "Hollywood Palace"; they received $4,000 for an appearance on Dean Martin's show. They also appeared on Ed Sullivan's show, earning considerably more than the "Lucy" show budget would allow. In addition, the group also made money from its own music publishing company, which was managed by William Howard, son of Dorothy Lamour and Bill Howard.

Lucy later optimistically remarked about Desi, Jr.'s quick success: "Fortunately, he knows now that this was just a phase. He realizes how fleeting fame and fortune are in today's teen-age music business. I'm glad that he does know, because teen-agers have enough problems without that."

Lucy had mixed feelings about Desi's success. "Of course she was thrilled that the public loved her son," notes a friend. "No mother could be more concerned with her kids being happy and succeeding in life than Lucy. But she was annoyed, too, because the kid didn't have to *earn* the rewards. There had been no struggle at all. Just as she had been flabbergasted by Streisand's nonchalance about 'making it,' she didn't want to see the same thing happen to Desi."

Although a trifle pudgy during his middle teens, Desi was proving to be the image of his father. In more ways than one. Lucy knew she was in for a few headaches. She said about the group, "they got all this adulation—this uncalled-for adulation—with the little girls screaming, and it's very hard when they come back home for us to get them back to normal."

She said that she was able to do it "by sticking to the rules. Telling him he's not going out during school months, no matter how big a hit he was with his group when he was out on the road." She meant it.

It was obvious that her children would have show business careers. "Nothing can stop Desi, Jr.," Lucy said. "I can't imagine him not making it from the way he acts. He's become a really great drummer. He plays the organ, the piano, the vibes. Lucie is a fine little actress, and she'll have a big career if that's what she wants to do."

As contract time for big Lucy rolled around again, it was no secret that whether or not she would renew would be determined by how well Desilu did in selling five new series pilots.

The studio had come up with several interesting shows. In addition to "My Son, the Doctor," Oscar Katz announced that CBS was considering a comedy, "My Lucky Penny," starring Brenda Vaccaro, Richard Benjamin, Joel Gray and Luana Anders. It was about two wives putting their husbands through dental school.

Desilu also had ABC interested in "Frank Merriwell," a series based on the famous turn-of-the-century dime novels. The show featured Beau Bridges and Tisha Sterling, daughter of Ann Sothern. Two other Desilu properties were: "The

221

Good Old Days," starring Darryl Hickman, and "Star Trek," starring Jeff Hunter and Peter Duryea, son of Dan Duryea.

None of the series sold. Lucille re-signed with CBS.

Although she enjoyed being president, associates noted that one aspect of the job that Lucy didn't relish was the annual stockholders' meeting. "Lucy didn't like being responsible to other people and having to explain her every business decision," an associate recalls. But since Desilu was a public company, she had no choice, and she no longer had Desi to "handle things" at these meetings.

Many times during business meetings Lucy would turn controls over to Milton A. "Mickey" Rudin, her whip-sharp attorney. Lucy, used to having people depend on her, depended heavily—and still does—on Rudin for business advice.

One of the problems she faced from many Desilu stockholders was that they had thought of Lucille Ball and Desi Arnaz as a one-unit institution, and those investors who had bought stock in Desilu on the basis of faith in the two stars no longer had that faith to fall back on. They respected Lucille, of course, but the directors of the company were merely businessmen and since Desi's departure stockholders began to take a keener interest in how their money was being spent.

There was quite a furor at the annual Desilu meeting in August, 1965, held at the little theatre on the lot. John Gilbert, a man who owned one hundred shares of Desilu stock and was described as "a person who makes a profession of attending stockholders' meetings and asking pointed questions," charged that Lucy's income—close to $500,000 a year —was equal to the loss the company sustained. He referred to the fact that the year's net profit of $455,000 was a drop from the almost $800,000 profit of the previous fiscal year. Gilbert and other shareholders were also upset that the stock had dropped from a high of twenty-nine to seven. They also noted that one director of Desilu did not even own any stock. And many protested the firm's no-dividend policy.

Gilbert was vehement, and several times his shouts interrupted the meeting. An attempt was made to rule him out of order, but he continued to toss charges at the company's management. Lucy had been conducting the meeting, but Mickey Rudin took over in her behalf. Rudin, who was also a company director and Desilu's chief counsel, ordered John Reeves, Desilu's chief of security, to toss Gilbert out.

Reeves and Gilbert struggled. Gilbert's glasses were knocked to the floor. The two men fell into the aisle and began wrestling. Lucy began shouting: "Leave him alone. Let him go back to his seat."

Gilbert was released and sat down.

But by now the melee involved most of the close to a hundred stockholders present. Lucy's flaming temper rose a number of times as she "stared knives" at Gilbert through most of the meeting. At one point she noted, "I've read about him. He's all that they say."

"Thank you," Gilbert retorted.

In defense of Lucy, Rudin noted that she was paid as both president of the company and an entertainer "and she is about two hundred per cent underpaid" in relation to other stars.

The main argument was about the lack of dividends. Lucille read from a written statement: "Use of cash for corporate purposes is needed. Directors have decided it is in the best interests of the company not to pay dividends. Our money is being used to support the company."

At one point the debate became so heated that one stockholder suggested a short recess so that things could "cool off." The recess was declared. Lucy huddled on stage with her aides and Gilbert remained in the audience surrounded by his "supporters." Lucy cracked: "Mr. Gilbert, do you mind if I go to the ladies room?" He graciously gave his permission and Lucy stormed out.

When the meeting was called to order, the bickering increased. The directors sat staring at the ceiling, becoming more red faced. Lucy chain-smoked and took some aspirin. "Bufferin and water on the house," she called.

When one stockholder suggested that company officers take only a dollar a year with their salaries going for dividends, Lucy snapped: "How long could I keep these valued advisers at a dollar a year? This isn't war—it's the TV business."

Gilbert had the last word. He summed up the meeting: "This has been a real show. Too bad it wasn't on television. It might have increased our revenues."

Several minority stockholders proceeded to file suit against Desilu, charging that Lucy's compensation had been excessive during the last three fiscal years. The suit charged that in 1962, before Lucy took over the majority of stock, she received $175,000 a year. Since then she received $375,000 in 1963, $735,000 in 1964 and $490,000 in 1965. The suit said that from the moment she bought out her husband, she had "engaged in a plan and scheme to use her control and dominance over the corporation to obtain for herself excessive and illegal compensation." The stockholders also maintained that Lucy had only been rendering part-time service to Desilu.

The company replied that Lucy had been paid $100,000 per year for services as president, and $390,000 for services as an actress, with sixty-seven per cent of the latter sum to be deferred for payment in later years. But Desilu would retain total residual rights of the new "Lucy" show, and Lucy would not share in any residuals. Thus, the company explained, her huge salary was not only justified but a bargain, since they had already secured substantial mimimum guarantees for reruns of the show.

In the fall of 1965 President Lucy authoritatively declared: "I don't like the way television programing is going. There is too much sameness, too much repeating of the old formulas. There is no real exploring of new avenues for entertainment."

224

She voiced concern over the networks' scheduling more movies during prime time hours. "It seems to me that the networks are abandoning their duty to create new entertainment for television. They are making of TV little more than a second-run movie house."

Insiders noted that as president of Desilu, which was finding it almost impossible to place shows with the networks, her concern was obviously corporate. While she was saying that "the public deserves more creativity from TV," the "Lucy" show rolled along predictably as ever.

For the 1965-66 season the "Lucy" locale was changed from Connecticut to California. Gale Gordon, Lucy's talented second banana who portrayed her cantankerous banker-boss, remained in strong support, Lucy's male Vivian Vance. Her TV daughter was all but written out of the script, and her TV son would appear in only a few shows.

Bill Frawley made a guest appearance on one episode, and with the absence of Vivian Vance other guest stars were used, including Milton Berle, Danny Thomas, Mickey Rooney and Art Linkletter.

Then, in the winter of 1966, Lucy announced she was quitting. She agreed to do two specials the following year, but wanted to drop the series. "I have things I want to do—specials and pictures." CBS programing chief Mike Dann commented: "CBS is certainly not happy about Miss Ball's decision." Industry gossip said this time Lucille wasn't bluffing. They based this prediction on the fact that she hadn't asked for anything.

But it seemed to others like a different version of the annual renewal ceremony. Lucy could parry like the best politician: "When it comes time for me next season, I'll ask myself again about doing a weekly series. I don't know what my answer will be. How long do I want to be bitten? But I'll tell you this: I'm not retiring. I have no intention of retiring."

Lucy had obviously tired of the annual allegations that she

225

"held up the network" to take Desilu's products. "No matter what the impressions may have been," she said, "I don't play games about the series. Look, I am a company woman—not just mine. I belong to CBS. I reserve my opinion for what's best for my company and CBS."

The network still needed her and Desilu signed a spectacular $12,000,000 deal with CBS in 1966. The package involved a renewal of the "Lucy" show; two one-hour Lucille Ball specials; and the purchase by CBS of reruns of "The Lucy Show," to be used as a daytime network strip (one a day) when the show ended its prime-time run.

Each new "Lucy" show was budgeted at $90,000. CBS agreed to put up $600,000 for development of pilots by Desilu Studios. In addition, part of the pact included Desilu supplying summer replacements for the "Lucy" show in 1966 and 1967. The trade noted that Desilu's unsold pilots were the most likely replacements.

In the spring, Lucy went to London to film a special, "Lucy in London," with guest stars Anthony Newley and the then red-hot Dave Clark Five. Discussing the special, Lucy said, "I've been around for fifteen years. I find getting out to new places is invigorating. My mind seems to work a little easier. I could think of lots of things to do for TV in different places."

The show, broadcast that October, was "not Lucy's finest hour," according to critic Jack Gould, but he noted "that she may have hit upon an engaging innovation." He referred to the use of gifted writers, directors and cameramen of British and European television. "It could lead to television that might be fresh and different," Gould concluded. It didn't.

Lucy was suffering from a slight case of laryngitis and was "saving her voice" so Mickey Rudin chaired Desilu's 1966 annual stockholders' meeting. Although revenues had slipped slightly to $18,897,000, the profit went up from $455,000 to $735,000. The ruckus at the last annual meeting obviously had figured in corporate thinking since the company declared a five per cent stock dividend on its common and class B common stock. It was the first dividend of any kind that Desilu had paid since 1961 and its initial stock dividend.

Lucille Ball and "The Lucy Show" were still the company's principal assets, although it was producing two other shows for the season and renting its facilities to other companies.

Desilu had sold 132 reruns of Lucy shows to CBS for a minimum of $6,600,000. Lucy's salary, though considerably reduced to $75,000 as president and $156,000 as an actress, again drew complaints from the stockholders.

John Gilbert was at the meeting again and proposed a resolution that would limit Lucille's salary to $90,000 in any year in which the company paid no dividends. Naturally, the resolution was defeated. Desilu contended that Lucille was underpaid and that other studios would pay far more for her services and talents.

Desilu had been buying its own stock and had acquired 136,569 shares during the fiscal year. Rudin told stockholders that the company treasury had more than 200,000 shares and Desilu would consider acquisition or merger through a stock swap only. He noted, "I should also explain the possibility that other companies may want to purchase the Desilu stock, but no discussions have been held." He added that Lucille Ball wouldn't sell her shares unless the same offer was made to all shareholders.

Was Lucy planning to sell Desilu, now that it seemed the company was rolling at last? For the new season, in addition to the "Lucy" show, the studio had sold "Mission: Impossible" to CBS. "Star Trek," which had failed to sell the year before, had been reworked and reshot with different stars, William Shatner and Leonard Nimoy, and Desilu sold it to NBC.

Lucy was furious with gossip that CBS had bought "Mis-

227

sion: Impossible" in order to persuade Lucy to sign. She claimed that the series had been purchased by CBS long before any agreement was reached with her. Desilu again stated they never at any time demanded that CBS buy a Desilu series as part of a price for Lucy's renewal.

Interestingly, "Mission: Impossible" did not fare well in the ratings initially. But it was "kept on the air" and later proved to be an enormous success, Desilu's most successful dramatic series since "The Untouchables."

Lucy's pressures at work were increasing. Despite the sale of the two new shows, Desilu was far from the leading producer for TV. When Desi was running the company in the late 1950s Desilu had been hailed as being responsible for more film production than several major motion picture studios combined. Now the stature and prestige of the company had slipped. And Lucy was getting tired, relatively speaking. "She was still energy-plus, and in good health, but the endless problems of running an empire were wearing her down," says a former associate.

Early in 1967, Gulf and Western Industries, which had acquired Paramount Pictures the previous year, made Lucy an offer for Desilu that they were hoping she couldn't refuse. The deal was in the neighborhood of $17,000,000 in stock. Lucy's share would be over $10,000,000, since she owned sixty per cent of Desilu stock.

At first, it wasn't easy to convince Lucille to sell, even though Mickey Rudin and others kept warning her that the day of the independent TV producer was drawing to a close. "You can't face the networks and buck the major studios alone," they had advised her.

Hollywood was in transition and although Lucy didn't want her people swallowed up by a conglomerate, "She could see the handwriting on the wall and Lucy was never one to miss the bus."

In February, while the Gulf and Western deal was pending, Lucille "fled" to Miami to try to talk Jackie Gleason into co-starring with her in a film about Lillian Russell and Diamond Jim Brady.

Rudin tried desperately to reach her by phone to get her to make a decision on the sale. The deal was being arranged so that Lucy would receive a substantial capital gain. It would relieve her of the headache of being Madame President. But on the other hand, part of her liked playing that role.

She was afraid of a corporate takeover. Desilu was one of the more pleasant and casual lots in town. She could be outspoken—she didn't think the creative end of the business should be left in the hands of people who sold cheese.

Rudin couldn't reach her by phone so he flew to Florida. Lucy has described ensuing events. "Everybody had heard about the merger. Panic! Still, I couldn't make up my mind. Mickey came down. He had to have an answer, he said. Twenty-four hours or we blow the deal!

"Well, we went over the whole thing again and I started to cry. 'I need an hour,' I told him, 'I've just gotta have an hour.' More thinking. I said to him, 'Do you know, Mickey, I haven't even seen this man?'" She was referring to high-powered Gulf and Western boss, Charles Bludhorn.

" 'Now Lucy,' Rudin said, 'I've told you about him. Will you talk to him on the phone?'

" 'No,' I said, 'I like to see a man's eyes, shake his hand.'

"Well, I talked to him anyway and do you know what he said? He said, 'Miss Ball, one of the things I am prepared to like about you is that you care.' I cried again. Then I said yes."

At the time of the takeover, Desilu stock was trading at about fourteen and a half. Bludhorn announced that Desilu Productions would continue as a separate corporate entity and Lucy would remain as president of the subsidiary.

Bludhorn said, "Miss Ball is one of the greatest artists of

229

our time. We are glad to welcome her to the Gulf and Western team. We look forward to a fine association with her."

When the shareholders, who always made Lucy a little uneasy anyway, voted overwhelmingly for the merger, it seemed she had made the right decision.

Observers noted that for Lucy, who was still paying off the almost $3,000,000 she had paid Desi, the $10,000,000 loomed large.

The merger clearly left her free to concentrate on acting activities. Hollywood insiders said part of the deal was a commitment from Paramount to star Lucy in one or two films each year, if she wanted to do them.

Lucy later met Charlie Bludhorn, but not until after the deal had been consummated. One afternoon, when he was at Paramount, the Austrian-born businessman-turned-movie mogul walked over to the Desilu lot.

Lucy got a charge out of the story that Bludhorn and his aides had a tough time getting into Desilu. A skeptical studio cop at first wouldn't let his new boss, whom he didn't know, through the studio gate.

About Bludhorn, Lucy said: "He travels fast, talks fast and acts on impulse. I just hope he stays alive."

With benefit of hindsight, it seems that Lucy sold Desilu at the wrong time. After years of not being able to sell pilots or hit with a successful show other than "Lucy," the year of the takeover Desilu had two hits: "Mission: Impossible" and "Star Trek," with a third winner, "Mannix," in preparation. In addition, *The Beardsley Story*, a script which had been lying around the studio for years, would prove to be a gold mine.

Now that corporate pressures were lifted from her shoulders, Lucy decided to go ahead and film *The Beardsley Story*, retitled *Yours, Mine and Ours*.

The Beardsleys are a real-life family from Northern California. Helen North, a widowed Navy nurse with eight children, met and married Navy lieutenant Frank Beardsley, a widower with ten children. The Beardsleys then proceeded to have more children of their own. The family had been written up in *Life* and Lucy, impressed, had bought the film rights for Desilu.

Melville Shavelson was signed to direct. He recalls, "At the time I was called in to do *Yours, Mine and Ours* no one really wanted to do a picture with Lucy. That's the reason it hadn't been made up to that time." Shavelson was referring to the fact that *Critic's Choice* had been a dud, "and Lucy's box office in movies was considered zero, even though she was one of the top TV favorites."

It was no secret that Lucille Ball would be difficult to direct in a film, since for the last dozen years she had, in effect, been directing herself and everyone else. Shavelson notes, "On her television show she runs everything and she likes that. And she doesn't want to do it any other way; she doesn't want to play second fiddle to anyone."

There were script problems from the beginning. Shavelson remembers, "When I came into the project Lucy had owned the story for years and they had about five screenplays. *All* of the screenplays were similar to the Lucy television show. They were farcical comedy shows with Lucy and seventeen kids. Well, that's a joke, not reality, and I said, 'Well, somebody really lived this life. Somebody better go talk to these people and find out how it happened.'

"They turned out to be very intelligent people, their reasoning and everything else made sense. And a great deal of material that was in the picture I got from the Beardsleys themselves. None of it had ever appeared in any script at all because nobody was interested in what the reality of the situation was."

Shavelson's main concern was that Lucille Ball had typed herself as the "Lucy" character and didn't feel confident playing any other character, especially after *Critic's Choice*.

231

The public wanted her as "Lucy" and she knew it, "so if you give the public something fresh or different, you run a big, big gamble," notes Shavelson.

When he started on the film, Lucy had him test her own children for parts. "I could've used Desi," notes Shavelson, "he has quality and ability. But I didn't use him because he was making more money with his group than I could afford to pay. Besides, I felt that if one of the kids in the movie was her real child it might subconsciously disturb the audience."

Shavelson didn't want to use little Lucie. "The girl was pudgy and had baby fat. She didn't look too good at the time and she didn't make a good test. I told Lucy I was rejecting her. I thought it would be a big struggle, but Lucille said, 'Okay.'"

Henry Fonda was signed to co-star, but not without an argument. Shavelson recollects, "Fonda was near the bottom of a career and he didn't want to make the movie. I spent a whole day talking him into his role. Fonda has always been one of my favorite actors.

" 'Please, nobody's going to believe me as a lieutenant,' Fonda said.

"So we made him a warrant officer," notes Shavelson.

Shavelson licked the problem of writing the Helen North character for Lucy realistically while retaining certain aspects of the comedy the public expected from Lucille Ball.

In the final script, the role was not typically "Lucy." "We knew she had to be a specific person and come alive as that person in order to make this picture work, because the film was about real people," states Shavelson. "Had it been Lucy playing 'Lucy,' the film would have had a certain audience, but it would have been fairly limited."

Rex Reed was an observer on the *Yours, Mine and Ours* set. He had been told, "Lucy's tough. You'll think you're talking to a man."

Reed noted that Lucy sounded tough, but she told him, "Don't believe that guff. I have enough trouble worrying about the studio during the day. When I get home at night, I take care of my family. I go home in this terrible heat and jump in the pool. After years of being in this routine, I've learned to budget my hours and my energies. I reserve. I don't let things tear me apart at the wrong times. The most important thing is what I have to do at the moment. If I'm driving down the street, I think of nothing but the wheel. If I'm making up, I think only of my lipstick. I only go to other people's sets in cases of extreme emergency; usually they come to me."

Shavelson had his hands full with Lucy. On one typical occasion on the set she commanded, "*Cut.* Let's do it again. There's a shadow on Hank's chin. Mel, move that light three inches to the left. Now stay where you are, Hank." ("She's the same girl she was at MGM," beamed co-star Van Johnson, observing her.)

She never hesitated to voice her opinions about how scenes should be shot, where things should go and on numerous other aspects of production, in front of the crew. "This undermines a director's relationship with the crew," remarked a director who has "been through it" with Lucy.

But, Mel Shavelson understood Lucy. According to him, "The biggest scene in the picture is where Lucy had to be drunk and crying and laughing at the same time. I felt it was a key scene in the picture. I had written the scene for Lucy and I knew she was capable of it. She felt she wasn't, and when it came time to do the scene she refused to do it. She wanted to change it to either one way or the other. I insisted that she go through with it and she finally did. It was tough, but she did a great job. I don't know anybody else who could have carried off both of those emotions at the same time. It's that mixture of the tragic and the comic simultaneously. Only a comedienne can do that, because a comedienne can play legitimate. But it's extremely hard for a legitimate actor to play comedy successfully."

The scene, in which Beardsley's children get their prospective stepmother drunk, was the highlight of the film.

During shooting, Lucy gave innumerable interviews. "You always got the feeling that she regarded the interviews as a chore," recalls an associate. "But as the star and co-producer she knew she owed it to the picture to help publicize it. It really was a chore, too, considering that under that 102-degree heat it was a real problem to preserve her heavy movie make-up."

She was continuing as president of Desilu until April of 1968. Lucy said she turned down offers more lucrative than Bludhorn's and noted, "I'd been assured that Mr. Bludhorn had no intention of razing Paramount."

She also said, "I sold everything to them because they want to propagate the species. Others just wanted the property, I suspect, to bulldoze everything and get into real estate."

Yours, Mine and Ours was an unexpected super-hit. It grossed over $17,000,000, and was the biggest box-office winner that Lucy has ever made. And she was furious about it. Mel Shavelson contends, "Lucy could never forgive me for not warning her in advance that this was going to be such a successful picture." She hadn't provided a tax shelter for her profits. Her share as an actress ran to over $2,000,000, but she didn't keep much of it.

In addition, Desilu's share went to the new Desilu owners, Gulf and Western. The conglomerate made millions they hadn't counted on from *Yours, Mine and Ours,* paying them back a considerable percentage of their total cost for Desilu.

11

ALTHOUGH DESILU was sold, Lucy's exclusive contract with CBS would run until 1970. "The Lucy Show" was under the Paramount TV banner for the 1967-68 season. Gary Morton took over as executive producer, a move that had been expected for years.

"Anyone married to me has an uphill climb," Lucy noted. "Gary and I coped by anticipating. We knew we shouldn't be separated eight, nine months a year, so he tapered off his act, found other things to do—making investments, building things. He plays the golf circuit, Palm Springs, Pebble Beach. . . .

"He didn't come into the business for six years. I didn't want to put him in a position in which he would be ridiculed. I could tell that he was grasping things—casting, story line. I said, 'You've been a big help to me. You should be paid for it.'"

Cleo became producer of the show. Lucy said, "I have

been after Cleo for five years to take this job because she is so good at it." And she added, "Cleo thought a long time before becoming producer, wondering if it wasn't overdoing family. 'Nobody seems to be suffering from it,' I told her."

Lucy liked to keep the program a close family operation. "Unlike a lot of comedy stars, Lucy is not gregarious," an associate explains. "It takes time to become one of Lucy's friends, but when the barrier is crossed you're a friend for life."

Audience warm-ups for the show were a family affair as well. Gary would do comedy bits, introduce Lucille's loyal and durable mother, who has missed only one or two of the "Lucy" shows filmed to date, and he would then introduce Cleo, who by this time had divorced Ken Morgan and married *Los Angeles Times* television critic Cecil Smith. Even Smith appeared on a couple of Lucy shows.

Little Lucie was attending Immaculate Heart High School in Los Angeles. Desi was at La Jolla High and later switched to Beverly Hills High. He wasn't a good student. "When he brought home two D's, he was grounded a month for each," Lucy remembered. "We pulled all the plugs out of the wall. There's nothing in Desi's room that can't be unplugged, and I go up and unplug. I worked so hard the first time I was exhausted and had to go to bed."

She also noted, "He couldn't have friends in and he couldn't go out. He knew we meant it."

Lucy pointed out that sending the kids to their rooms without unplugging was no longer punishment, since they had TV, stereo, tape recorder, *et al.* About young Lucie, Lucy remarked that she got B's, and occasionally an A, "which indicates she's a talented girl. But she's just getting along in her studies."

Lucy's theory was that many children don't work up to their potential because they're afraid of being called "egghead." She noted that Billy Hinsche, of the Dino-Desi-Billy

236

trio, was an egghead, but "they let him in the group because he plays drums so well."

Lucy had always been concerned with her children doing well in school. Like most teen-agers, Lucie and Desi weren't particularly concerned with such things, despite Mama's insistent nagging.

There have been times when Lucy has swatted her kids. And there have been those other times, experienced by all parents, when she was heartbroken because they wouldn't let her do the things she wanted to do for them.

As might be expected, Lucy supervised all their early dates. Little Lucie was fifteen before she was allowed to ride in a car with a boy. The story goes that Lucy had them tracked all the way down to Sunset Boulevard. Desi was allowed to date officially when he was fifteen, but neither was allowed to go out during the week. Furthermore, their parents had to know who they were with, where they went, what time they'd be back. About these early dating years Lucy said, "They have to call me if they are late or if there is any change in plans. They don't have the freedom to do just anything they want."

Lucy brought up her kids the way she had run her life, in an understanding, no-nonsense fashion. In Hollywood circles the children were well liked and had the reputation of being well behaved.

When she was sixteen, Lucie met young Phil Vandervort Menegaux on the set of a TV show. She told a friend that when he drove her home and dropped her off, he said, "So long. See you in five years." She knew he meant it, so she called the TV station, got his telephone number and tracked him down. They started dating.

At first, Lucille and Gary were concerned, because Phil was much older than Lucie—he was twenty-two.

Even though she was dating, Lucie still "stuck close to

237

home." Lucille has told of the time when her family wanted to screen some films at home. "So up went the paintings and on came *Thunderball*. Five adults and a few kids sitting around. Well, the blood is spurting, the bullets are flying, the sharks are biting, and then this 007 guy climbs into bed with this dame and I yelled 'Stop the film! What the hell kind of picture is this?' My daughter, who is sixteen now and in the middle of a big romance, said, 'Oh Mother, my God—we've seen it three times!' So I showed *Blow-Up*, that awful Italian thing. Well, that was worse. I said, 'I have had it, get me a western.' And so help me they're in the fort, see, with the Indians coming through the gate, and I'll be damned if the girl doesn't make the sign of the cross, rip her clothes off and climb on top of this cowboy—Rod Taylor or somebody—and they're crawling all over each other in bed like there's no tomorrow! Ugh! Everybody's taking their clothes off but me. You'll never catch me in the buff, kiddo."

Despite the hassles, the pressure-cooker existence, "Being a tycoon wasn't that difficult," reflected Lucy after the Desilu sale. "Actually, if you're successful, people think you know the answers anyway."

At production meetings for the TV show, she usually had most of the answers. Gary Morton sometimes tried to suggest a one-liner. Once, Lucy asked, "Where did that line come from?"

"I was just thinking by myself over here," answered Gary.

"No, darling," said Lucy.

At staff meetings she never hesitated to coldly analyze a script's deficiencies. "That's just radio exposition," she declared to head writer Milt Josefsburg at one meeting. "I kept hoping there'd be a joke coming up, not just a lot of words! Let's go! Don't just sit there with your chin on your expensive hand!"

One time while Lucy was being interviewed, Gary called to her from outside her office window: "Lucy, Lucy, can you come out and play?"

"I'd like to come out and play, but I have to do the dishes," replied Lucy in her little-girl voice.

"Your mother said it's all right," he pleaded.

"Later, sweetheart," she answered, turning her attention back to work.

Though Desi, Sr., was now mostly on the outside of Hollywood and out of the public eye, he made a few headlines in the late 1960s which seemed to support stories that he was still a hot-headed, temperamental Latin.

In 1966, when he was annoyed by beach bums in front of his Del Mar home, he attempted to scare them away by "shooting blanks at them." Desi called the sheriff, but it was he who was arrested, not the beach bums.

"Del Mar has been harassed the last couple of years by hordes of these beach characters with long hair," complained Desi. "There was one murder last summer, and two nights ago I found a bunch of them on my front porch drinking."

Desi later explained that he was in his bathrobe, preparing to eat dinner at about 9 P.M. when nine youths started a ruckus in front of his house. Little Lucie and a girl friend were visiting, and Desi said that he went out to try to talk to the "beach bums" creating the disturbance. "All they did was to holler and cuss at me. I put a .38 revolver in my bathrobe pocket, loaded with blanks. I thought I could scare them by shooting into the sand at my own feet. I fired two shots. The shots didn't even faze them. They just hollered and cussed more, even louder. Then I went into the house and called the sheriff myself. I was sitting on my front porch when the sheriff's car drove up."

According to Desi, when he said "Thank God you're here!" the deputies said: "You're under arrest."

The deputies later reported that Desi had approached a parked car and told the young men in it, "I've got a .38 and I'll shoot your tires and car."

Then he fired one shot past one of the boys and another at

his feet. One of the sheriff's deputies said, "Arnaz apparently thought the boys were on his property and wanted to scare them off." He noted, "The car was on public property."

The gun had been a present to Desi from the cast of "The Untouchables," and he commented: "I have never aimed a gun at anybody in my life."

Desi was freed on $1,000 bail and later released.

Another publicized incident concerned a multi-million dollar suit against Desi, pending in the courts for several years, which was finally settled in 1967. The suit involved one Jack Young, a former maintenance man at the Thunderbird Club in Palm Springs, and his wife. They sued Desi for the staggering sum of $34,000,000 for "orally and physically assaulting" them back in 1964. The suit was later revised down to $100,000, and famed attorney Melvin Belli represented the Youngs.

Supposedly Desi, his wife Edie, and Jimmy Durante and his wife had gone to the country club to find Desi's mother. The Youngs claimed that Desi became enraged when Young took what Desi thought was too much time to respond to a request for information. They accused Desi of hurling an ashtray at Mrs. Young, hitting Young and verbally attacking both.

At the trial, Young testified that Desi had described working people as "low-down dirt under my feet." A witness for the defendant was comedian Durante and after hearing the evidence the jury deliberated about ninety minutes. Their verdict: Desi was innocent.

Desi suffered a freak accident in the summer of 1967 which would affect his health for years. Desi and Edie had taken Lucie and Desi, Jr., on a boat trip to Baja California, Mexico. They were visiting the tiny (about eight hundred people) village of San Juanito and at one point Desi and the family sat on a veranda. A heavy man came along and sat on the same porch. It broke in half and they all fell to the ground.

But Desi, unfortunately, fell on a broken tree, which pierced his left side.

A doctor was flown in from the States immediately, giving Desi temporary first aid to stop the heavy bleeding. He was then flown to La Jolla's Scripps Memorial Hospital, outside of Del Mar and operated on at once to remove several clots.

A few weeks later Desi announced plans to build a $250,-000 hospital for San Juanito, in gratitude to "the Man away up there."

"Desi realized that God had been good to him," notes a friend. "He was lucky that when he had that stupid accident he had the means to fly a doctor in and then be flown to a hospital. Desi wanted to do something for the poor people in that little village."

Desi was ready to get back into show business. He had found a book he wanted to make into a film and flew to New York to arrange financing. Then, according to an account related by Desi, "I got a call from Bill Paley, the head man at CBS. He says, 'I hear you're going back to work but not in TV. . . . You have something against TV?' he says. 'How can I have anything against TV,' I say, 'when I borrow fifty thousand and make ten million?' . . . So anyway, Paley talked me into coming back. Funny thing is that after all that my show ends up on NBC."

Desi's idea for a new TV show was a situation comedy, "The Mothers-in-Law," starring Eve Arden and Kaye Ballard in the title roles, with Herb Rudley and Roger C. Carmel as their husbands.

There had been stories that Desi was not only an ex-tycoon but worse—a Lucy-less ex-tycoon. "What could he do without her?" asked show business pundits.

Eve Arden was not a clown like Lucy. "No," Desi said, "Eve is more a Rosalind Russell, more an *It Happened One Night* comedienne. I don't know anyone who can deliver a line like Eve." Desi had seen Kaye in night clubs and liked

241

her, knowing her broad comedy style would blend well with Eve's.

Although Desi and Edie had many residences—a house in Palm Springs, one in Del Mar, a breeding farm in Corona and a resort hotel in La Paz, Mexico—they took an apartment at the studio, where they lived while Desi was working. Desi was now saying, "I never said I was going to quit forever, because I love show business."

"The Mothers-in-Law," whose competition was the second half of Ed Sullivan's top-rated show on CBS and "The FBI" on ABC, was not a big hit. NBC renewed it for a second season, but the renewal was based on the cast's working for their first season's salary. Roger C. Carmel objected to this, since his contract called for a large raise. Desi fired him and hired Richard Deacon. The show was left in its tough Sunday night time slot and never saw a third season.

Desi, as always, survived. Many people voiced the opinion that he had reentered TV because he needed the money. Arnaz, according to one long-time friend, has gone through more money than most bank tellers. Desi discounted the rumors. "I'm not a multi-millionaire the way I should be, but I have enough left so I can do only the things I want to do, not just something everybody else is doing."

Although Desilu was now owned by Paramount, at contract time the trade still accused Lucy of "holding out" so CBS would "consider" purchasing other Desilu products.

Little Lucie has explained, "At the end of every season, mother comes in and says, 'Well, kids, it's the last TV show I'm doing,' with a tear trickling down her cheek. So down to the studio Desi and I have to go. Everybody cries. The band plays 'Auld Lang Syne' and that's it for another year."

This season, however, Lucy was annoyed at bad publicity she received as a result of "Mannix" replacing "Gunsmoke." When it was announced that the long-running western favorite was going off the air, Desilu bore the brunt of the adverse reaction from the public.

"When I heard that I was being blamed I called CBS and they said it wasn't so," said Lucy. "That Jim Arness was making a lot of trouble about wanting to retire and not giving so much time to the show. I told them that if they took it on themselves to put 'Mannix' in, they shouldn't blame it on me."

"Gunsmoke" was moved to a different time slot and continued to flourish.

When Lucy ceased being president of Desilu and the company was fully incorporated into Paramount-TV, Lucy formed a new company and rented space on the Paramount-Gower lot, formerly Desilu.

The new company, Lucille Ball Productions, had Lucy as president, Gary as vice president. Lucy revealed, "When Paramount bought out Desilu they also bought out the format of 'The Lucy Show.' It became theirs completely. So I either had to negotiate with them to use the format or I had to find a new one."

She found a new one—"Here's Lucy"—and also announced that her new company would plan motion pictures, films for TV and television specials.

Since Lucy was finding it more and more difficult to keep her kids under supervision, she decided to take action. Unlike most working mothers, she had a unique solution: take the children to work with her.

Mel Shavelson says that it was after filming *Yours, Mine and Ours* that Lucy made the decision to incorporate her children into her television program. In Shavelson's opinion, she did it because "she was worried about what was happening to Desi, Jr., and also what might happen to Lucie. If she could bring them onto her TV show she could watch them all the time."

Lucy offered another explanation: "Lucie and Desi had

been wanting to work with me. The idea fitted in to the scheme that I had long had for them. I feel that too many kids nowadays go right into college without knowing what they want to do. For many of them, the experience is wasted."

After putting them on her show, Lucy noted, "Now they are able to work and carry on their high school education at the same time. Their grades have improved tremendously with a private tutor. I feel that when they do go to college—and I think it's very important to do so in today's world—they will have a much better idea of what they want to do."

In "Here's Lucy," Lucille played a widowed secretary, Lucille Carter; Desi, Jr., her son Craig; Lucie, her daughter Kim. Her brother-in-law was portrayed by Gale Gordon. When the show premiered, some critics were unimpressed with the Arnaz offspring. *Women's Wear Daily* was positively negative, saying not only did the kids have "no talent" but the show was pure "treacle." Even the trade paper, the *Hollywood Reporter*, called it "one giant marshmallow."

Lucy's reaction: "Listen, that's a *good* review. I usually get okay personal notices, but the show gets knocked regular."

The *New York Times*, however, noted: "The youngsters know how to trade lines with the veteran star. And Miss Ball should have a ball trying to bridge the generation gap."

Desi, Jr., of course had been a successful professional for some time. Lucie had appeared in several of her mother's shows and a few school plays before undertaking regular duty.

Lucy admitted that she really worried about whether or not the kids would work out on the show. Someone on the scene says, "The kids hated it but they did it."

Why had Lucy deliberately taken the kids out of school? They were, after all, in good schools. Lucy's reasons were down to earth. "I didn't like that scene. It was the usual—pregnant girls, drugs. A lot of girls who boarded there were unhappy misfits, and Lucie was already working in the nunnery. All the friends she brought home were the rejected. I'm that way myself."

Lucy denied that the kids objected to her stage-managing their lives. "They were as sick of that weird high school scene as I was," claimed Lucy. "I made them a proposition— told them to think it over for a month. Do you want to be on the show? I told them the salary would be scale, that most would be put in trust. They'd be tutored and not able to graduate with their classes. They both thought they were going to coast, but working with a tutor, they really got turned on by books for the first time." And she admitted, "They wanted to be in show business and I wanted to keep an eye on them."

Both Lucille and the kids were aware that they were in a unique position. Her prescription for them, to keep their feet on the ground, was to keep them busy. Lucy's value system is that work brings fulfillment. She wanted to instill this in her youngsters and made a point of the fact that they wouldn't be in the TV series as "adornment" but as hard-working actors. She was true to her word.

Desi didn't like to practice in front of his mother, or anyone else. "He doesn't want to work out the kinks while anyone is watching," stated Lucy. "He's very self-conscious." Observers agree. They recall that Desi's self-consciousness was evident at rehearsals for the show. He would become upset when he missed a cue or did something wrong.

"I've been a tough taskmaster with them," Lucy told a friend. "My children have the discipline and desire to work hard and learn." But she added, "It isn't always easy. Especially with Desi."

Lucy gave the kids three-year contracts, subject to annual options, and each would receive $17,600 the first year, $20,-400 the second year and $25,200 the third. Twenty per cent of the money paid to them was put into government bonds. Forty per cent was set aside for taxes.

Lucy insisted that bringing the kids on the show brought

245

the family closer together. She told friends, "We each had our own interests before. Now we get home and begin to talk —not only about the work we've been doing all day, but about politics and everything else."

However, Desi, Jr., gave a clearer picture of the *true* situation when he revealed, "These were difficult times with my mother. My sister and I had two quite different relationships with her: parent-child at home and employer-employee at work. It isn't a very good arrangement. She would treat us— rightfully so—as cast members at work, but we would still take things personally that probably weren't intended that way. When most people are hassled at work, they can blow off steam when they get home. But it didn't work that way for us because we just continued the same arguments when we got home. My stepfather was always the peacemaker."

Desi, Jr.,'s allowance went up from five to fifteen dollars a week. But, as Lucy noted, "He had to pay for his own lunches." Lucie didn't have a regular allowance, but she did have a credit card to buy clothes. "So far," her mother said, "she's never taken advantage of it."

However, Lucie's friends did. Lucy remembered, "They would admire some clothes and little Lucie would say, 'Go ahead, take it.' I had to put a stop to that in a hurry, particularly since half the time she was giving away my things."

Lucy admitted that her children were spoiled. But she noted that the triumph was that they lived through being spoiled. "They had to learn who their real friends are and who are the leaners, the phonies. They've been terribly hurt several times." Lucille described a time when Lucie cried to her, "The only reason she liked me was that you're my mother."

At first, Lucie had been the harder child to raise. Lucy noted, "They go through stages. First it was the girl, then it was the boy. I have a feeling that possibly from now on it will continue to be Desi."

How right she was!

246

Desi was harder to control, since he had had a taste of "freedom" while traveling with his group. In addition, his sparkling personality and charm and lust for life made it difficult to discipline him.

Lucy had tried sending him to a military academy. "Actually, it was his idea," she said. "He had seen the uniforms and the band and the drums, but soon he had nightmares when he came home and, boy, I got him out of there fast. I didn't dig all those thirteen-year-old generals. And those disciplinary rules! Once he got a demerit for bending down to tie his shoelace when he wasn't supposed to."

An extremely bright boy, Desi, Jr., has summed it up. "My school years were chaotic. I went to seven different Catholic schools and a military academy before I settled down. I spent the second grade in New York. The real trouble started when we got back to California. I really wasn't cut out for the military academy—a point on which the people who ran it would agree—but I also found out when I went back to Catholic grade school that I wasn't cut out for that either. I was overweight and confused about the Catholic faith—which even then was difficult for me to accept—and so I made up for all my insecurities by being the class clown. Only the school people didn't think I was very funny. I did things like writing a paper on religion using all the dirty words I could think of and sneaking a snare drum into a concert and tangling repeatedly with the priests and nuns over points of theology that didn't make sense to me."

The greatest problem that Lucy had was one that she shared with millions of other parents—a lack of communication with her children. Lucy's lament: "You try to keep close. You travel together, laugh together, do everything together. But the kids won't really confide—won't ask you things."

When Lucy brought this to her daughter's attention, Lucie's answer was, "There's nothing I want to know, Mom."

Lucie was a typical teen-ager—lots of clothes, messy room, friends, dating. Desi was more organized. "His room looked like an office," a friend recalls. "It was neat and uncluttered. There was a large desk, and he took the responsibility of running his music publishing company seriously." "I've got all these companies but no money," he moaned as a teen-ager.

Lucy kept him on a strict budget. She tried to make a point of not letting their wealth go to the children's heads. "I told them it won't always be this way," she said. "People in show business don't have real money like people in Boston or Pasadena. I've tried to teach them moderation."

The kids admit that they were always made to appreciate what they had and were instilled with the idea that they weren't unusual. A friend of the family notes, "Both of them are really practical kids. Not temperamental or spoiled. Neither was ever overbearing or demanding like the stereotype Hollywood child."

Lucy told friends, "I can lock the doors, rip out the TV and they still won't go to sleep." Lucy reacted like the typical mother in many situations and her children reacted like typical teenagers, with responses like, "Oh Mom, please!"

Both kids, however, loved Irene Burke, their tutor on the set of "Here's Lucy." They contend that they learned more from her than they could have possibly learned in regular school. Although Lucy had often expressed the wish that the kids go to college, it always was highly unlikely that they would.

They simply didn't have to; their careers were mapped out for them. Their TV appearances with Mom made them ational celebrities. "People go to college to prepare for ca- ers," notes an associate of Lucy's. "The kids not only had ir careers determined for them, they had a head start on yone else; and they had, thanks to Lucy, the spunk and -how to cope and survive. All in all, she has done a good job bringing them up."

ourse the kids had all the material possessions one xpect. Lucie had a Mercedes sports car. Desi had an rtin. Both had all the clothes and paraphernalia

8

they could possibly use. Lucy herself drove a silver Rolls Royce, which she had bought for $8,000 from Hedda Hopper's estate. She drove the car herself, never feeling comfortable in chauffeur-driven autos.

Although the kids had come to accept and appreciate Gary, he never for one moment was considered a father replacement. Both Lucie and Desi, Jr., love their father and have spent a lot of time with him in the last few years.

In the opinion of a prominent producer, another reason Lucy wanted the kids on her show was to get them involved in *her* life so they would be with her and not Desi.

"They are close to their father," Lucy admitted. "They visit him at Del Mar in the summer and at Palm Springs and Corona at his horse-breeding ranch in the winter, and they enjoy that thoroughly." But she pointed out, "Their father has an easier life with them because it is usually vacation time and more fun for everyone. In Beverly Hills it's school and homework; early to bed and not so many dates, just on weekends."

Desi, Sr., took over The Candy Store, a popular Hollywood discotheque, for Desi, Jr.'s sixteenth birthday in 1969. When Desi, Sr., was asked if he was going to buy his son a car for this birthday, he laughed "Are you kidding? That kid made more money last year than I did."

In recent years, Desi and his son have been extremely close while Lucie has remained closer to her mother. Desi, Sr., was determined to have as close a relationship with his son as he had with his own father.

For his sixteenth birthday, Desi wrote his son a touching letter containing a lot of the same advice his own father had given him:

> Dear Desi,
> Well pardner, you are now sixteen, and in my book that means you are no longer a child; you are a man.
> You will get your driver's license and you will drive your

own car. A note of warning about driving, particularly about driving on the road that lies before you—the one we all have to travel, the road of life.

It is very much like the road from Las Cruces to La Paz. There are stretches that are so smooth and beautiful that they take your breath away, and then there are others that are so ugly and rough that you wish you had never gotten on the damn thing, and you wonder if you will ever get through.

Somewhere during the way, you will get into a particularly bad spot that presents a very difficult problem, and you may not know exactly what to do. When that happens, I'd advise you not to do anything. Examine the situation first. Turn it upside down and sideways as many times as you have to. But then, when you have finally made up your mind, do not let anything or anybody stop you. If there is a mountain in your way, go through it.

Sometimes you will make it; sometimes you will not. But if you are honest and thorough in your decision, you will learn something either way. We should learn as much from our mistakes as we do from our successes.

And when you do come up with a minus, try to convert it into a plus. You will be surprised how many times it will work. Use a setback as a stepping stone to better times ahead.

And don't be afraid to make mistakes; we all do. Nobody bats five hundred. Even if you did, that means you were wrong half of the time. But don't worry about it. Don't be ashamed of it. Because, that is the way it is. That is *the* bag.

Remember, good things do not come easy, and you will have your share of woe—the road is lined with pitfalls. But, you will make it, if when you fall, you try and try again. Persevere. Keep swinging. And don't forget that the Man Upstairs is always there, and all of us need His help. And no matter how unworthy you think yourself of it, don't be afraid to ask Him for it.

Good luck, son.

Love,

DAD

It is plain that Desi Arnaz, in his way, follows basically the same tenets as Lucille—belief in God and in yourself, hard work and perseverance.

250

Desi, Jr., recently noted about his father, "On the way up he lost sight of the things that were really meaningful to him. So there was a bad period when his values were all scrambled. But now he's found them again. Now he can admit his own mistakes and tell me how to avoid them. Now he has a wife geared to those attitudes and a new way of life and a house in Mexico and a boat, and he works as much as he has to. I see a good deal of him, and the only absolute condition of our relationship is that we always tell each other the truth as we see it."

Lucy played a different role in the children's lives as they grew older. She admitted being "strict about their friendships. There are certain homes where they're *not* allowed to go; the atmosphere is entirely too free, not enough discipline, no parental supervision. There have been times when either one or both of the children were never going to forgive me—like when I separated Lucie from the girl who had been a lifelong friend for no more reason than that they'd been born in neighboring bassinets at Cedars. I had to barge in when it became apparent that Lucie's life and her choice of friends were being determined by the other girl's thinking. Lucie was being ridiculously pushed and pulled, but when I ended it, she was bitterly resentful and I was, for a little while, 'the enemy.' "

Lucille was happiest when her children's social life centered around home. The kids liked to entertain, and Lucy noted that she and Gary didn't "intrude on their parties, but we're at home, in attendance from a distance. I learned a long time ago that my joining the party spoils it. 'Shhh, here *she* comes!' If I do come out even just for a moment, I always call out first, 'Just checking if you need anything.'

"There's a difference between being concerned and being nosey, but it took me a while to convince Lucie and Desi of *that*. They finally understood and that helped in our little matter of communication, too."

251

Lucy has always been proud of the fact that Lucie and Desi have talent. "I fervently hope they realize their potential," she often said, "and I think being with me on my new show will help. I'd like to see Lucie go to Northwestern to college because they have such a fine drama school, but I haven't pushed that yet. Right now I'm pushing grades. For both of them." But she was serious with remarks like, "They either cut the mustard or they'll find themselves written out of the script. Both my kids are inclined to settle for 'just getting by.'"

Lucy must be given credit for viewing her children objectively. Many show business personalities don't want their children to enter the field, either because they feel their children have no talent and would make fools of them (the parents) or because their egos can not withstand competition from younger members of the family. Unlike Jackie Gleason, Ray Milland and many others who did not encourage or help their offspring to break into the business, Lucy gave her kids every opportunity to succeed once it was obvious they wanted show business careers.

Was there a rule book of do's and don'ts for Lucille's kids? "I don't set up rules for my kids. I never said a word to them against their father. They've come to know that he's not easy to understand, but he's much better now. . . . I'm observing now, watching to see how much of my philosophy of life has rubbed off on my kids. I'm a twelve-hour-a-day watcher."

"I've been as good a mother as I know how to be," she told a friend. "And so far they have not disappointed me. The only thing I ever missed was little Desi's graduation from grade school. Or maybe a Little League baseball game now and then, but my mother or Gary is always there. I keep up with the times through them."

Even Lucy's enemies admit, "She's a truly good mother in her own way. At least she's worried enough about her kids."

Lucy was now taking the show on location around the

country and the cost of each episode had spiraled to $110,-000 each. The location shows would cost around $200,000 apiece. Old-time director George Marshall, who had directed movies starring some of cinema's comedy greats—Laurel and Hardy among them—was signed to direct.

"We want to bring something a little different to the show," Lucy said. "It will be the kind of thing with which American families can identify—a trip in a camper." She said her kids were deciding whether they wanted to continue their show business careers. "Now they're finally experiencing the tough discipline working on location."

By this time, Lucie was dating Phil Vandervort steadily and wanted to move out and get her own apartment. Lucy, like any mother, was horrified. The universal cry—"What can you do in your own apartment that you can't do here??"

There are two versions of events which occurred at the time of Lucie's moving to her own apartment. At the time Mama Lucille's version for public consumption was calm and intelligent: "Thank heavens she broke it to us gradually. She kept buying little pieces of furniture here and there and led us into her announcement. Then she cooperated by moving into the neighborhood we wanted and the type of building that is protected well. It had to come and I'm glad she handled it the way she did."

"Young Lucie has her own apartment now," Lucy said in February, 1970. "She's learning to cook her own meals, budget and run her own life. I believe in this. You're obligated to teach a child how to stand on his own feet."

She then referred to the eccentric young millionaire who had just made national headlines. "Look at that Michael Brody character inheriting all that money. You don't give a twenty-one-year-old that much money. They don't know what to do with it. If all I had to my name was forty cents, my children would get ten cents a year."

Desi, Jr., however, later told the real story of the

anguished scenes when his eighteen-year-old sister moved out. "By the end of the first year of the show, we were on the point of breaking up, and it was clear that we were going to have to make some adjustments at home. So Gary became the mediator, and we managed to work together and live together pretty well until my sister turned eighteen and announced she was cutting out to set up her own apartment. My mother didn't see it that way, and things got pretty tense. There was a big scene when my sister left, but two weeks later everyone had a great revelation and the whole emotional thing seemed rather silly to me."

At the start of the 1970 season, Lucy hired Jerry Paris, noted as one of the best directors in the TV industry. Paris's credentials were impressive. He had won an Emmy and directed the top TV comedies: "The Dick Van Dyke Show," "That Girl," "The Partridge Family," "Love American Style." The opening segment of the Lucy show was going to co-star Elizabeth Taylor, Richard Burton and the sixty-nine-carat Burton diamond.

How did Lucy land the Burtons for her show? She met them at a party in Hollywood. Elizabeth and Richard were great fans of Lucy's, and Burton casually suggested, "Why don't you have Elizabeth and me on your show sometime?"

Lucy was flabbergasted. Never one to miss an opportunity, she said, "Love to have you on the show. When can you do it?"

The Burtons' only available time was immediately, so Lucy flew into action. She had her writers whip together a script centering around the Burtons and Elizabeth's fabulous solitaire.

Lucy was "in awe" of the Burtons, like everyone else. "You can't help being in awe of them," she laughed. During dress rehearsal, Richard had a line that was supposed to get a guffaw, but instead received only a mild twitter from the audience. Lucy, naturally, didn't command the Burtons the way she did the rest of her cast and crew. However, she couldn't stand by and let Burton lose the laugh. She suggested to him that he punch the line across with more force.

Burton stared at her, sort of a "thanks, kid, I'll think about it" expression on his face. However, came the air-show taping, Burton took her advice. The line got the big laugh it should have, and Richard Burton had learned a bit about comedy from the red-headed maestro.

It was the casting coup of the television decade and the Burton-Taylor show was used to launch Lucy's new season. The rating was tremendous and although Lucy's competition, "Laugh-In," was then at its peak as the number one show, Lucy managed to give them the roughest possible competition.

Jerry Paris, however, was extremely unhappy. He and Lucy split up after the first half-hour confrontation, although he was initially signed to direct three more segments. Paris said at the time, "It wasn't Lucy's fault. The other shows were supposed to be filmed in Hawaii. CBS didn't want to spend the money to go there."

He was being diplomatic, but later he was outspoken about Lucy, saying she was her own woman, and man, and director, as well as star. "She runs her own ship," he noted. "Here's my analysis of it in a nutshell: Lucy has been left alone with so few directors after the divorce from Desi that she's had to work back of the camera as well as in front of it.

"That's a pity," he observed. "Lucy is the finest comedienne in the world. But it's very hard for a performer to see herself that way—from the back of the camera. Experienced actresses as well as apprentices need good directors. I think if she'd given it a chance more with me, we'd have swung together. But she's not used to a good director, so she didn't recognize one."

A cameraman who has worked on both Marlo Thomas's

"That Girl" as well as "Here's Lucy" notes, "If Marlo Thomas has a velvet glove, Lucy has an iron fist. She's a hard-working burlesque comedienne and on that set she has total authority."

Lucie and Desi stayed with their mother's show for three seasons, after which Desi dropped out and Lucie continued.

Desi was going to attend the California Institute of Arts, to study music and drama. It was obviously a move to please his mother, who was always concerned with appearances. He has explained, "The basic concern of my mother and step-father has been protection of the family name—don't do or say anything that might expose us in a bad light. I never felt it was all that important—and neither did my Dad, who hasn't done too well on this score. I guess that's one big reason I feel such a powerful bond of affection with my Dad —a bond that has actually grown since my parents were divorced. Temperamentally, we're much alike. My father is Latin and terribly sentimental. Simple things like home and family and honesty turn him on. Business doesn't, so when he got totally hung up in things that were fairly low on his scale of importance, he ended up hating himself—and that's when he got in trouble."

If Lucille's major concern was "protection of the family name," she was in for a few jolts in the new decade. Desi, Sr.'s romantic hijinks as a young man were, in the words of a friend, "chopped liver" compared to the approach taken by his offspring.

Desi, Jr., was fast becoming Hollywood's most famous Lothario. If Lucy had been worried that Desi would follow in the footsteps of his older, sophisticated friends, she had reason to. With his charm, good looks and incredible zest for living, Desi didn't miss much.

Barely seventeen, he saw actress Patty Duke at a Merv Griffin show, liked her and called her for a date. It was not unlike his parents' first meeting. Desi's description: "Right off, we fell in love."

Patty was six years older than Desi—the same age difference as between Lucille and Desi, Sr. She had been married at eighteen and was recently divorced from Harry Falk, Jr., a young director. She already had won an Academy Award and countless other prizes for her superb performances on the stage and in films.

But her personal life had always been desperately unhappy. Her father, a cabdriver, had deserted the family when Patty was a baby. She was raised by guardians, John and Ethel Ross, who were also her theatrical agents. Early publicity said Patty was an orphan who had been adopted by the Rosses, but in fact her mother was living.

Desi and Patty began steady-dating. They were sophisticated children of show business and Desi has recalled that shortly after their affair began she told him she was convinced she was incapable of getting pregnant. "At least the doctors told her that there was a forty to fifty per cent chance of her never having babies because she had previously miscarried," said Desi.

Naturally, like most young people in love, Desi and Patty talked about having children. However, Desi later explained, "I didn't want to get married. I wasn't financially secure. . . . I couldn't afford marriage and I didn't want to get married in any event. I know it sounds young, illegal, immature and all the rest of it, but maybe if two people love each other and they can live happily together, maybe they don't need that marriage contract."

Desi explained his attraction to Patty. "Patty is a lot like my mother, the same drive, and strong will, a perfectionist. . . . But I'm never going to get married. Marriage is unrealistic, expecting you to devote a whole life unselfishly to just one person. Do you know people age unbelievably when they marry? From what I've seen, eighty-five per cent of married couples are miserable; fourteen per cent just average; one per cent happy."

With statements like these, Desi was expressing the views of the new generation. But his mother was from the old generation, and, in the words of a friend, "Lucy was horrified, upset and worried. She didn't want him to throw his life away. Not only was Desi living the life his father had led, but he was being vocal about it! Even though Desi was still underage, he was as strong willed as his mother and he wasn't afraid to stand up to her."

Desi accompanied Patty to the Emmy Awards, where she won the Best Actress award for her performance in the motion picture for television, *My Sweet Charlie*. All America watched as Patty, receiving the Emmy, thanked the Academy and then—looking straight at Desi Arnaz, Jr.—said, "And . . . thank *you*."

The affair had become inescapably public.

In August, Desi got his first movie role, a starring one in Hal Wallis's production for Universal, *Red Sky at Morning*. It would be filmed on location in New Mexico and before Desi left Hollywood, "Patty told me that she thought she was pregnant. We had had some false pregnancy alarms before, so we weren't quite sure."

He and Patty must have quarreled, since, as he said, he didn't want to get married and even if he did, he was underage. Desi went to New Mexico for the film, and Patty resumed her career.

"We were sort of uptight during this period," Desi remembered. "But we talked all the time and when I got back from New Mexico, she was in Palm Springs and she was five months pregnant."

Patty was emotionally distraught. She suddenly eloped to Las Vegas with a rock music promoter named Mike Tell. She had known him for one day. "A week later," Desi said, "she announced her pregnancy, not by him but by me."

Nineteen days after her elopement Patty announced that she was divorcing Tell. Desi's reaction was one of "mixed emotions." "I was happier than I had ever been before in my life," he said. "Patty was also happy. She was more tranquil, more at peace with herself than I'd ever seen her. People didn't interfere with us during this period, and we were happy. We were looking forward to the birth of our child, a child who was innocent."

Every fan magazine in the country had a field day and was making Lucille Ball out as "the wicked witch of the west" by not allowing her son to marry Patty Duke and legitimize his child.

Desi subsequently contended that both his mother and father stood by him and Patty during the trying ordeal. "My mother was great about everything. She had Patty over to the house. She looked after her. She was gentle. Yet all the while the fan magazines made my mother furious. They conjured up such fictions as 'Lucy Throws Patty Out of House . . .' 'You're Not Good Enough for Desi, Cries Lucy,' 'Keep Away From My Son, Warns Lucille Ball.' It was sickening, infuriating. . . ."

"The truth was that Patty and my mother got along beautifully. And my Dad, Desi. Patty and I went down to his place in Baja California, and he was magnificent. 'Be honest with yourself,' he advised. 'Do what you think best. I am behind you a hundred per cent.'"

The furor increased before the birth of the baby. It was almost impossible to pass a newsstand without noticing piles of fan magazines with pictures of Lucille, Patty and Desi, Jr., on the covers. The headlines: "Why Lucille Ball's Son Is So Bitter About His Own Mother"; "Patty Duke Begs Desi, Jr., to Believe Her: You Made Me Pregnant." The implication was that Desi, Jr., wanted to marry Patty; Desi, Sr., would have gone along with it; but Lucille absolutely refused to give her permission.

259

On January 19, 1971, Desi celebrated his eighteenth birthday with a party at the Luau. Although Gary Morton and Lucie were on hand, Lucille was not. And beaming, pregnant Patty was very much in attendance.

A month later, on February 25, she gave birth to a son.

Lucille has been candid in describing the entire Patty Duke episode. "I worked for years for a quiet personal life and to have it personally impinged upon, with no recourse, is hard. I brought Patty to the house, feeling very maternal about her, saying look at this clever girl, what a big talent she is. Now, I can thank her for useless notoriety. She's living in some fantastic dream world, and we're the victims of it. Desi being the tender age of seventeen when they met, she used him. She hasn't proved or asked for anything. I asked Desi if he wanted to marry her and he said no. My daughter helped outfit the baby, which Patty brought to the house, but did she ever say thank you?"

Some reports quoted Patty as replying, "Lucy never brought me into her house. Sean was two months old before I ever even spoke to Lucy—and then the only reason I was at their house was because Desi had begged me to come. Let me tell you something—Desi may have been seventeen, but he knew the score. She makes it sound like I led him down the garden path and that's not the way it was. Not at all. That other thing is totally untrue, too. Lucie Arnaz did go shopping with me. We went to Saks in Beverly Hills. She helped me pick out clothes, but every penny went on my charge. And I even paid the bill for the lunch we had afterwards, I think. I don't know what Lucy means by 'I never thanked her'—what was I to thank her for, for shopping with me?"

Desi, Jr., visited his son the day after he was born and described the experience. "It was an incredible sensation. He looks just like me." The baby was born by caesarean and weighed only five pounds. Patty named him Sean Patrick

Duke. "That is the name she wants," Desi said, "but he is my son and I love him just as I love his mother."

"But the relationship between Patty and me has altered," he noted after the baby's birth. "Our passion is not as tempestuous as it once was."

At first Desi, Jr., visited his son two or three times a week —"as frequently as I can." And he also stated, "I am prepared to do what is best for all of us."

Young Arnaz didn't like to talk publicly about his son, but finally revealed his views on Patty and the baby because he was annoyed with the fan magazine approach to the situation. "The magazines day after day are filled with the most incredible articles," he noted. "The writers, especially in fan magazines, seem to create their own dialogue. I am constantly amazed when I read what I am supposed to have said.

"I would avoid the subject completely if it weren't for the fact that my mother in this whole thing has been turned into a heavy.

"Supposedly, my mother doesn't want me to acknowledge our child. She doesn't want me to see Patty again. I'm supposed to forget that whole unmarried-father bit. Patty isn't good enough for me. Supposedly, Lucille Ball has barred Patty Duke from entering our house, threatening to ruin her, tried to buy her off. All lies! My mother has been the kindest, most gentle, most understanding mother any son could ask for. She and my Dad have treated Patty with love and respect and great tenderness. They think the world of Patty Duke. However we want to work out our problems, it's okay with them."

Desi, Jr., took Patty and Sean to visit with Desi and Edie in Mexico.

Patty bought a house in Bel-Air and then came another surprise. In Desi's words: "Because she is an honest and decent and forthright girl," Patty told him that she had

261

fallen in love with some other "lucky young man" and planned to marry him. At the time, Desi said, "Naturally, my male vanity is a trifle shattered that she has fallen out of love with me and in love with someone else. But, at the ripe old age of eighteen I feel sure that I will be able to overcome it."

Desi, Jr., had said earlier, "I have no intention of bugging out from home just because my parents can no longer legally hold me." Referring to his sister's departure from Lucy Manor he noted, "I don't want to go in an atmosphere of hostility or recrimination. I want to work out any problems I have with my parents beforehand, resolve our disagreements and leave—when I do leave—because the time has come.

"I'm sure I feel this way because I had a taste of living away from the family when I traveled with my musical group and also because I saw the emotional wrenching that took place when my sister left. I don't think that has to happen in any family, and I hope it doesn't happen to me."

After the Patty Duke affair, Desi obviously felt his "time had come," and he moved out of the Roxbury Drive mansion and into his own apartment off the Sunset Strip. Friends said he moved out because he wanted to avoid embarrassing his mother any further. He said, "It's just time for me to be on my own."

A top movie director says about young Desi, "He's very much like his father. He likes girls, good times, fast cars and has the talent and looks to write his own ticket professionally. And he's got a big head start on his father, having the money and position his father never had at the beginning. Yet he's a nice kid. Again, just like his father, he doesn't have any kind of swelled head about him. He knows he has everything lying there in front of him and he's picking it all up."

Lucy has admitted, "Yes, he's very much like his father— too much, sometimes. I just hope he has Desi's business acumen."

262

12

LUCY'S TWENTY-YEAR exclusivity contract came to an end in 1970, but her series continued on CBS. "I've never given them a hard time," she said. "They just like to make it sound that way."

Meanwhile, Desi, Sr., had returned to performing. He was delighted with his children's success and was anxious to work with them. "Lucy worked with them, why shouldn't he?" asked Desi's friends, adding, "He didn't work with them for the same reasons Lucy did. With Desi it was strictly for the kick of performing with them."

Arnaz starred on the Kraft Variety Hour on NBC with Desi, Jr., Lucie and Vivian Vance. One of the highlights was father and son whamming away at bongo drums for a Latin-rhythmed duet. Desi Sr. did a comedy sketch with his daughter. Afterwards he noted, "We did a bit together that Lucy and I did years ago. Big Lucy was in the audience. Afterwards I said that Lucie had done it better than her mother had. And big Lucy agreed.

"You know, it's funny, but big Lucy and I get along better now than we did when we were married. I've been fortunate about my kids. Strangely enough, despite the divorce, we're all very close."

Desi, Sr., also made a guest appearance on an episode of Universal's "The Men From Shiloh," the updated version of their long-running "Virginian" TV series. His hair showed wisps of grey amidst the shock of jet black. It was Desi's first western and he said he had taken the role because he was "getting tired of seeing Ricardo Montalban and Fernando Lamas in all these Mexican roles."

There had been rumors for several years that Desi Arnaz was seriously ill. He had had several operations and seemed to age a great deal overnight. When there are rumors of a "serious illness" they usually refer to one dread disease.

"Everybody but everybody was sure I had cancer," Desi told a friend. "The reason they thought I had the Big C is because they heard I had surgery four times during the last two years." He could laugh about it, admitting, "I haven't been around much." Nonetheless, friends said that despite his bouts with the knife he looked fit, even though he had gotten a bit paunchy. The hospital stays had been for diverticulitis and a hematoma that developed after he took a nasty spill on his power boat.

"Only high class people like L.B.J. get diverticulitis," joshed Desi. "No really," he added, "it's very common. And neither of the difficulties had anything to do with cancer. Actually, I haven't felt better in fifteen years. I've put on about twenty-five pounds, but that's because I haven't been doing anything but fishing and drinking beer since I sold my interest in Desilu."

Desi has expressed hope of someday doing a film with his son. Many people feel this is Desi's prime reason for continuing to perform.

However, Desi, Jr., offered the explanation, "Dad still feels some compulsion to business activity, so he can't turn away

264

from it completely. But he'll never be consumed by it again, and that's the way it has to be with him." Comparing his parents the young Arnaz continued, "My mother is entirely different, and I suppose it was impossible that they could ever reconcile two such divergent approaches to life. There's an innate quality some people—and especially Latins—have that makes it easy for them to see past the superficial and realize finally that there are only a few things that really count. It took Dad a very long time to get there."

In the last few years Lucille Ball has been trying to learn to relax. Although it has always been Desi Arnaz who bore the brunt of bad publicity concerning his drinking habits, Lucy did not entirely escape such rigors of superstardom. She was recently described by nationally syndicated columnist Walter Scott as "a good, stiff, two-fisted drinker."

By the 1970s Lucy decided she wanted—needed—a private hideaway. She found the spot in Snowmass, Colorado, where she bought a house, a rough-beamed structure deep in the woods. "It's her new, old passion," says a relative, "a throwback to her childhood in upstate New York. She likes to read. She takes up lots of books and scripts with her. She's even learned how to ski."

"She loves the snow," said her son. But whether in Beverly Hills or Snowmass Lucy remained her old intense self. Once when family and friends were visiting Lucy insisted on cooking every night. Desi Jr. remembered, "I told her I wanted to fix the dinner and she said no, she'd handle it. We tried to compromise but couldn't agree on any of the dishes. So it ended up with the two of us pushing one another around the kitchen and cooking two different dinners. We had ten guests, and it must have been a pretty confusing dinner because mother and I were each pushing our own dishes on them and competing for customers, right down to the dessert."

Desi, Jr., enjoys his mother best when they're "just family" and not co-workers. But he sadly concluded, "Then the mood passes and she gets itchy and we're back in the old work syndrome again.

"But the other side of her—the side that loves to be with her family and yearns for a cabin somewhere in the snow—is the one so few people know. And the one I love."

It is no secret that Gary, however, is happiest not in a winter haven but in Palm Springs playing golf. Lucy remarked that Gary often goes to the Springs and "tolerantly lets me stay at Snowmass for weeks. Sun just doesn't agree with me."

On her nineteenth birthday, Lucie Arnaz had staged a colorful gypsy dance at the Roxbury Drive mansion. She asked a friend, "Gee, what can I do to top that?"

She thought of something. The following year, three days after her twentieth birthday, on July 20, 1971, Lucie married twenty-six-year-old Phil Vandervort. It was the Hollywood society wedding of the season.

Although Lucie seemed young to be getting married, especially as far as her mother was concerned, she was actually a very mature young woman. Mama had done her job well. Both her children had been brought up to make decisions and lead their own lives. Lucie had grown up in an adult world and her outlook on dating was more sophisticated than an average teen-ager's.

Her new husband was described as a documentary film maker.

The young couple had to weather the expected bombardment of gossip and innuendos about Vandervort being attracted to Lucie "because of her fifty-million-kilowatt personality—worth about $1-a-kilowatt according to estimates of the Ball fortune."

The Saturday afternoon wedding and lawn reception took place at the Roxbury Drive estate. Crowds of people gathered outside, straining to catch a glimpse of celebrities. Lucy's neighbors turned on their sprinklers to keep the crowds off their lawns.

More than two hundred guests attended, including columnist Rona Barrett, Beau Bridges, Lloyd Bridges, Carol Burnett, Ken Berry, Dino Martin Jr. and his wife Olivia Hussey, Ruta Lee, the Ross Martins, Buddy Hackett, Jack Carter, Virginia Graham.

The bride wore a dress she had designed herself. "We've Only Just Begun" replaced "I Love You Truly" as the wedding theme, and a grey-haired teary-eyed Desi Arnaz Sr. gave his daughter away.

Lucie's maid of honor was Wanda Clark, big Lucy's secretary. The four bridesmaids were Lisa Pharron, Cindy Barnes, Alice Brittingham and Naomi Parry. Cee Cee Durante, Jimmy's daughter, was the flower girl and Lucie's cousin Marcus, son of Cleo and Cecil Smith, was ring bearer.

Dick Gautier (Conrad Birdie in the film version of *Bye Bye Birdie* and currently a TV show emcee) was Vandervort's best man. Ushers were Ed Hall, Steven Hitter, Ben Stone and Desi Arnaz Jr.

Lucie was radiant, but brother Desi, without trying, almost stole the show. He was incredibly handsome in his tux and those on the scene recall he was a meticulous host, visiting with friends, chatting with business associates. Women at the party were "swooning" over him and everyone gossiped about the eighteen-year-old's current romance, a rumored on-again, off-again affair with the estranged wife of a "major, major" figure in show business. "Shades of *The Graduate*," laughed a family friend.

One of the highlights of the reception was when Desi Sr. danced with Lucille. Gary Morton cut in. "That's the second time you've cut in on me," Desi kidded.

Vandervort joined Lucille Ball Productions as a production associate soon after his marriage.

267

While Lucy's television series continued successfully with its usual devoted audience, a major policy change was on the horizon at CBS. A talented, tough new young programing vice president, Fred Silverman, held the reins. Silverman was outspoken, an unusual trait for an executive in his position. He said Rod Taylor's expensive CBS "Bearcat" series, "looks chintzy, even with all the money we're spending." And he called Doris Day "too Pollyannaish, too saccharine."

Perennials like Red Skelton, Ed Sullivan and Jackie Gleason (who wanted to do a variety show but CBS only wanted him to do weekly "Honeymooners" episodes) had top ratings, but, in the eyes of the network, they had no long-range future. Their fans were dependable but growing older, and new, youthful fans were not watching.

Lucy knew who made up her TV audience. "Kids watch me during the day. Women and older men at night. Teenagers no. They look at 'Mod Squad.'"

Although Lucy was high in the ratings, talk filtered through that her show was on Silverman's "cancel" list. There were reports that Silverman made off-the-cuff comments about Lucy's show which Gary overheard and a verbal battle ensued.

Gary later said, "Lucy and I read a blind item in a west coast column which said, 'Which top CBS star is trying to get Fred Silverman fired?' Lucy turned to me and said, 'Who's the top CBS star?' She had no idea the item was referring to her."

Morton told friends that Silverman's reputation was riding on three yet-to-debut shows: "Funny Face," with Sandy Duncan; "Cannon," with William Conrad; and Sonny and Cher's summer series.

It was indeed true, as Gary Morton implied, that Silverman's future was on the line with the three series in question. However, they all proved to be resounding hits.

Whatever differences Lucy and Silverman had, the situation was resolved. Lucille Ball remained with CBS. It seems

268

clear that "Here's Lucy" will continue as long as Lucille wants it to, which appears to be indefinitely.

In the words of Desi, Jr.,: "Mom is still hung up on the excitement of what she's doing. Not that it isn't meaningful, she gives a lot of pleasure to millions of people every week. But sometimes, it seems to be making up for a void somewhere. The great entertainers I know—including my mother —have so much of whatever is inside them that it has to come out, and so they work it off in show business. This compulsion drives her to be doing things that right now are really unnecessary, because she doesn't have to work that hard anymore."

Lucy's marriage to Gary has endured eleven years. Morton told a pal after a recent anniversary, "Do you know how many bets were lost about our marriage lasting?" And he confided, "I've slept on the couch only once."

While marriage never dulled Lucy's career drive, for a while after Lucie Arnaz's marriage, young Lucie was less career oriented. She made a pilot for her own TV series and the industry buzzed that big Lucy was pushing hard for a sale. However, Lucie didn't appear too disappointed when the pilot didn't sell. "She's happily married and never really cared that much about a career anyway," said a girlhood friend a bit prematurely. "It's fun for her, but she doesn't have the drive her mother has."

Lucie could have a big career *if* she wanted one. But unlike her brother, a career on her own wouldn't come easily. In the opinion of a top producer, "Lucie is personable and has a certain sparkle, but nobody's going to beat down doors for her services. It's Desi who has so much style and charisma that even if he didn't want a career in show business, it would be inevitable."

It is certain that Desi Arnaz, Jr., will become a major star. Even though he is only nineteen, his sophisticated private life has overwhelmingly captured the interest of the press and public.

A close family friend notes in what is undoubtedly an understatement, "Desi, Jr., seems to gravitate towards women who have certain qualities that Lucy has—ambition, drive—but usually lack her other qualities, like stability and discipline."

"It's obvious that a certain 'helpless' quality in a woman is irresistible to him," conjectured another one of his pals. "A gamin quality—little girl lost—these things turn him on."

Desi was turned on instantly by saucer-eyed, twenty-six-year-old Liza Minnelli. It was an immediate attraction for both. Once again he had chosen a girl with a successful career, but with a garbled private life and from a family background totally dissimilar to his.

True, Liza was from a show business family. Her parents, Judy Garland and Vincente Minnelli, were two of Hollywood's brightest luminaries. However, they divorced when Liza was four and the child's formative years were spent in a somewhat less-than-stable atmosphere with lots of love from her parents but no structured home life.

Liza's romance with Desi immediately became front-page news. Reporters eagerly recounted Liza's previous exploits—her stormy marriage to young singer Peter Allen, the man her mother wanted her to marry, which ended in divorce; her affair with Rex Kramer, guitarist in the group from her night club act. (In an extremely candid appraisal of the Liza-Kramer affair, Peter Allen said: "Rex was exactly the opposite from me. He was a country boy who hated the city and loved girls.")

Liza's affair with Rex ended amidst an outburst of bad publicity. His ex-wife sued for $500,000, charging alienation of affections. After the brouhaha subsided, Liza said she realized all along that Rex was not really in love with her but was in fact using her.

Liza's romance with French singing star Charles Aznavour was, according to Aznavour, "amitie amoureuse." "I had it with Piaf and I have it with Liza. It's less than love and more than friendship. It's better than romance."

It seems to be old-fashioned love between Desi and Liza, although they haven't exactly raced to the altar. They have exchanged wedding bands which symbolize, in Liza's words, their "bond of union and understanding."

Liza has further described their relationship. "Desi understands the need for calmness the way I do. He has a steadiness that's very important to me. I hate abrupt changes of emotion, and I can't live in that kind of atmosphere."

Early in 1972 Liza spent time with Lucy at Snowmass, "skiing."

"Lucy wanted to make sure that she and Liza understood each other," according to one intimate. "Lucy has accepted the fact that Desi, Jr., is a 'chip off the old block' and she's trying to make the best of it."

Lucy understands Liza's background and realizes Liza's need for a family. "I was one of the first to ever see Liza," remembered Lucy. "I was in the hospital with Judy within hours because we were such good friends. Liza spent one summer with us because Judy was on the road. Liza thought I was her mother."

How did Lucille view the relationship between Liza and Desi, Jr.? "They're engaged," Lucy told a friend. "But they're not getting married. They're too busy."

Will they ever be married? In Lucy's words: "Who can tell? We've always been very fond of her. She would be welcome in our family anytime."

As far as young Lucie was concerned, "I love Liza. Listen, he could do a lot worse—and he did!"

At that point, big Lucy cut in: "Okay, cut her off."

On another occasion, Lucy stated that Desi and Liza "are wildly in love and that's all I know."

271

Lucy was still bitter about Patty Duke. "She made a career of magazines for a year," Lucy told writer Kay Gardella. "She went every way—up, down and around—and then suddenly it all stopped and she revamped her stories. They changed every day and it was really something for awhile. It was a real barrage and it had very little to do with us." (By the summer of '72 Patty had married actor John Astin and had signed to star in "Love Child," an episode of Universal's "Owen Marshall" TV series in which she'd play a girl whose out-of-wedlock baby becomes the subject of child custody litigation.)

Desi Arnaz, Jr., and Sr., accompanied Liza to the world premiere of *Cabaret* in New York in the spring of 1972. Desi, Jr., then flew to Puerto Rico to be with her while she tried out her new night club act. They were also together at the Oscar ceremonies in April. Then young Desi flew to Tokyo for his second film, *Marco Polo.* Liza joined him later on.

"Desi will never marry her," says one Hollywood wag. "Why should he?" But others note that Desi is capable of impulsive and romantic actions.

In any case, Lucille is "thankful that Liza's not giving out interviews at Desi's expense," according to a close friend.

As this book goes to press, Liza has stated that she will probably marry Desi in December 1972, adding "Desi wants to get married in Baja, Daddy wants a wedding here at home and I'm in the middle."

By the summer of 1972, their first anniversary, Lucie Arnaz's marriage was in trouble. Lucille Ball's cover-up statements—"It's very tough the first year . . . ," describing the split as "an amiable separation for awhile . . . a little spat . . . everything is very amiable . . . ," didn't make it any easier for her to accept her daughter's situation.

Much to Lucy's displeasure, young Lucie has become

272

more outspoken since separating from her husband. She is tired of the "little Lucie" tag. When a friend recently telephoned Lucy and Lucie answered the phone, the caller asked, "Is this little Lucie?"

"No," answered the girl. "This is *young* Lucie. Do you want to talk to my mother?" Lucille picked up the phone. "This is *old* Lucy speaking," she snarled.

Lucie's complaint is that "To most people I'm still *little* Lucie. Almost everybody I meet starts out by asking me about my mother. The last time I was interviewed the reporter wanted to know if my mother wasn't going to appear on the show in the fall season because of her broken leg, would I replace her No, I told him, because no one could replace her! What's more, I wouldn't want to. I only wish that after five seasons on her show, somebody would be interested in me instead of always asking questions about Mother and Dad and Desi. People even ask me why I don't have red hair. Well, I don't because my mother's hair color comes in a little bottle. Mine is a combination of the auburn hair my mother used to have and my father's one-time black hair."

Lucie has also "had it" concerning her reputation for being shy. "Me? *Shy?* Only when I do something professionally, and that's because my brother always outdid me. When we went to mother's taping and were introduced to the audience, it was Desi who stood up and bowed and bowed and bowed. I just grinned sheepishly. Oh, how Desi loved all the attention!"

After the split, Lucie Arnaz was being squired around town by female impressionist Jim Bailey, who, ironically, rocketed to stardom via his extraordinary impersonation of Liz Minnelli's late mother, Judy Garland.

Where does Lucille Ball go from here? Often asked "Suppose your rating should drop, what would you do?", she

273

replies she has no idea. "Might take a trip on the Inland Waterway from Boston to Florida." Lucy has moved her production company from Paramount to Universal. "In my deal with Universal, I can make specials, other movies, TV pilots. I wouldn't have to ski 'spooked' at Snowmass."

"Honey, I have to be careful," she said. "If I break a leg five hundred people are out of work."

Lucy did break her leg skiing and was laid up for several weeks. Undaunted, she had her writers whip together scripts with the Lucy character laid up with a broken leg.

It was, in fact, a serious break, known as a butterfly shatter, requiring months in a brace and four silver screws in her leg. "The doctor tells me that I will never be able to ski again, and I love the sport."

Lucy's sense of humor didn't desert her when, with Gary on the sidelines, she described her ordeal in the hospital to a group of friends. "It was like a scene from *M.A.S.H.*"

Gary interjected, "That place was really very nice. Next year we'll go back so Lucy can break the other leg."

Lucy forced a smile.

Lucille Ball and work. They're synonymous.

In a revealing statement, her son said: "At work she is totally engrossed, a perfectionist to whom nothing else matters at that moment. As a businesswoman, she's good instinctively but not technically. She knows this and surrounds herself with sharp people. Her contribution is to serve as a motivating force. She's a great unifier of people toward worthwhile objectives."

In Lucy's words: "Your first goal must be as diligently pursued as the later and bigger goals. The habit of having a goal is the important thing." But she noted the size of the goal unimportant. "Listen, it never occurred to me, in life, that I'd fail ever, because I always appreciated small successes. I never had a big fixed goal."

About "Here's Lucy" a top writer says, "The Lucy character is really an ingenue, and Lucille is getting away with it—she's playing an ingenue. As you know it is completely acting. The Lucy that she plays in the Lucy show has nothing to do with Lucille Ball. In most cases television is an X-ray and you can't exist very long unless you're playing yourself. She's done it. She's playing somebody else."

Regarding her "Lucy" scripts, Lucy noted, "I need a strong father or husband figure as a catalyst. I have to be an inadequate somebody, because I don't want the authority for Lucy. Every damned movie script sent me seems to cast me as a lady with authority, like Eve Arden or Roz Russell, but that's not me."

Lucy has analyzed herself and what she has become. "I don't think I'm too versatile, but that's sort of beside the point. If millions like this, it would be pretty silly of me to go astray. I've learned a lot about my trade over the years. I have a knowledge of physical comedy, my timing is reliable and I'm believable. People laugh where they should and they don't think I'm unbelievable, because I believe it all the way. I do what I do with all my strength and heart.

"What comes to my mind immediately is what the characters around me must not do. Their reactions to me have got to be in a certain vein . . . If we are in a dangerous spot, the audience mustn't think I'm hurt—not really. There's a funny way to cry and a funny way to be hurt and a funny way to be angry and that's what I've learned. And the attitude of those around me must be the same as it is toward a child—one of tolerance."

After all these years, she hasn't wearied of the Lucy character. "No, I'm a rooter, I look for ruts. My cousin Cleo is always prodding me to move. She once said Lucy was my security blanket. Maybe. I'm not erudite in any way like Cleo. But why should I change? Last year was big TV relevant year, and I made sure my show *wasn't* relevant. Lucy deals in fundamental, everyday things exaggerated, with a

275

happy ending. She has a basic childishness that hopefully most of us never lose. That's why she cries a lot like a kid— the WAAH act—instead of getting drunk."

Lucy pooh-poohs any deep psychological analysis of why she is a comedienne. "Listen, honey," she told a friend, "have you heard me say anything funny? I tell you I don't *think* funny. That's the difference between a wit and a comedian. My daughter Lucie thinks funny. So does Steve Allen, Buddy Hackett, Betty Grable.

"Dean Martin has a curly mind. Oh, I can tell a funny story about something that happened to me. But I'm more of a hard-working hack with an instinct for timing, who knows the mechanics of comedy."

Associates point out that Lucy is so work oriented that when she isn't busy on one of her own projects, she runs all over the country doing guest stints on other people's shows.

Knowing her trade has made Lucille Ball a multi-millionaire. Her wealth has been reckoned at $50-to-$100-million. She has down-played this. "Hah! Like Sinatra, I owe about three-and-a-half-million bucks all the time. That figure is ridiculous. All my money is working."

"I do have a respect for money," Lucy has admitted. "But I think I can honestly say that I've wanted only enough to take care of my own, and to help others, and to have some around for emergencies. No one can deny that you need some money to create happiness. But the oldest tag line in the world is so, so true: Money is *not* everything."

Everybody knows Lucille Ball isn't working for the money. Someone is always asking Lucy why she's still working—"as if it were some crime or neurosis. OK, I'll say, it's for my kids. But I like a routine life. I *like* to work."

On another occasion she explained, "One of the reasons I'm still working is that people seem grateful that Lucy is there, the same character and unchanging view. There's so much chaos in this world, that's important. Many people, not only shut-ins, depend on the tube, too much so—they look for favorites they can count on. Older people loved Lawrence Welk. They associated his music with their youth. Now he's gone. It's not fair. They shouldn't have taken off those bucolic comedies; that left a big dent in some folks' lives. Maybe we're not getting messages anymore from the clergy, the politicians, so TV does the preaching. But as an entertainer, I don't believe in messages."

What is Lucy's opinion of controversial TV shows like "All In The Family"? "I don't know . . . it's good to bring prejudice out in the open. People do think that way, but why glorify it? Those not necessarily young may not catch the moral. That show doesn't go full circle for me."

By "full circle," Lucy meant, "You have to suffer a little when you do wrong. That prejudiced character doesn't pay a penance. Does he ever reverse a feeling? I'm for believability, but I'm tired of hearing 'pig,' 'wop,' 'Polack' said unkindly. *Me, I have to have an on-the-nose moral.*"

Lucy is aware of all trends, and their ramifications, in show business today. She saw *No, No, Nanette* on Broadway. "Listen, I studied that audience," she told a friend. "I saw people in their sixties and seventies enjoying themselves. That had to be nostalgia. The thirties and forties smiled indulgently, that Ruby Keeler is up there on the stage *alive*, not dead. For the below thirties, it's pure camp. I don't put it down, but it's not warm, working nostalgia, but the feeling 'Ye gods, anything but today.' "

Lucy believes in "right now." She works as hard now as she did as a young starlet. Thursday night show time remains as tense as ever. Gary warms up the audience, filled with out-of-town tourists, with jokes such as "Lucy started out with another fellow, can't remember his name. . . . What is home without a mother? A place to bring girls." Lucille then explodes on the scene, gorgeously coiffed, made-up and gowned. "For God's sake," she tells the audience, "laugh it up! We want to hear from you . . . Gary, have you introduced my mom?" (DeDe is eighty now but her hair is the same shade as Lucille's.)

Lucille still takes the show home with her. "I'll tell you about Lucy," an old friend observes. "It's all work now. She was a warm, passionate, loving woman, years ago. She was crazy in love with Desi. She's been hurt. Hurt for years and years. It's frozen her. There's a lot of kissing and calling people darling, but really underneath, it's cold. The warm part of her is hidden down, down, where nobody can ever hurt it again."

"I learn from my mistakes," Lucille has often brusquely noted about her personal life. "I don't admire people who beat their heads against the same mistakes over and over again. I don't like people who flounder too long. I don't admire these everyday martyrs, the pitiful drunken messes, the hysterical floundering women, the Beats shouting 'the world owes me a living'—all these people who cling to you, who need your help. You help them up to a point, but after a while you wish they'd go cry on somebody else's shoulder.

"I like people who love their work, love their families, love life—people who, fundamentally, love themselves—nothing is more important than being able to stand on your own feet."

Lucy's philosophy is "learn the art of taking care of yourself and remember that there is a very fine distinction between being selfish and taking care of yourself. If you take care of yourself others won't have to."

Lucy remains a follower of Dr. Norman Vincent Peale. On her bathroom wall, she has a memo scotch-taped: "Get Smart with N.V.P."

"I still adhere to his way of thinking because he preaches a day-to-day religion that I can understand. Something workable, not allegory. Like how to get up in the morning and just get through the day."

Does Lucille believe in Women's Lib? "I don't know the

278

meaning of women's lib. I never had anything to squawk about. I don't know what they're asking for that I don't have already. Equal pay for equal work, that's okay."

Although Lucy doesn't profess much interest in current events, she commented: "Maybe I'm more concerned about things than I realize. I told you politics is definitely not on my agenda—I got burned bad, back in the forties, signing a damned petition as a favor. Just say the word 'politician' and I think of chicanery. Too many subversive angles today. But I must be one of millions who are so fed up, depressed, sobbing inside, about the news . . . the atrocities, the dead, the running down of America. You can't obliterate the news, but the worst dream is that you feel so helpless."

Will Lucy make any more films? She is scheduled to begin "Mame" in January, 1973. She's certainly perfect for the role and despite the problems of make-up, lighting and now her broken leg, she is definitely going ahead with it.

"But making a film is tedious work and lacks the spontaneity of a live audience, which Lucy thrives on," notes a friend.

Lucille Ball, at sixty-one, is still a striking-looking woman on the television screen. But there are virtually no close-ups on her show. A friend of Gary's relates, "Once my parents were coming to Los Angeles and were dying to meet Lucy. Gary's a doll. He's always ready to please and he said he'd see what he could do."

However, when the elderly couple went backstage to meet Lucy they were only allowed to see her from a distance. "She waved to them from across the set," says Gary's friend. "He later told me she wouldn't let them get any closer because she doesn't like her friends to see her close up and be disillusioned."

A famous actress who has worked with Lucy claims that "Lucy has had her face lifted, but everybody should look that good after a face lift. I've seen a lot of those women who've had their faces lifted, but their bodies look like they

279

have to be carried to get in and out of a car. Lucy's got a good body. She works so hard her body is always tuned up. I've never seen her get sloppy fat. She's always kept herself in good shape.

"She's still glamorous in her way. I mean, my God, I don't know of anybody that's had a span of years like that woman has had. Let's face it. How long has she been on the screen? At least forty years."

Lucy has been in the public eye for over forty years. She has never in all that time been shy or coy with the press. When an interviewer touches on a topic Lucy doesn't want to discuss, she fixes a steely blue-eyed stare at him and declares: "How about another question?"

Naturally, Lucille has been accused of being an egomaniac. "You can get bawled out for having too little ego too," Lucy has pointed out. "Once, years ago at a cocktail party in Philadelphia, somebody said to me, 'Be nice to that man over there. He's with a local paper.' I went over to him and said, 'I'm Lucille Ball,' and he said sarcastically, 'You don't say!' and I just died, because all I'd wanted to be was friendly.

"I guess he thought it was like Jimmy Durante coming up to him and saying coyly, 'I'm Jimmy Durante,' only Jimmy wouldn't have been coy about it, and even if he had, the man should have said, 'You don't have to tell me, Jimmy, I recognized you,' or something human, instead of being nasty. Anyhow, the next day his paper tore into me as an example of fake humility, while actually all I was trying to do was to tell the man who I was. The people I'm most grateful for in this world are those who just stick out their hand and identify themselves."

In the opinion of a prominent actress, who has known Lucy for years, "Lucy's greatest characteristic is inner strength. She's a showman. It's her whole life. I think everything revolves around it. I know she's in love with Gary Morton, but if something should happen I don't think it would interfere with her career. It's in her blood and that's it.

"Imagine pursuing a career for forty-five years? And keeping herself on top? She's done it."

In Desi Jr.'s words: "She's found the thing she's best at and sticks to it. As long as she has Snowmass, she has an escape, some reality. I realize she lives half in a man's world, and that must be tough on a woman. My father worked hard for years, and then he'd had it. This is silly, weird, he felt. . . . I'm like him. I feel life is very short."

Will Lucille Ball ever retire? She's answered that question herself: "Yes. When I drop in my tracks."